HIKING THE ADIRONDACK 46 HIGH PEAKS

Sunrise from Algonquin, one of the best places to watch the sunrise in the High Peaks.

HIKING THE ADIRONDACK 46 HIGH PEAKS

Jonathan Zaharek

ESSEX, CONNECTICUT

FALCONGUIDES®

An imprint of Globe Pequot, the trade division of
The Rowman & Littlefield Publishing Group, Inc.
4501 Forbes Blvd., Ste. 200
Lanham, MD 20706
www.rowman.com

Distributed by NATIONAL BOOK NETWORK

British Library Cataloguing in Publication Information available

Library of Congress Cataloging-in-Publication Data

Names: Zaharek, Jonathan, 1997- author.
Title: Hiking the Adirondack 46 high peaks / Jonathan Zaharek.
Description: Lanham, MD : Prometheus, [2024] | Includes index. | Summary:
 "Hiking the Adirondack 46 High Peaks is the guide to everything hikers
 need to know about summiting each of the 46 high peaks of the Adirondack
 Mountains. Whether you are a veteran hiker looking to register as an
 official "46er" by checking all the summits off your list or a more
 casual hiker looking to sample some of the most impressive summits in
 the Adirondack high peaks, this guide will deliver invaluable
 information"—Provided by publisher.
Identifiers: LCCN 2023041727 (print) | LCCN 2023041728 (ebook) | ISBN
 9781493070084 (paperback) | ISBN 9781493070091 (epub)
Subjects: LCSH: Hiking—New York (State)—Adirondack Mountains—Guidebooks.
 | Adirondack Mountains (N.Y.)—Guidebooks.
Classification: LCC GV199.42.N652 Z34 2024 (print) | LCC GV199.42.N652
 (ebook) | DDC 796.5109747/5—dc23/eng/20231020
LC record available at https://lccn.loc.gov/2023041727
LC ebook record available at https://lccn.loc.gov/2023041728

CONTENTS

ACKNOWLEDGMENTS   ix

MEET YOUR GUIDE   x

INTRODUCTION   1

BEFORE YOU HIT THE TRAIL   29

MAP LEGEND   30

THE HIKES

Cascade Range
  1. Cascade and Porter Mountains   32
  2. Porter Mountain from Marcy Field   36

Giant Mountain Wilderness
  3. Giant and Rocky Peak Ridge   42
  4. Rocky Peak Ridge from New Russia   48

Big Slide
  5. Big Slide Mountain   53

Lower Great Range
  6. Upper and Lower Wolfjaw Mountains   58
  7. Gothics and Armstrong Mountains   63
  8. Sawteeth via the Scenic Route   69

Upper Great Range
  9. Saddleback Mountain   75
 10. Basin Mountain   79
 11. Mount Haystack   84
 12. Haystack, Basin, and Saddleback Loop   91

Mount Marcy

   13. Mount Marcy   96

MacIntyre Range

   14. Wright Peak   103
   15. Algonquin and Iroquois Peaks   107

Street and Nye

   16. Street and Nye Mountains   113

Phelps and Tabletop

   17. Phelps Mountain   119
   18. Tabletop Mountain   123

Lake Colden Region

   19. Mount Colden   128
   20. Mount Marshall   136
   21. Mount Redfield and Cliff Mountain   141
   22. Mount Skylight and Gray Peak   146

Whiteface and Esther

   23. Whiteface and Esther Mountains   154

Colvin Range

   24. Mount Colvin and Blake Peak   162
   25. Nippletop and Dial Mountains   167

Dix Range

   26. Dix Mountain   173
   27. Macomb Mountain, South Dix, Grace Peak,
       and Hough Peak   177
   28. Grace Peak   181

Santanoni Range

   29. Santanoni, Panther, and Couchsachraga Peaks   186

Seward Range

30. Seward, Donaldson, and Emmons Mountains   193
31. Seymour Mountain   197

Allen Mountain

32. Allen Mountain   201

Overnights and Traverses

33. Great Range Traverse   207
34. Pinnacle Traverse   212
35. Bob Marshall Traverse   216
36. High Peaks Wilderness Traverse   220
37. Cold River Loop   224

Bonus Hikes

1. MacNaughton Mountain—The Lost 46er   229
2. Sawteeth and Blake Peak Loop   233
3. Indian Head   235
4. Mount Jo   238
5. Mount Adams Fire Tower   240
6. Noonmark Mountain   242

HIKE INDEX   245

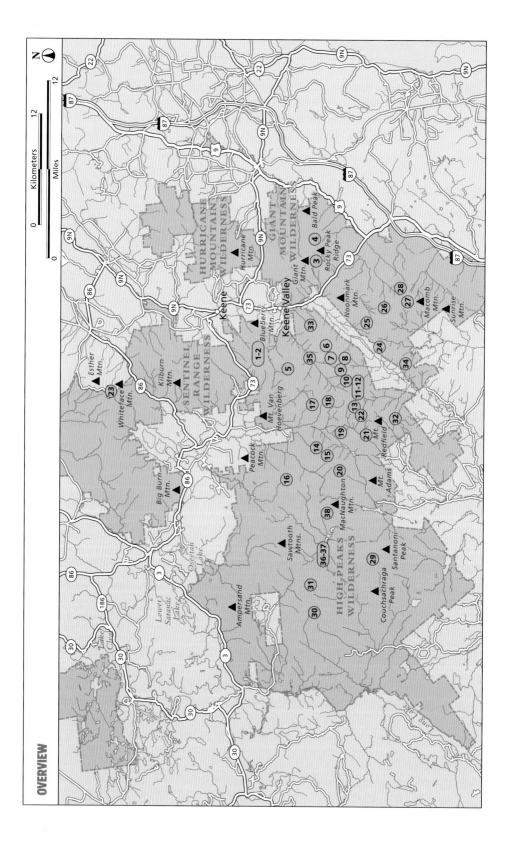

ACKNOWLEDGMENTS

I am deeply honored to present this guide, a culmination of my passion for the Adirondack High Peaks, and a reflection of the countless hours spent exploring their majestic beauty. This guide is as much a love letter to these peaks as it is a resource for you, the reader, in hopes that you too will come to cherish this remarkable place. My journey to creating this guide has been shaped by many influences. I am forever grateful to my parents for introducing me to this incredible region during my youth and fostering my love for adventure, the outdoors, and the pursuit of my passions. I also extend my gratitude to those who have come before me, inspiring and guiding me along the way. I must thank God for instilling in me the passion and desire to explore His magnificent creation, rejoice in His faithfulness, and share this love with others. It is through His grace that I have been granted this extraordinary opportunity.

Throughout my years of hiking in the Adirondacks, I have learned countless lessons. My hope is that this guide will serve as a distillation of those experiences, helping you avoid the mistakes I have made and ensuring your success in the backcountry. To those who have followed my journey for years, I extend my deepest appreciation for your continued support—you know who you are. Adirondack Park would not be the treasure it is today without the dedication of the pioneers who blazed the trails, the Adirondack Park Agency, the NYS DEC Rangers, the caretakers, volunteers, and stewards of this land. Their efforts have preserved this place as Forever Wild and ensured the protection of public lands.

During the creation of this guide, I found myself home in Ohio, studying music and worship at Cedarville University, taking a hiatus from the Adirondacks. Crafting this guide helped me maintain my connection to the region and kept my passion alive. There have been many sources that have helped me in the creation of this book as well, such as *Heaven Up-h'isted-ness!*, which was created by the 46ers, various Paul Smith's professors, several local historians, and some writings by Erik Schlimmer. It was my goal to make sure that all historical information in this book is as accurate and up-to-date as possible. By the time you read this, I hope to have returned to the Adirondacks, ready to continue my journey wherever it may lead. Should our paths cross on the trails, please do not hesitate to introduce yourself, as I genuinely enjoy meeting fellow hikers. In closing, I hope you find this guide to be an invaluable resource on your own Adirondack adventures.

—Jonathan

MEET YOUR GUIDE

Jonathan Zaharek, originally born in Ohio, was raised visiting the Adirondacks through frequent vacations during his early years. This connection with the park spans four generations. Jonathan made the permanent move to Lake Placid in 2019, allowing him to fully dedicate himself to his hiking and photographic career. Since 2019, he has endured many hiking feats within the High Peaks. He has traversed over 4,000 miles of the High Peaks Wilderness, accomplished eleven full rounds and three winter rounds of the 46, completed the entire High Peaks Wilderness Red Line in both summer and winter, undertaken the Bob Marshall Traverse solo in both summer and winter seasons, and notably covered twenty-five high peaks in a twenty-five-hour stretch. Jonathan has solidified his reputation as a professional photographer, guide, and YouTuber in the region. He has a notable digital presence on Instagram and YouTube by creating content designed to inform, motivate, and resonate with the Adirondack community. His written contributions can be found in such publications as *LOCALadk*, *Embark*, *Adirondack Life*, and *PEEKS Magazine*, while his photography is shown in the Lake Placid Center for the Arts at Gallery 46. For those eager to embark on a visual journey through the Adirondacks, you can keep up with Jonathan's adventures on Instagram and YouTube.

Jonathan on the summit of Porter.

INTRODUCTION

Welcome to the *Hiking the Adirondack 46 High Peaks* guidebook, your comprehensive companion for exploring the majestic Adirondack High Peaks. These mountains, nestled in the heart of New York's vast Adirondack Park, provide a unique and challenging experience for hikers seeking adventure in the Northeast. These peaks are undoubtedly some of the hardest, remote, and most beautiful mountains in the Lower 48. (I know that is a bold statement, but I believe this from experience.) The Adirondack High Peaks are steeped in history and tradition, with a legacy that spans many millennia. Over the years, more than 15,000 people have followed in the footsteps of the first 46ers, seeking to climb each peak and earn the coveted title of a 46er. But the true essence of this challenge lies not in the title or status it confers but in the opportunity to connect deeply with nature and to discover your own strengths and resilience.

As you traverse these rugged landscapes, climbing peaks that may vary in elevation but all offer breathtaking panoramas, you will undoubtedly develop a profound respect and love for these mountains as I have. The journeys to each summit will challenge you both physically and mentally, yet the rewards will be immense. From the awe-inspiring views from the Upper Great Range to the densely forested topped peaks of the Seward Range, you will find yourself transformed by the experience. This guidebook is designed to be your trusted companion on this journey, providing you with detailed descriptions of the routes to each of the forty-six high peaks, as well as essential information on maps, GPS coordinates, and resources. My aim is to ensure that you are well-prepared to tackle these mountains safely and confidently, armed with the knowledge and tools you need to make the most of your adventure.

Throughout your 46er journey, you will encounter a diverse range of terrain, from dense hardwood forests to alpine zones with flora and fauna reminiscent of more northerly climates. These mountains will test your endurance, skill, and determination, but the memories you forge along the way will be unforgettable. Whether you are hiking solo, with friends, with family, or even a dog, the shared experiences on these trails will create bonds that will last a lifetime.

Bear in mind that the true essence of this endeavor lies not in conquering the mountains themselves, but in overcoming yourself and limitations. These towering peaks stand unwavering and unyielding, embodying the power of nature and the indomitable spirit of human exploration and achievement. Your sojourn among these giants offers an opportunity for personal growth, a chance to broaden your horizons, push your boundaries, and cultivate a profound appreciation for the splendor of the natural world. As you embark on this adventure, my hope is that this guidebook ignites your curiosity and inspires you to break free from your comfort zone, fully immersing yourself in the wonders of the Adirondack High Peaks. Stay safe, cherish the journey, and hold dear the memories that will etch themselves into your heart and soul as you traverse these magnificent mountains.

WHAT ARE THE FORTY-SIX HIGH PEAKS AND 46ERS?

New York State is home to two very distinct locations in the United States. It is home to the largest city in the entire country as well as the largest park in the Lower 48. For a state to have both the densest population area and one of the most remote parks in the country is quite a dichotomy. New York is one of a kind. This "largest publicly protected area" is known as the Adirondack Mountains. It boasts a whopping 6.1 million acres—larger than Yellowstone, Grand Canyon, Glacier, Yosemite, Great Smoky, and Rocky Mountain National Parks combined and is larger than six other US states. It is huge.

Located in the heart of this park is a place well known and loved called the High Peaks. This area is the crown jewel of the Adirondacks—truly a one-of-a-kind place on earth. The Adirondack High Peaks consist of forty-two mountains that are 4,000 feet above sea level. A "high peak" is any mountain in this region that has an elevation of 4,000 feet or greater. Although these peaks have a low elevation when compared to some of the topography out west, they range from anywhere between 2,000 to 4,000 vertical feet of prominence. This is a higher hiking prominence than many 14ers in the Colorado Rockies. Now, you may be asking yourself "*Wait, I thought there were forty-six high peaks?*" That's correct, but many of the high peaks were first climbed before they were officially measured by the USGS. Some sub-4,000-foot peaks were erroneously considered to be above the 4,000-foot mark way back in the 1800s and were added to the list. Since the first 46ers, Herb Clark and Bob and George Marshall in 1925, these peaks ultimately remained on the list as tradition. These four sub-4,000-foot peaks (Cliff, Blake, Nye, and Couchsachraga) are the only sub-4,000-foot peaks on the entire Northeast 115 list of mountains. But despite this, we still love them and fully count them as high peaks. Over the course of your 46er journey, you'll meet these mountains. And just like tens of thousands of people before you, you will come to know and "love" these four peaks for their indistinguishable, lasting impact they will have on your "peaks I least enjoyed" list.

Climbing all forty-six of these high peaks has been on the hearts of many for over 100 years. The 46ers started in 1936, when Edward Hudowalski (#6) and Ernest Ryder (#7)

Aerial photo over the Great Range.

View of Colden (left) and Algonquin (right) from the Plains of Abraham on Adirondack Loj Road.

formed it. Back then, it was known as the Troy 46ers. Eventually it was recognized by the state of New York as the Adirondack 46ers in 1948. Since then, over 15,000 people have become 46ers. (I'd assume that you are hoping to become one, too!) However, for some, hiking these peaks is not about the title or status of the accomplishment—not that taking pride in the achievement is a bad thing. I believe it is respectable and understandable to hike all forty-six peaks and to not register as a 46er. At the end of the day, this is your own journey and should be used to develop *your* relationship with these peaks and *your* passion for the outdoors. I would encourage you to challenge yourself and find true love and connection to these mountains. If you look hard enough, you'll find it. And you may just fall in love and respect these mountains to the same degree as the explorers did hundreds of years ago. Remember why you hike. Remember that these mountains are not to be "conquered." They cannot be. They will only "let you" climb them. The only thing to be conquered is yourself and the journey. The mountains, at the end of the day, remain steadfast and immovable.

To learn more about the 46ers, visit www.adk46er.org.

LIST OF THE FORTY-SIX HIGH PEAKS BY ELEVATION

Rank	Mountain	Elevation (feet)	Rank	Mountain	Elevation (feet)
1	Marcy	5,344	7	Gray	4,840
2	Algonquin	5,114	8	Iroquois Peak	4,840
3	Haystack	4,960	9	Basin	4,827
4	Skylight	4,926	10	Gothics	4,736
5	Whiteface	4,867	11	Colden	4,714
6	Dix	4,857	12	Giant	4,627

Rank	Mountain	Elevation (feet)	Rank	Mountain	Elevation (feet)
13	Nippletop	4,620	30	Lower Wolfjaw	4,175
14	Santanoni	4,607	31	Street	4,166
15	Redfield	4,606	32	Phelps	4,161
16	Wright Peak	4,580	33	Donaldson	4,140
17	Saddleback	4,515	34	Seymour	4,120
18	Panther	4,442	35	Sawteeth	4,100
19	Tabletop	4,427	36	Cascade	4,098
20	Rocky Peak	4,420	37	South Dix	4,060
21	Macomb	4,405	38	Porter	4,059
22	Armstrong	4,400	39	Colvin	4,057
23	Hough	4,400	40	Emmons	4,040
24	Seward	4,361	41	Dial	4,020
25	Marshall	4,360	42	Grace Peak	4,012
26	Allen	4,340	43	Blake Peak	3,960
27	Big Slide	4,240	44	Cliff	3,960
28	Esther	4,240	45	Nye	3,895
29	Upper Wolfjaw	4,185	46	Couchsachraga	3,820

It should be noted that these elevations reflect the 1953 USGS map. Recent surveys have provided evidence that supports the superior accuracy of the contouring in the 1953 USGS series of topographic maps compared to the later 1979 metric series, which inaccurately portrayed a 4,000-foot contour on MacNaughton and many other peaks near this height.

A trail runner scrambling his way up Mount Haystack from Panther Gorge.

LIST OF NOT-SO-HIGH PEAKS: A CLOSER LOOK

The general rule of elevation in the Northeast is 200 feet of rise to determine a mountain. The Adirondack High Peaks list, which was established by Herb Clark, Bob and George Marshall in the early 1900s, created their own criteria prior to the current standards. Their custom criteria included a minimum elevation of 4,000 feet (and) a prominence rule of 300 feet rise on all sides (or) a distance rule of 0.75 miles away from neighboring mountains. However, several peaks on this list don't actually fulfill the criteria set by its creators. According to these guidelines, the following peaks do not qualify as high peaks:

Gray Peak (4,840 feet)—135 feet rise/0.65 mile

Wright Peak (4,580 feet)—280 feet rise/0.65 mile

Armstrong (4,400 feet)—161 feet rise/0.65 mile

Donaldson (4,140 feet)—171 feet rise/0.70 mile

South Dix (4,060 feet)—190 feet rise/0.60 mile

Blake Peak (3,960 feet)—Below 4,000 feet

Cliff (3,960 feet)—Below 4,000 feet

Nye (3,895 feet)—Below 4,000 feet

Couchsachraga (3,820 feet)—Below 4,000 feet

These Peaks DO make the cut, but only because of an equal to or greater distance of 0.75 mile from its neighboring peak:

Iroquois Peak (4,840 feet)—190 feet rise

Redfield (4,606 feet)—270 feet rise

Panther (4,442 feet)—276 feet rise

Upper Wolfjaw (4,185 feet)—260 feet rise

Phelps (4,161 feet)—190 feet rise

Emmons (4,040 feet)—135 feet rise

Dial (4,020 feet)—190 feet rise

The reasons behind including some of these peaks and excluding others are not entirely clear, but it seems that this is mainly due to too much assumed data. Russell Carson pushed for Gray Peak's inclusion because of his admiration for botanist Professor Asa Gray. Bob and George Marshall initially disagreed, but eventually conceded after further observations and discussions. Conversely, peaks like Little Marcy, Yard, Boundary, and an unnamed peak southwest of Redfield, which technically meet the criteria of distance while being above 4,000 feet, were not considered high peaks due to their perceived lack of historical importance.

Using the more general Northeast rule of 200 feet of rise, peaks such as Yard (next to Big Slide), Tabletop Middle Peak, and even MacNaughton, which is believed to be 4,000 feet but not considered a high peak, would be classified as high peaks. However, the Adirondack 46ers organization has decided to preserve the original list, despite the inconsistencies. With these inconsistencies in mind, it makes you wonder how peaks such as Green Mountain and McDonnel Mountain weren't considered at first.

It's worth mentioning that for most of these peaks, the trails do not start on the side with the sub-300-foot prominence marks. This means that hikers still need to ascend more than 300 vertical feet to reach the summit in most cases.

LIST OF THE THIRTEEN STEEPEST TRAILS IN THE HIGH PEAKS

This list of trails is in order of overall factors distance over vertical gain ratio. This is not necessarily in order of most difficult, but only the steepest overall grade of these hiking sections. Seymour Ascent and Lilian Brook Trail are tied for third, at 43.6%/23.6°.

#1 Macomb Slide (Macomb Mountain)
900ft/0.35 miles = 48.7%/26°

#2 Gothics Cable (Gothics)
500ft/0.2 miles = 47.3%/25.3°

#3 Seymour Ascent
1,030ft/0.45 miles = 43.6%/23.6°

#3 Lilian Brook Trail (Dix Range)
530ft/0.23 miles = 43.6%/23.6°

#4 Saddleback Cliffs (Saddleback Mountain)
220ft/0.10 miles = 41.62%/22.6°

#5 Haystack from Panther Gorge
1,050ft/0.50 miles = 39.7%/21.7°

#6 Allen Mountain Ascent
1,050ft/0.50 miles = 39.7%/21.7°

#7 Mount Colden South Side
1,200ft/0.60 miles = 37.8%/20.75°

#8 Dix via Round Pond (after slide)
1,500ft/0.75 miles = 37.8%/20.75°

#9 Nippletop from Elk Pass
1,100ft/0.6 miles = 34.5%/19.2°

#10 Elevator Shaft (Blake Peak)
1,400ft/0.8 miles = 33%/18.3°

#11 Whiteface via Connery Pond
1,700ft/1.0 miles = 32.2%/17.85°

#12 Boundary Peak Ascent
1,600ft/0.95 miles = 31.9%/17.7°

Hiker ascending the cliff section on Saddleback.

WEATHER AND SEASONS

One of my personal favorite attributes of the Adirondack High Peaks is the ever-changing weather and seasons. I believe these fluctuations add a unique and special charm to the mountains, making each visit a new adventure. Let's dive into the wild wonders of the High Peaks' weather and learn how to embrace the excitement it brings! Summer in the Adirondacks can be deceptive, with temperatures ranging from a chilly 20°F to a balmy 90°F. What's more, you might experience a high of 72°F and a low of 35°F all in a single day. Keep in mind that there's usually a 15-degree difference between the base and summit temperatures, so pack accordingly. Remember to consult multiple reliable sources for weather updates, and be prepared to dance to Mother Nature's tune.

Hiker ascending the Santanoni Express Trail in February.

While the High Peaks may not hold the record for the highest wind speeds, don't underestimate the gusts that sweep through these mountains. Winter winds can send chills below -100°F, while summer heat, sun exposure, and scarce water sources deep in the wilderness can quickly turn a hike into a life-threatening situation. The key to a safe and thrilling adventure lies in having the right gear (no cotton, please), knowing your body's limits, and being well-informed about the terrain and conditions. Each season in the Adirondacks is a beautiful performance, with the long, icy winters setting the stage for vibrant springs, lush summers, and awe-inspiring autumns adorned with vibrant foliage. As hikers, we get to be part of this spectacle, experiencing the unique challenges and rewards that each season offers, from snow-covered trails to verdant forests and colorful canopies.

Autumn and winter collide in October in the MacIntyre Range.

The Adirondack High Peaks' weather and seasons are a dynamic and captivating aspect of these mountains. To truly appreciate and enjoy their beauty, we must respect the mountains and adapt to their ever-changing conditions. Stay informed, be prepared, and immerse yourself in the High Peaks' seasonal wonders, forging unforgettable connections with the natural world and creating lasting memories in this extraordinary landscape.

SAFETY, GEAR, AND PREPARATION

The title says it all! When it comes to hiking the High Peaks, safety should be your top priority. With the right gear and preparation, you can ensure a memorable and enjoyable experience. This guide provides essential information on gear, attire, and important tips to keep you safe and sound in the great outdoors.

Suit Up for Success

Wearing proper gear and attire is crucial for a comfortable and safe hike. Opt for moisture-wicking synthetic fabrics that keep your skin dry and help regulate body temperature. Avoid cotton, as it retains moisture. Layered clothing is recommended, even in summer. Light-colored clothing makes it easier to spot ticks (although not common in the High Peaks), and waterproof, sturdy shoes or boots are a must. I also recommend mesh trail runners that wick fast and keep you light on your feet. Don't forget a watch or time-keeping device, and consider using trekking poles to reduce leg fatigue and joint pain. Remember that you get what you pay for. Investing in the right gear will not only make your outing more enjoyable, but safer. Your gear will also last longer when you invest in quality materials.

The Ten Hiking Essentials

Pack these essentials in a daypack for a safe and enjoyable experience:

- Navigation: map, compass, GPS system, and extra batteries
- Insulation/rain gear: waterproof/windproof jacket, hat, gloves, thermal undergarments, wool socks, goggles (winter), and face mask (winter)
- Light: headlamp, flashlight, lanterns, and extra batteries
- First aid supplies: use a premade kit or build your own
- Emergency kit: whistle, signal mirror, duct tape, pocketknife/multi-tool, bright colored cloth
- Fire: matches in a waterproof container, lighter, fire starters
- Nutrition: high-protein and high-calorie items, and extra food
- Water: at least 2 liters per person, carry more than you think you need and a water filtration or purifying system
- Sun and insect protection: sunglasses, sunscreen, hat, bug repellent, bug net
- Emergency shelter: tent, space blanket, tarp

Plan and Inform

Use maps, guides, or the Department of Environmental Conservation's (DEC) website to plan your trip. Leave trip plans with family or friends and update them with any changes. Be realistic about your fitness and skill level, and choose trails accordingly. Check the weather forecast and current conditions before setting out. Be aware of thunderstorms and take necessary precautions if one occurs. Weather conditions can affect your health; prevent hypothermia by staying warm and dry, and avoid heat exhaustion and heat stroke by wearing sunscreen, slowing your pace, and drinking water frequently. Hike in a group, pace your hike to the slowest person, and monitor conditions to know when to turn back. In case of emergencies, know what to do and be prepared. *Stick together and avoid splitting up* (which is a very common problem). At the trailhead or parking lot, conceal valuables, lock your vehicle, and sign trail registers. On the trail, drink water regularly, rest and snack occasionally, and keep track of time. Turn off

Two hikers near Haystack as the sun goes down.

cell phones or switch to "airplane mode" to conserve the battery. Remember that your phone should never be a primary safety or light device.

In Case of Emergency

If you're lost or injured, stay calm and assess your situation. Call DEC Dispatch (1-833-NYS-RANGERS/1-833-697-7264) if you have cell service or 911. If not, find a visible location for searchers. Prepare for survival by building a fire and shelter if necessary.

Hiking the High Peaks can be a thrilling and rewarding experience with the right gear, preparation, and safety measures. Follow these guidelines to make the most of your adventure while staying safe and enjoying the beauty of the High Peaks.

RULES AND REGULATIONS

It is *very* important to understand and adhere to the strict rules of the High Peaks. Things are different here than other places in the Northeast. The High Peaks Wilderness, covering 275,460 acres, is the largest wilderness area in New York State and the second-largest east of the Mississippi. As a protected area, it is essential for visitors to follow specific rules and regulations to ensure the preservation of its natural beauty and unique habitats. In 2018, the High Peaks Wilderness Complex Unit Management Plan proposed a series of changes, addressing rezoning and regulations by the DEC, which involved alterations to local regulations. The key changes included the renaming of the Eastern High Peaks to the Central High Peaks Zone, while the Western High Peaks and several new land acquisitions, such as the former Dix Mountain Wilderness, Boreas Ponds Tract, and MacIntyre East Tract, became the Outer High Peaks Zone. Additionally, bear canisters were changed to May 1 to October 31, instead of the previous April 1 to November 30 time frame. Lastly, the requirement for skis and snowshoes was updated to apply when there is 12 inches or more of snow off-trail, as opposed to the previous 8 inches. Keep in mind that these rules (as of 2023) have not been officially implemented, but they will be in the near future.

Please follow these guidelines when visiting the High Peaks Wilderness:

1. No campfires are allowed in the Central Zone of the High Peaks Wilderness.

2. Group size maximums: day trips, fifteen people; overnight trips, eight people.

3. No camping on summits or above 3,500 feet, except at lean-tos or designated sites.

4. Do not camp in areas with "No Camping" signs present.

5. Camp in designated sites whenever possible. If necessary, at-large camping must be at least 150 feet from any road, trail, water body, or waterway.

6. Bear canisters are required for all overnight campers in both the Central and Outer Zones of the High Peaks Wilderness between May 1 and October 31.

7. Carry out what you carry in. Dispose of waste properly and pack out all gear and garbage.

8. Dogs must be leashed at all times in the Central Zone. In the Outer Zone and Adirondack Canoe Route, dogs must be leashed at all trailheads, campsites, and above 4,000 feet. *Note:* Dogs are not allowed on Adirondack Mountain Reserve (AMR) property.

9. Bikes, drones, and ATVs are prohibited in all wilderness zones.

10. Skis and snowshoes are required to be worn when snow depths are at least 12 inches off trail.

11. Adirondack Mountain Reserve (AMR) Rules: Reservations are required for parking, daily access, and overnight access between May 1 and October 31. No camping, dogs, drones, or off-trail travel allowed on AMR property.

12. Adirondack Canoe Route: Overnight groups between nine and twelve people need to get a camping permit from the local forest ranger. Campfires are permitted in designated firepits.

Always check the Adirondack backcountry information for the High Peaks region for important general notices and updates before planning your trip. Please remember to practice Leave No Trace principles when recreating in the Adirondacks, and always be prepared with proper equipment, maps, and guides.

LEAVE NO TRACE: A CRUCIAL RESPONSIBILITY

Preserving nature is an essential responsibility that falls upon each of us when we venture into the outdoors, especially in places like the High Peaks. As we immerse ourselves in the beauty and serenity of this unique region, it's critical to understand the importance of leaving no trace behind. After all, the Adirondacks are a precious treasure, and our actions directly impact the landscape and the experiences of future hikers.

The Leave No Trace seven principles provide a valuable framework to ensure we minimize our impact on the environment while exploring the High Peaks. By following these guidelines, we can help preserve the region's natural beauty and biodiversity for generations to come.

WILDERNESS REGULATIONS

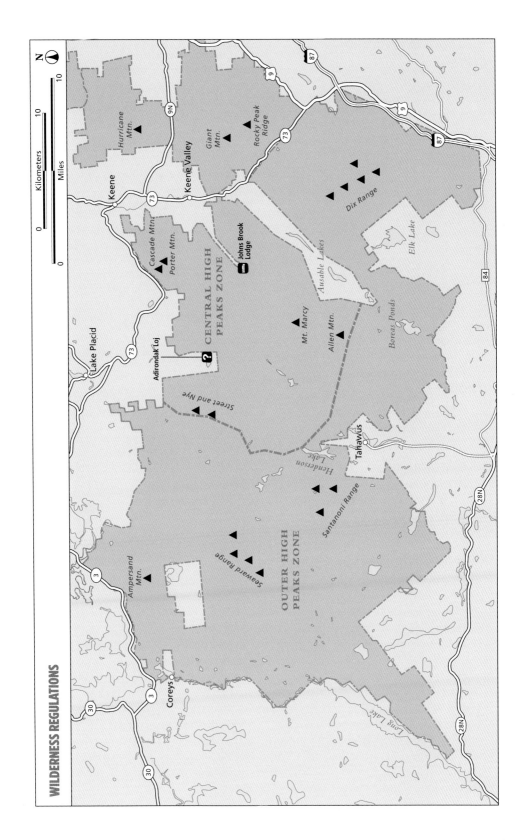

Hiker at Rainbow Falls in the fall season. DAVID WARD

Plan ahead and prepare: Research your destination and understand its regulations. Be ready for weather changes and emergencies. Aim to visit during off-peak times and keep your group small.

Travel and camp on durable surfaces: Stick to established trails and campsites, respecting delicate ecosystems. Always walk through mud or hop over rocks to avoid trail erosion.

Dispose of waste properly: Pack out all trash and litter. Dispose of human waste responsibly and use biodegradable soap when washing, scattering dishwater at least 150 feet from water sources.

Minimize campfire impacts: Use lightweight stoves and lanterns. If a campfire is necessary, ensure it meets DEC guidelines, using established fire rings and keeping fires small.

Leave what you find: Do not touch or remove any cultural, historical, or natural artifacts, and avoid introducing non-native species to the area.

Respect wildlife: Observe animals from a distance and never feed them, as this can harm their health and disrupt natural behaviors. Store food and trash securely, and control pets at all times.

Be considerate of other visitors: The Adirondacks are meant to be enjoyed by all, so it's essential to be respectful of other hikers. Yield to others on the trail, give space to fellow campers, and maintain a quiet presence to allow nature's sounds to prevail.

PUTTING THE WILD IN WILDERNESS

What is the essence of wildness? To better understand this, we must first distinguish between "wilderness" and "wildness." Wilderness, a concept that often generates division among people and the lands they inhabit, primarily refers to an area of unspoiled nature. In the Adirondacks, for instance, most of our forests are classified as wilderness. This designation can lead to conflicting beliefs, with people vying to preserve these areas according to their own convictions. Rather than fostering unity, the concept of wilderness can create discord. In contrast, wildness is a unifying force, transcending the divisiveness associated with wilderness. The primary difference between the two is that wilderness is a place, while wildness is a process. Wilderness involves demarcating and protecting public land, typically viewed as a positive, preservation-worthy act. In urban settings, people often advocate for zoning laws that allocate specific areas for biodiversity and human spiritual growth, and others for commercial development. They seek to limit human intrusion in order to encourage reflection on our relationship with the natural world and the ways in which we interact with it daily.

Wildness, however, encompasses more than wilderness. The term "wild" can also imply "will" or the willpower of a person or entity. Wilderness embodies a form of wildness, exemplified by its unyielding nature. Wildness is about renewal and restoration, signifying a mutual growth between humans and the landscapes they inhabit. It emphasizes living in harmony with the land, responding to its needs rather than solely imposing our will upon it. The focus is not only on maintaining nature but also nurturing it to flourish and regenerate. The distinction between wildness and wilderness is evident in the differing approaches of conservationists and environmentalists. Conservation, defined as the prudent management and official supervision of natural resources such as rivers and forests, contrasts with environmentalism, which advocates for the protection of air, water, plants, animals, and other natural resources from pollution and its effects. Both concepts share similar goals, yet their methodologies can sometimes diverge. In embracing the notion of wildness, we foster a deeper connection with the natural world, working in harmony to ensure its preservation and revitalization.

The stars in the High Peaks are incredible. The Milky Way as seen from Indian Head over Lower Ausable Lake.

Henry David Thoreau said it like this:

Today, wilderness is usually considered to be something good and in need of preservation.

The beauty and awesomeness of it dominates our attention.

We are attracted by wilderness, the Otherness of it, the sense it is something inevitably outside of us. To apprehend it, we cannot be naked enough.

But within Wildness is the preservation of the world.

HIKING TIPS AND SUGGESTIONS

Whether you are taking a stroll to Marcy Dam, or doing the Great Range Traverse, embarking on a hiking adventure in the High Peaks is a thrilling experience. These tips are just for your considerations, but highly suggested. Let's talk about footwear first. I know from experience that finding the right balance between comfort and support is essential. Some hikers opt for sturdy boots with ankle protection and rigid soles, while others prefer lighter shoes for increased maneuverability (such as myself). Whichever you choose, ensure you've tested them on shorter hikes before tackling more significant trails. Hiking with untested boots is a surefire way to end up with painful blisters. The less your skin and feet hurt in them, the better of a fit they are. Make sure you know your foot type, arch, and width. This can be a crucial understanding to your shoe selection. Toe socks are also key to clean feet and blister reduction.

Next are hiking poles. Let me straight up settle the debate. Hiking poles are not for the "weak and elderly" as some might assume is their primary usage. They are much more than that. As a strong advocate for hiking poles, I believe they can benefit every hiker. Poles distribute energy to your upper body, protect your knees on descents, and provide stability when crossing rivers or navigating uneven terrain, which is exactly what these trails are. What's more, modern poles are lightweight and easily collapsible, making them a convenient addition to your gear. I would highly recommend buying "Z" poles or a clamp lock. Do not get twist locks, as these are highly unreliable.

I have to confess, I'm a bit of a daredevil when it comes to drinking water from alpine streams. While I personally don't always filter, I have had some fantastic experiences with crystal-clear runoff. I'll never officially recommend doing the same. (Generally the cleaner water sources are not coming from a stagnant source where there are many contaminants possible.) Now, let's talk about alpine water sources. Stagnant water from alpine lakes should never be consumed unless properly filtered, as it can harbor harmful microorganisms. Some high alpine streams, on the other hand, may present surprisingly clean water. Even so, individual comfort levels vary, and legally, I'm obliged to advise you to bring a filter for your own safety. Just remember that although I've enjoyed my filter-free adventures, it's always better to play it safe and filter your water to ensure a healthy and enjoyable hiking experience.

Remember that time flexibility is key when it comes to hiking. Sometimes, things don't go according to plan, and that's okay. Embrace changes in weather or other unexpected situations as opportunities to explore new trails or activities in the area. Or simply save it for another day. With the wilderness offering such a diverse range of experiences, you're bound to find something enjoyable and safe. Don't underestimate the time it takes to complete a hike.

The full moon rising over the Sawtooth Mountains.

Lastly, if you end up using your smartphone's GPS capabilities for navigation, please be very careful. (Always have a physical map.) Pre-downloading maps and tracking your hike in airplane mode will conserve battery life. I can't emphasize enough how helpful it is to have a record of your route in case you get lost or find yourself hiking after dark. Again, the smartphone can most certainly be a helpful tool, but please take caution. Know where you're going and don't put your life into the hands of an unreliable piece of technology.

PHOTOGRAPHY TIPS AND TRICKS

As some of you may know, I'm a huge fan of photography. In fact, I do it for a living! It's the reason I started exploring the High Peaks in the first place. Over time, I've picked up numerous tips and tricks that I'm eager to share with you, regardless of your photographic experience or equipment. So, let's dive right in.

- **Embrace patience:** In photography, patience is crucial. Sometimes, you may need to wait for the perfect light or for the right subject to come into frame. Don't rush the process; instead, embrace the art of waiting and observing your surroundings, as this can lead to incredible shots. Remember, some of the most stunning images are captured when you least expect it, so stay alert and be ready to seize those unexpected moments.

- **Master light and camera settings:** Light is the essence of photography, and mastering it is a vital skill in outdoor photography. Understand how to use your camera's settings to capture the best possible exposure and avoid relying solely on auto mode. Familiarize yourself with aperture, shutter speed, and ISO, and practice adjusting these settings to achieve the desired effect in various lighting conditions. As you become more comfortable with your camera's controls, you'll be able to adapt to changing light conditions and capture stunning images no matter the circumstances.

- **Accessibility and gear:** A Cotton Carrier system is a fantastic way to keep your camera accessible during your hikes. This is a durable camera system that keeps your camera on your chest. With your camera at the ready, you won't miss any fleeting opportunities for stunning shots. Personally, I don't bring a tripod unless I'm taking night shots, but this is a personal preference. Assess your own needs and plan your gear accordingly. Don't forget essentials like extra batteries, memory cards, and a lens cloth to keep your equipment in top shape. Check out Cotton Carrier systems online and use my code (JonathanZaharek) for 10 percent off.

- **Seek out the extraordinary:** The High Peaks region never fails to present amazing photographic opportunities; it's up to you to be ready for them or to seek them out. My favorite subject is sunrises, and I highly recommend capturing them over sunsets. Sunrises often offer cleaner air and less atmospheric haze, which can result in more vibrant colors and sharper images. Moreover, I prefer starting my hikes in the dark rather than finishing in the dark, as it's easier to navigate and feels safer.

- **Composition and post-processing:** It's important to shoot in RAW format, as it allows you to capture more data and have greater flexibility in post-processing.

Jonathan taking landscape photos near the Flowed Lands.

Learn to use your scene effectively for composition, and experiment with techniques like the rule of thirds or leading lines to enhance the impact of your images. In post-processing, explore various editing tools to bring out the best in your photographs and truly convey the emotions and beauty of the scene.

Photography is a beautiful art form that, when done right, can convey powerful and evocative messages to others. By embracing these tips and honing your skills, you'll be well on your way to capturing breathtaking outdoor photographs that showcase the beauty and excitement of the High Peaks.

WEBSITES AND RESOURCES FOR WEATHER AND TRAIL CONDITIONS

"Know before you go." I've gathered a list of my favorite and most recommended websites and resources for weather and trail conditions in the High Peaks region. These sources have proven to be reliable and accurate, helping me plan my trips and stay safe on the trails.

Mountain Point Forecast: Not to be confused with "Mountain-Forecast," The Mountain Point Forecast is a highly accurate 36-hour weather forecast specifically for the High Peaks region. This resource, provided by the NOAA, is tailored to the unique conditions found in mountainous areas. Visit their website at https://www.weather.gov/btv/mountain.

Mountain-Forecast: Mountain-Forecast is a popular resource for high peak–specific weather forecasts. However, it should be noted that this website can have some inconsistencies with visibility and precipitation, but is overall a good source. It provides weather predictions for different elevations, which can be particularly helpful for hikers and climbers planning their trips. Check out their forecasts at https://www.mountain-forecast.com/.

My YouTube channel: My YouTube channel can be an excellent source of information on hiking conditions in the High Peaks area. I will sometimes provide frequent weekly updates and provide valuable insights into trail conditions, weather, and other important factors that hikers should be aware of: https://www.youtube.com/JonathanZaharek.

DEC Adirondack Backcountry Information: The New York State Department of Environmental Conservation (DEC) maintains a webpage dedicated to Adirondack backcountry information, including access, outdoor recreation infrastructure, and conditions. Visit their website at https://www.dec.ny.gov/outdoor/7865.html.

You can also sign up for weekly updates with the DEC for a DEC Adirondack Outdoor Recreation Bulletin found at https://www.dec.ny.gov/public/65855.html. You can also find the weekly ranger reports for rescues here as well.

These resources provide a comprehensive overview of weather and trail conditions for the High Peaks region. Always check multiple sources before heading out on a hike to ensure you have the most accurate and up-to-date information for a safe and enjoyable outdoor adventure.

MAPS, GPS, GUIDES, APPS, AND RESOURCES

While this guide offers a solid foundation for planning your Adirondack High Peaks hike, you'll undoubtedly need additional resources, such as topographic maps displaying trails and distances. To ensure a well-rounded hiking experience, you may also want to explore other books. In today's digital age, having access to online resources and maps is essential for any hiker. These tools not only aid in planning your trips but also offer valuable information to enhance your overall hiking experience.

Here are four excellent online resources for Adirondack High Peaks hiking:

AllTrails: AllTrails is a widely used app and website offering comprehensive trail information for Adirondack trails, including distance, elevation, difficulty, and user

The path up to Avalanche Lake is very rocky.

reviews. The app's offline map download feature ensures you have access to vital trail data even when out of cell service range. Even though this is the most popular, you should always cross reference the data on this site with another source for accuracy. Visit their website at https://www.alltrails.com/ or download the app to your smartphone. (Please note that this is only recommended for planning your hike, and not to be used as a primary navigation tool in the backcountry.)

Caltopo: For those interested in a more advanced customization to their maps, Caltopo is an invaluable resource. This online mapping tool lets users create tailor-made maps of the Adirondack region, featuring layers such as topographic lines, satellite imagery, and slope angle shading. Caltopo is especially helpful for back-country navigation and trip planning. Explore their website at https://caltopo .com/.

Natural Atlas: A hidden gem and another excellent online resource, Natural Atlas provides information on Adirondack trails, campgrounds, and other rare points of interest within the High Peaks region. Users can explore the area, create their own maps, and contribute to community-sourced data on this platform. Check out their website at https://naturalatlas.com/.

46 of 46 Podcast: For a more personal touch, visit the 46 of 46 Podcast website, which features the best Adirondack podcast channel and an e-book guide *From 1-to-46: A Complete Guide to Climbing the 46 High Peaks* by James Appleton. The podcast offers a docuseries that follows one local hiker's Adirondack adventures, complete with summit session conversations, Adirondack campfire stories, and more. Learn from James, a seasoned hiker and good friend, by visiting https://46of46.com/.

A view from the trailless peak TR Mountain in the Central High Peaks. Mount Marcy can be seen as well as Indian Falls to the left.

As far as maps go, I really can only endorse one:

> The Adirondack Mountain Club (ADK) High Peaks Trail Map is a highly recommended alternative to the National Geographic version due to its accuracy and consistent revisions. This waterproof and tear-resistant map encompasses the Lake Placid and High Peaks regions of Adirondack Park.

Before diving into GPS options, it's worth noting that some hikers prefer stand-alone GPS devices for their rugged construction and extended battery life. Personal locator devices like SPOT Gen 4 and Garmin InReach/Mini offer tracking capabilities and an emergency rescue button for those in distress. Garmin InReach even provides a screen for preloaded maps and satellite texting, but bear in mind that a subscription service is necessary.

In addition to maps and GPS devices, there is a wealth of books to expand your knowledge of the Adirondacks. *Heaven Up-h'isted-ness!* by the 46ers is a comprehensive history of the Adirondack 46ers club and the High Peaks.

Erik Schlimmer is another author with numerous historical books on the region. He is a Colorado-based disabled veteran, writer, and huge hiker. He has authored ten books on outdoor adventure, history, and exploration. Some of his ADK works include *History Inside the Blue Line, My Adirondacks,* and *Among the Cloud Splitters.*

Online communities can also be incredibly helpful for hikers. Facebook groups like Aspiring 46ers and Adirondack Backcountry Hikers provide a platform to connect with others, ask questions, and share experiences.

Hiring a professional guide can provide the necessary guidance, expertise, and reassurance you need to enjoy your experience. There are several reputable guiding services

A cloudy day at Marcy Dam with Mount Colden in the distance.

in the Adirondack region that cater to various interests and skill levels. Here are a few recommendations:

- Guide ADK: Guide ADK is an Adirondack-based service offering a wide range of outdoor experiences for visitors with different abilities. From hiking and camping to climbing, paddling, and winter sports, their professional guides will ensure your adventure is enjoyable and memorable. Explore their offerings at https://guideadk .com/.

- The Mountaineer: A renowned outdoor specialty store located in Keene Valley, New York, The Mountaineer offers not only a wide selection of high-quality mountaineering and outdoor equipment, but also professional guiding services to help visitors of all skill levels safely explore and experience the stunning Adirondack wilderness. Discover their guiding services at https://mountaineer .com/guides/.

- The Scenic Route Guiding Services, LLC: Guiding services that champions the philosophy that knowledge is an invaluable piece of gear on the trail. Dedicated not just to guiding you to the summit, but also instilling the skills and education essential for independent ventures, they emphasize the fun in research and preparation. Their offerings range from tranquil sunset treks to demanding ultras. Tailoring experiences, whether it's pursuing a hiking challenge, acquiring a patch, mastering outdoor skills, or seeking tranquility, they're poised to guide your journey: https://adventurewiththescenicroute.com/.

- High Peaks Mountain Guides: Established in 1983 by Karen and Brian Delaney, HPMG has helped lots of people discover the High Peaks Wilderness. Their team of guides is committed to providing exceptional service, education, and experiences while promoting environmental stewardship. Visit their website at https://www.hpmountainguides.com/.

- Your author: While my availability for guiding is limited, I am also an option for those seeking a guide. However, I recommend considering a full-time guiding service first to ensure the best possible experience. Reach out to me on my Instagram or website.

DRIVING, PARKING, AND TRAILHEADS

One thing about the backroads of the High Peaks region is that there are not many. In fact, there is only one main route that circumnavigates nearly 500,000 acres of wilderness that has no towns or roads. Within this region, you will find seventeen primarily used trailheads to access the forty-six high peaks:

- Adirondack Loj
- South Meadows
- The Klondike
- Mount Van Hoevenberg Center
- Marcy Field

- The Garden
- Rooster Comb
- AMR/St. Huberts
- Zander Scott
- East River

- Upper Works
- Coreys Road
- The ASRC for Whiteface
- Elk Lake/Clear Pond

- Giant Mountain East
- Santanoni Range
- Round Pond

There are certainly more trailheads that can be used for High Peaks access, but these are the most common. Unlike the White Mountains, there is not a universal pass for our trailheads, but some require payment or a permit/pass such as the Adirondack Loj (Lake Placid), the Garden (Keene Valley), or the Ausable Club (Keene Valley). Each trailhead, aside from the Ausable Club, is first-come, first-served on arrival.

The High Peaks trailheads are known for being packed. Infrastructure has been slowly growing over the years, but is still a concern with the millions of visitors each year to the region. Some trailheads, like the Adirondack Loj or AMR, have over seventy parking spots, while trailheads such as Round Pond and Elk Lake have less than twenty. Please plan accordingly when arriving at these locations. If you are parking at the Adirondack Loj or the Garden, bring cash to pay for parking. Generally, the busiest trailheads such as the Adirondack Loj, the Garden, and Elk Lake, fill up well before 7 a.m. on weekends. It is crucial to make smart choices when parking on the sides of roads. Please keep in mind traffic and where you are not allowed to park. Tickets are steep and your life is not worth saving 5 minutes of walking. Please park responsibly in the same way that you hike responsibly.

Adirondack Loj

The Loj sits on a private protected area of 706 acres owned and managed by Adirondack Mountain Club. Pronounced "Adirondack Lodge," the Loj is located on Heart Lake and was built in 1927. The Loj is the most popular trailhead for High Peaks recreators and is also home to many campsites and accommodations where hikers and tourists can come to "get away." It is beautiful and also has a new sister property in the former Cascade XC Ski Center on NY 73.

Although the Loj has many parking spots, it is not uncommon for parking to fill up before 6 a.m. on busy weekends. When overflow occurs, hikers are to park about a mile from the entrance starting at South Meadows Road and walk in. During overflow, cars can be backed up to 4 miles long on Adirondack Loj Road. During overflow, there is also a secondary parking place that you can hike into Marcy Dam from. This is at the end of South Meadows Road at the Klondike Notch Trailhead. From there, hikers can easily access the same areas as the Loj with only an added 0.5 miles via the Marcy Dam Truck Trail. Parking at the Loj starts at $15 for all-day parking, but members of the ADK Mountain Club can get $7 day passes or even a $50 annual parking pass.

Learn more at www.adk.org.

Adirondack Mountain Reserve/Ausable Club

The Adirondack Mountain Reserve (AMR) is a privately owned 7,000-acre land parcel in Keene Valley, New York, that allows for limited public access through a conservation easement agreement with DEC. This club was founded in 1887 and is there to preserve and protect the forests, lakes, mountains, and wildlife on the property. This trailhead is a High Peaks hub where hikers can enjoy hiking to places like Indian Head, the Lower

The old and rustic AMR gate for Lake Road.

Great Range, Colvin Range, and Nippletop. In 2021, the AMR implemented a free, first-come, first-served reservation system from May 1 through October 31 for parking, daily access, and overnight access to trailheads and trails on AMR property, and is not required at any other time of the year. If it is your goal to hike from this location, please check their website for all your other questions and RSVP information. Unlike all the other trailheads, dogs are not allowed on this property at all.

Please be respectful of this property and abide by their access guidelines as found on their website.

Learn more at www.hikeamr.org.

FLORA AND FAUNA

In the heart of New York State, the Adirondack High Peaks region presents a diverse and fascinating array of flora and fauna. This area is home to a multitude of ecosystems that support a wide variety of plant and animal species. Beginning in the lower elevations, mixed-hardwood forests are predominant, featuring sugar maple, yellow birch, and American beech trees. As you climb higher, you'll encounter the transition to coniferous boreal forests, where balsam fir and red spruce become more prevalent. Finally, reaching the highest elevations, you'll experience the rare alpine ecosystem, a unique environment characterized by dwarf shrubs, grasses, and sedges, with conditions more akin to those found in Arctic regions.

Among the mammals you may encounter during your exploration of the High Peaks, the white-tailed deer is perhaps the most commonly sighted at lower elevations. These graceful creatures can often be seen browsing on vegetation near the forest's edge or occasionally crossing roads and trails. Moose, although more elusive, can be found throughout the region, typically in mid-lower elevation forests. Like their counterparts in the White Mountains, moose in the Adirondack High

Labrador tea plant at Lake Colden.

Peaks are also grappling with the devastating effects of the moose tick, which has contributed to a significant decline in their population. Black bears are another prominent mammal in the area, and while sightings are rarer, it is crucial to be bear aware when hiking or camping. Ensure that you store your food in bear canisters to avoid attracting these curious creatures to your campsite. While generally nonaggressive, black bears can become dangerous if they feel threatened or if they perceive you as a risk to their young. Smaller mammals, such as the red squirrel, snowshoe hare, and North American porcupine, can also be observed throughout the High Peaks region. These animals, although less imposing than their larger counterparts, contribute to the complex ecosystem and are an essential part of the region's biodiversity.

Bird enthusiasts will not be disappointed either, as the area boasts a rich variety of avian species. You may spot wild turkeys roaming the forest, as well as the startlingly loud grouse, which can often cause a surprise as they burst from their hiding spots. Thrushes, nuthatches, and even birds of prey such as owls and hawks can be observed in the region, providing ample opportunities for birdwatching and photography. Insects and amphibians also have a strong presence in the Adirondack High Peaks. The region's ponds and marshy areas are home to frogs and brightly colored eastern newts in their juvenile red eft stage. Insect life abounds, including an array of butterfly species that add splashes of color to the landscape. However, it is essential to be prepared for less welcome insects, such as mosquitoes and black flies, which can be persistent nuisances during the warmer months.

The diverse plant life of the Adirondack High Peaks is a spectacle in itself. As you traverse the various ecosystems, you'll encounter numerous types of lichen, including the yellow map lichen, orange sunburst lichen, and target lichen, which grows in concentric rings. Old man's beard, a wiry branching lichen, can often be seen hanging from tree branches, while mosses, such as the bright

An eastern tiger swallowtail on some common milkweed.

green peat moss, cover the forest floor. Mushrooms and fungi are abundant throughout the region, and hundreds of flower species can be found, particularly in the alpine zones where they create a dazzling display of colors during certain times of the year. In the forests, springtime ushers in a spectacular array of blooms, with various trillium species taking center stage. These distinctive flowers are easily identifiable by their three large leaves and three brightly colored petals. If you're fortunate, you may also come across the rarer and strikingly beautiful jack-in-the-pulpit, with its hooded sheath, and the pink lady's slipper, a native orchid species. It's important to note that the delicate alpine flora of the Adirondack High Peaks is particularly vulnerable to human impact. Many of these plants have a limited growing season and can take years to recover if damaged. As you explore these environments, be sure to practice Leave No Trace principles, staying on designated trails and avoiding trampling on fragile vegetation. The Adirondack High Peaks region is a treasure trove of biodiversity, and its flora and fauna are an integral part of the area's appeal. As you journey through these diverse ecosystems, take the time to appreciate the intricate web of life that they support. From the smallest insects to the largest mammals, the plants and animals of the Adirondack High Peaks contribute to a rich and vibrant natural tapestry that is worth protecting and preserving for generations to come.

GEOLOGY

The Adirondack Mountains are truly a wonder to behold. Their unique circular dome structure sets them apart from other mountain ranges like the Rockies and the Appalachians. This massive dome, which is about 160 miles wide and 1 mile high, is actually made up of ancient rocks that have been molded into a relatively new formation. As a result, the Adirondacks are often referred to as "new mountains from old rocks." The geology of the Adirondacks has been profoundly influenced by the glaciers that once

The bottom of the Trap Dike opening at Lake Colden.

covered the region. When the Earth was cooler, the snow that fell during winter didn't entirely melt in the summer. Over time, the accumulated snow turned into ice, forming glaciers that eventually moved and shaped the landscape. As the glaciers advanced, they scraped soil and rocks from the ground, smoothing and sculpting the land as they went. In their wake, they left behind various geological formations, such as erratics—large rocks deposited in seemingly random places, which can be seen throughout the Adirondacks today. One of the most striking features of Adirondack geology is the presence of alpine glaciers. These smaller glaciers formed on the upper slopes of the mountains and left their mark on the landscape. For example, the distinctive summit of Whiteface Mountain was shaped by alpine glaciers that carved bowl-shaped amphitheaters, called cirques, into the rock. As the ice receded, it created a diverse range of landforms. Kettle holes and kettle ponds were formed when large chunks of ice broke off, eventually melting and leaving depressions in the ground (such as Lake Arnold, Avalanche Pass, and Chapel Pond). Eskers and kames were created by meltwater streams flowing within the glacier, leaving winding ridges and mounds of sediment in their wake.

The soils in the Adirondacks are quite young, having developed since the glaciers retreated. These soils are generally thin, sandy, and acidic, and they are often found in the forested areas. A combination of mineral and rock particles, decayed organic matter, live organisms, and space for air and water make up the soil, which provides an essential foundation for the region's abundant plant life. As the glaciers melted, they formed rivers, lakes, and ponds that are now an integral part of the Adirondacks. The region is dotted with thousands of these bodies of water, each with its own unique ecosystem. The rivers and streams in the Adirondacks serve as vital habitats for a wide range of fish and wildlife, as well as providing transportation and power for human activities. The Adirondacks offer a fascinating glimpse into the Earth's geological history. This beautiful region, with its rich geology and diverse ecosystems, is not only a testament to the power of nature but also a place of endless adventure and exploration.

HISTORY

The Adirondack Mountains have been home to various Native American peoples for millennia, with archaeological evidence demonstrating their presence dating back thousands of years. The more recent inhabitants included the Haudenosaunee, such as the Mohawk and Oneida, and Algonquin-speaking peoples like the Abenaki and Mahican. These indigenous communities relied on the abundant resources of the Adirondacks for hunting, fishing, and gathering. Caribou, deer, moose, and beaver were common game, and the lakes and rivers were rich with fish. A significant aspect of the Indigenous history in the Adirondacks is the probable existence of an intricate network of trails that connected settlements and facilitated trade. According to remaining Abenaki tribe locals within the region, they referred to the High Peaks, including Mount Marcy, as "White Mountains" for centuries. Indian Pass, a well-known feature in the High Peaks, was originally designated "The Great Adirondack Pass." Later, it was renamed "Indian Pass" by historians who sought to acknowledge the contributions of Native American tribes in the area. While it was once believed that only a limited number of tribes ventured deep into the Adirondacks as a whole, recent evidence has shown that Indigenous people indeed visited the High Peaks. The renaming, therefore, turned out to be more historically accurate than initially thought. This shift in understanding is part of a broader pattern that

Mount Haystack. From Upper Ausable Inlet, a 1880 lithograph by Verplanck Colvin and Weed, Parsons & Co., captures three guide boats, surrounded by lush forests and towering Mount Haystack. Featured in the "Report on a topographical survey of the Adirondack wilderness of New York," Plate 18.

reevaluates the involvement of Native American tribes within the park. Supporting this perspective, archaeologist Tim Messner's discovery of flint flakes near Lake Colden (over 2,700 feet) highlights the likelihood of Indigenous presence in higher elevations and throughout the area. Additionally, it is reasonable to assume that early Indigenous hunters followed caribou into these high elevations, as archaeological findings in North America's northwest region reveal ancient projectiles amid layers of caribou dung. Recent discoveries of old dugout canoes in the Adirondack uplands provide compelling evidence of Native American presence within the uplands region. Notably, two dugouts from Twin Ponds were crafted by Indigenous artisans using traditional techniques.

The larger canoe, up to five centuries old, is potentially the oldest known watercraft in the uplands area. Its substantial size and weight indicate long-term use at the site, challenging the notion that Indigenous people did not inhabit the Adirondack uplands. These findings shed light on the transportation methods employed by the region's early inhabitants and underscore the rich history of Native American presence in the area.

In the 1800s, the Adirondacks experienced significant changes due to the arrival of European settlers. The region's natural resources attracted loggers, miners, and trappers, leading to environmental degradation. Expansive forests filled with valuable timber attracted loggers and sawmills, leading to the rapid deforestation of the region. As a result, the logging industry significantly impacted the environment, wildlife, and local communities. In response, the New York State government established Adirondack Park in 1892, a pioneering conservation effort that covered the 6 million acres. This initiative set the stage for the creation of the Adirondack Park Agency in the 20th century. The Adirondacks saw a transformation into a popular vacation destination during the late 19th and early 20th centuries. Wealthy families built "Great Camps," such as Camp Pine Knot and Camp Santanoni, showcasing the area's rustic charm. The construction of the Adirondack Northway (I-87) in the 1960s further increased accessibility to the region, attracting tourists from far and wide. During the Great Depression (1929–1939), the Civilian Conservation Corps (CCC) played a significant role in improving the region's infrastructure. They constructed trails, bridges, and fire towers, many of which are still in use today.

As the park's popularity grew, the Adirondacks became a hub for winter sports, such as skiing and snowshoeing. The region hosted the Winter Olympics twice, in 1932 and 1980, which further increased its fame as a winter sports destination. The Adirondacks have experienced a rich and diverse history over the last 500 years. From the early Native American presence onward to the environmental challenges of the 1800s to the growth of tourism and the establishment of the Adirondack Park Agency, the region has evolved while retaining its commitment to conservation and natural beauty. Today, the Adirondacks stand as a testament to the enduring legacy of the Native American peoples who first called these mountains home and the importance of protecting the Adirondacks for future generations.

The stars as seen from Lake Jimmy.

An aerial view of the
Chubb River and Sawtooth
Mountains at sunset.

BEFORE YOU HIT THE TRAIL

As a fellow hiker who has experienced the challenges and rewards of these trails, I've crafted this guidebook to serve as a personal companion, designed to help you navigate and enjoy the Adirondack High Peaks to the fullest. This guidebook contains detailed information on thirty-two hikes, covering at least one route to each of the forty-six high peaks, along with seven extended traverses for a more challenging experience. The layout of this guide is based on the geography of the region and the hikes are not meant to be hiked in order. Each hike entry begins with an overview and hike specs providing essential information such as trailhead location, elevation gain, summit elevation, distance, difficulty level, approximate hiking time (moving time), and more. Keep in mind that difficulty is subjective, and my ratings are based on factors such as terrain, elevation change, and trail conditions. As you gain experience, you'll develop a better understanding of what different difficulty levels mean for you personally. Following the hike specs, the finding the trailhead section provides detailed driving directions and GPS coordinates for each trailhead, ensuring you start your journey on the right path. GPS coordinates are provided in the degrees, minutes, and seconds format (e.g., 44.14970°N / 73.76806°W). If your application requires decimal degrees (e.g., 41.40338, 2.17403), you may need to convert the coordinates using a free online GPS converter.

In the main section, **The Hike**, you'll find insights into the overall trail environment, including details about the terrain, recommended footwear, and any potential challenges you may encounter. This section is followed by **Miles and Directions**, turn-by-turn directions for the hike with key points and distances. A map is also included with each hike. Lastly, don't forget to explore the resources in the "Maps, GPS, Guides, Apps, and Resources" section of How to Use This Guide for additional tools and information to ensure a safe and unforgettable adventure. As you venture into the Adirondack High Peaks, I hope this guide serves as a trusted resource, offering guidance, encouragement, and insider knowledge to make your experience as enjoyable and fulfilling as possible. May it foster a deep appreciation for the cherished mountains we all love and admire.

MAP LEGEND

Municipal

≡(00)≡ Freeway/Interstate Highway

≡(000)≡ US Highway

≡(00)≡ State Road

═(00)═ County/Paved/Improved Road

───── Leader Line

Trails

------ Featured Trail

------ Trail or Fire Road

Water Features

◯ Body of Water

〜 River/Creek

≋ Waterfall

Land Management

National Park/Forest

State/County Park

Reservation Area

National Monument/
Wilderness Area

Symbols

✗ Airport

■ Building/Point of Interest

▲ Campground

▲ Campsite (backcountry)

× Elevation

⊟ Inn/Lodging

▲ Mountain/Peak

🄿 Parking

✕ Pass/Gap

🚻 Restroom

◧ Scenic View/Overlook

⛷ Ski Area

○ Town

① Trailhead

❓ Visitor/Information Center

CASCADE RANGE

Morning light on Cascade's Summit Ridge with Big Slide and the Great Range in the background.

1 CASCADE AND PORTER MOUNTAINS

Often recommended as the first mountains to hike of the forty-six, these two mountains do not fall short of an Adirondack high peak. These two peaks have recently gone under rerouting with a new trail but are still considered the most accessible and popularly hiked in the High Peaks. They still offer breathtaking views and wilderness, but with a challenge. Whether you are starting your journey as a 46er or simply looking to take your friends or family on an incredible hiking experience, this is the hike to do just that.

Start: Mount Van Hoevenberg Rec Center
Elevation gain: 3,300 feet
Summit elevation: Cascade Mountain, 4,098 feet; Porter Mountain, 4,058 feet
Distance: 12.9 miles
Difficulty: 4 out of 7, moderate
Hiking time: 5–7 hours
Seasons/schedule: This is good all year round but still may be considered for the summer and fall months.
Fees and permits: None
Canine compatibility: Great for dogs if they can handle the distance. They must be leashed.
Trail surface: Beautiful packed dirt and stone. Good for most outdoor footwear. The beautiful thing about this trail is the incredible new construction method used to build it. You just might fall in love with it.
Land status: Central High Peaks Wilderness
Nearest town: Lake Placid, NY
Water availability: Start with max water. There are few streams.

Amenities available: Mount Van Hoevenberg Rec Center and privy up high.
Maximum grade: 500 feet/0.7 miles: final stretch to Porter col
Special considerations: This guide is an unconventional approach to Cascade and Porter. In 2018, the NYSDEC underwent plans to create this new trail from the Mount Van Hoevenberg Rec Center (MVHC). It should be noted that when this guide is published in May 2024, this trail may or may not be completed yet. It will be open sometime in 2024–2025. Please check out the NYSDEC's website for up-to-date information regarding the status of the new trail. The old trail is to be closed and to become obsolete. Once the new trail is open, parking for the old trail will become limited, signage will be put in place, and the trail will begin deconstruction.
Sunrise or sunset: Both.
Route type: Out-and-back
Views: Both summits provide outstanding views in every direction.

FINDING THE TRAILHEAD

Mount Van Hoevenberg Rec Center is located on NY 73, 6.5 miles southeast of Lake Placid. Turn onto Bobsled Run Lane. Parking for hikers is at the end of this road on the left in Lot B. **GPS:** 44.21887°N / 73.92274°W

THE HIKE

Cascade Mountain gets its name from the infamous waterfall that flows into the Upper and Lower Cascade Lakes. This can be seen from NY 73 driving past the lakes. Cascade Mountain used to be part of the formerly known Sable Mountains, which included

A cloud inversion in October on Cascade Mountain.

Porter as well. The first ascent of this 4,098-foot peak can be attributed to Lon Pierce circa 1872, who supposedly set a bear trap on the summit, caught a bear, then later killed the bear. Although the first established trail for this mountain wasn't until after 1872, Lon and Charles Goff are known to be the first recorded individuals to climb this mountain nearly 80 years after the first recorded ascent of any high peak. To this day, these two mountains are the most sought-after high peaks.

This guide references two trails: the old trail and the new trail. As this guide is published amid the transition period between the closing of the old trail and the opening of the new trail, a brief summary of the old trail can be found under the Other Routes section. For today's hike, we start at the Mount Van Hoevenberg Rec Center (MVHC), nestled at the base of the bobsled run which hosted the 1932 and 1980 Olympics. Starting from the end of Lot B, head toward the rec center with the trail commencing behind this building. Yellow trail markers and signs guide you toward Mount Van Hoevenberg, paralleling the bobsled ramp, leading you to the official trail start. The trail continues along the Mount Van Hoevenberg route for 0.8 miles until a fork directs you toward Cascade and Porter to the left. From this point, the trail remains fairly consistent over the next 4.7 miles. After the fork, the trail gradually descends past High Notch and crosses the Mr. Van Ski Trail 0.5 miles later. The initial approach is gentle, with the terrain seeming more of a leisurely walk than a steep climb. The more challenging ascent begins approximately 2.7 miles from the start, also marking the halfway point. Another 2.7 miles later, you'll find yourself at the Porter col.

From here, it's 0.4 miles to the right to reach Porter, and 0.5 miles to the left to reach Cascade. Since you'll return via the same trail, you can choose either peak to start with. The trail between these two peaks is part of the old system and might appear more rugged, possibly muddy, rocky, and strewn with roots. Once you're done exploring the ridge, retrace your steps 5.5 miles back to the MVHC from the Porter col.

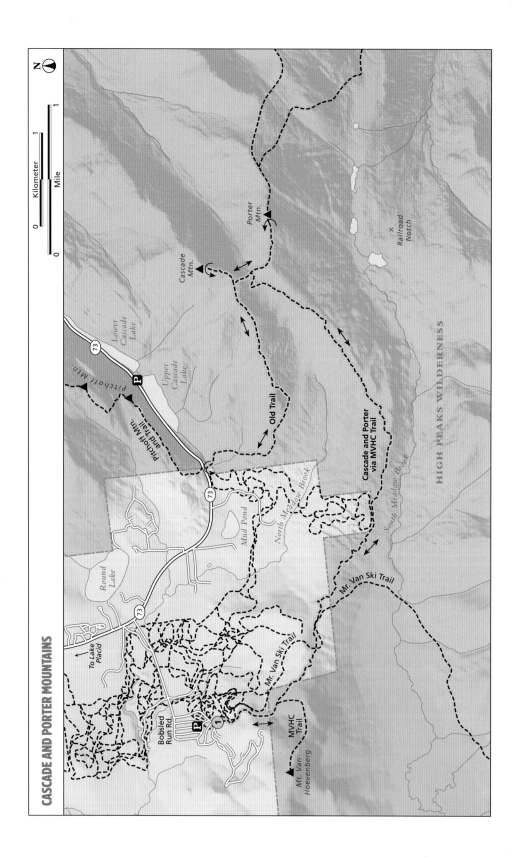

CASCADE AND PORTER MOUNTAINS

N

Kilometer

0   1

Mile

0   1

To Lake
Placid

Round
Lake

Pitchoff Mtn.

Lower
Cascade
Lake

Upper
Cascade
Lake

Pitchoff Mtn.
and Trail

73

73

73

73

Mud Pond

Bobsled Run Rd.

Cascade
Mtn.

Porter
Mtn.

Railroad
Notch

Old Trail

Cascade and Porter
via MVHC Trail

North Meadow Brook

South Meadow Brook

Mr. Van Ski Trail

Mr. Van Ski Trail

HIGH PEAKS WILDERNESS

Mt. Van Hoevenberg

MVHC Trail

MILES AND DIRECTIONS

0.0   Start at the trailhead sign-in located behind the MVHC.

0.8   Turn left at fork, following signs to Cascade and Porter Mountains.

1.3   Cross over the Mr. Van Ski Trail.

2.7   Begin gradually hiking steeper at the halfway point.

5.5   Reach the end of the "new trail" at the Porter col, turning right for Porter first.

5.9   Summit of Porter, return and head to Cascade.

6.6   Reach old intersection, turning right to Cascade.

6.9   Reach summit of Cascade, returning to the Porter col.

7.4   Return to Porter Col to descend back to the MVCH.

12.9 Arrive back at the MVHC.

OTHER ROUTES

OLD TRAIL VIA CASCADE LAKES—6.4 MILES, 2,400 FEET

This approach is only to be hiked if it is still open. This original/old trail is what used to be the main way up these mountains. Following its closure, the trail will become obsolete, blocked off, and will be deconstructed to begin its vital revegetation process. However, if it is still open, one can arrive at the Cascade Lakes across the street from the Pitchoff Trailhead to find the beginning of this hike. It is 2.3 miles from here to the summit of Cascade. The trail is highly eroded, rocky, and muddy.

2 PORTER MOUNTAIN FROM MARCY FIELD

This mountain is generally paired with Cascade Mountain. However, if you want to hike this mountain from a different approach and have an entirely different experience, then this is the way to do so! This alternate route up Porter Mountain is certainly not the most popular, but offers a wide range of trail diversity, views, and challenges. It is highly recommended to hike Porter this direction if you would like a challenge and a unique experience. Keep in mind that this is a more difficult approach to this mountain than the more popular route.

Start: Marcy Field via Blueberry Mountain Trail
Elevation gain: 3,700 feet
Summit elevation: 4,059 feet
Distance: 8.9 miles
Difficulty: 4 out of 7, moderate. Vertical feet over this shorter distance, mixed with many scrambles and less-used trails, makes this hike more difficult than other hikes with similar distance.
Hiking time: 6–7 hours
Seasons/schedule: This hike is best in June–Oct. It should be avoided in winter due to the infrequent foot travel.
Fees and permits: None
Canine compatibility: Okay for dogs. Leashed dogs are permitted; off-leash dogs permitted in some areas.
Trail surface: This trail is unmaintained.
Land status: Central High Peaks Wilderness

Nearest town: Keene Valley, NY
Water availability: There is one possible river source 1 mile in.
Amenities available: No privies.
Maximum grade: 1,200 feet/0.7 miles: ascent up to Blueberry Mountain
Special considerations: This trail is noted to be very wet at times and slippery. It is not used much and is definitely for the more experienced hiker. Not a first-time hike. Make sure you have good footwear because this is a very rugged and rocky trail. There are also not many places to refill water. Be prepared for a difficult but rewarding outing.
Sunrise or sunset: Neither for this approach (Blueberry Mountain for sunrise).
Route type: Out-and-back
Views: There are multiple 180-degree panoramic views along the way.

FINDING THE TRAILHEAD

Marcy Field trailhead is between Keene and Keene Valley, off NY 73 at the Marcy Field airstrip, 1.6 miles past The Mountaineer store. There is ample parking and it serves as the hub for the Garden Trailhead bus. **GPS:** 44.21844°N / 73.78994°W

THE HIKE

This trail is the gateway to Blueberry Mountain and Porter Mountain, but generally Blueberry Mountain is more commonly hiked via this approach. Formerly known as West Mountain in the 1800s, Porter Mountain was first summited in the summer of 1875 by Noah H. Porter Jr. and Ed Phelps. The name of this mountain was changed to Porter Mountain shortly after this first ascent. Russell Carson suggested to the town of

Keene Valley that the name be changed for this reason.

As noted multiple times, this is a difficult hike. This approach to Porter Mountain certainly is not for the faint of heart and is not suggested as a first high peak ascent. The reason for it being so difficult is due to its low starting elevation and sometimes challenging trail navigation. Even though this is one of the shortest high peaks on the list, Porter from this approach has over 3,500 feet of climbing. Most other mountains that have this much vertical gain are mountains within the top ten highest elevations in the region. So, it certainly can catch you off-guard if not prepared appropriately. This hike is comparable to hiking Algonquin Peak in the MacIntyre Range and Giant Mountain. To put it into perspective, this has nearly the same elevation gain as hiking Mount Marcy, but in just over half the distance.

Upon starting at the trailhead, you will find yourself walking on a very wide gravel path for about 100 yards. This gravel path

A crisp autumn morning overlooking railroad notch from the top of Porter Mountain.

takes you to other trails that have smaller loops on this lower ridge. After walking the gravel path for this short distance, you are met with a quick turnoff to the left. Generally, there is a small sign indicating Blueberry or Porter Mountain, but that can easily be missed. Once veering left onto this trail, you will briefly dip down and then slowly start making your way up a short but steep section to a smaller plateau.

After 0.5 miles from the trailhead, you are met with the real starting base of the mountain. From here, it will be nothing but uphill for 1.3 miles until Blueberry Mountain. Approximately 1 mile in, you will be met with a riverbed. At this riverbed, the trail crosses over and bears right. From this point, you will be met with one of two uphill crux sections. Over the next 0.7 miles you will climb 1,200 feet to the summit of Blueberry Mountain. Upon this 0.7-mile section, you will be met with beautiful forests and multiple exposed viewpoints. The summit of Blueberry Mountain has a gorgeous 10-foot-tall glacial erratic sitting right on top of it. You will know you have reached the top once you see this beautiful rock. When you have successfully reached this point, take a deep breath, eat some food, drink some water, and prepare yourself for the next half of your journey to the summit of Porter.

Carefully analyze the trail as at this moment you will be dipping downhill briefly. Look for the rock cairns and trail markers indicating the trail and start walking toward the next closest hill seen in the distance. Upon looking up to the ridge, you cannot quite see the true summit of Porter. It is hiding behind the farthest point visible, which is Porter Mountain's East Peak.

The summit of Porter from the summit of Cascade.

Navigating from here can be somewhat confusing at times but there are multiple trail indications to make sure that you stay on the path. Of course, this being a well-marked trail, keep an eye out for the trail disks on the trees marking where to navigate next. From Blueberry Mountain, you will drop approximately 100 feet into the col between the next ridge. After 0.2 miles, you will start ascending again until it flattens out for a short amount of time. Approximately 0.6 miles from Blueberry Mountain, you will be met with the second crux uphill section of the day. Over the course of the next 0.5 miles, you will climb approximately 700 feet. This will be the steepest and hardest section of the day. This section will consist of some scrambling, tree grabbing, and narrow trails. After this relentless 0.5-mile section, you will be 70 percent of the way to Porter Mountain!

At this point, you are 3,650 feet above sea level. You will also be at the summit of Porter's East Peak. From here, it is 1.4 miles to the summit of Porter. As you crest over Porter's East Peak, you will descend down about 100 feet and start ascending up to the next ridge. Most of the difficult climbing is over by this point. Over the course of the next 1 mile, you will be met with a few ups, a few downs, and some awesome views. Make sure to not lose the trail when stopping to see some of these views. About 0.25 miles after the East Peak, you will be met with a beautiful view out to the north. From here, you can see Cascade Mountain's rocky summit with Laramore Mountain just to the right and the Sentinel Range to the north, beyond Cascade. You can also see the remainder of the hike from this vantage point. Be careful not to lose the trail here as well.

Once you have reconnected to the trail, you will follow the ridge for another 0.75 miles where you will reach the intersection with the Little Porter Trail. Although there are multiple "trail closed" signs, the trail itself to Little Porter is not closed and is still an officially marked DEC trail. However, there is no trail exit from the Little Porter down to the Garden anymore, which is why it is closed. It is also in bad shape and not maintained

PORTER MOUNTAIN FROM MARCY FIELD

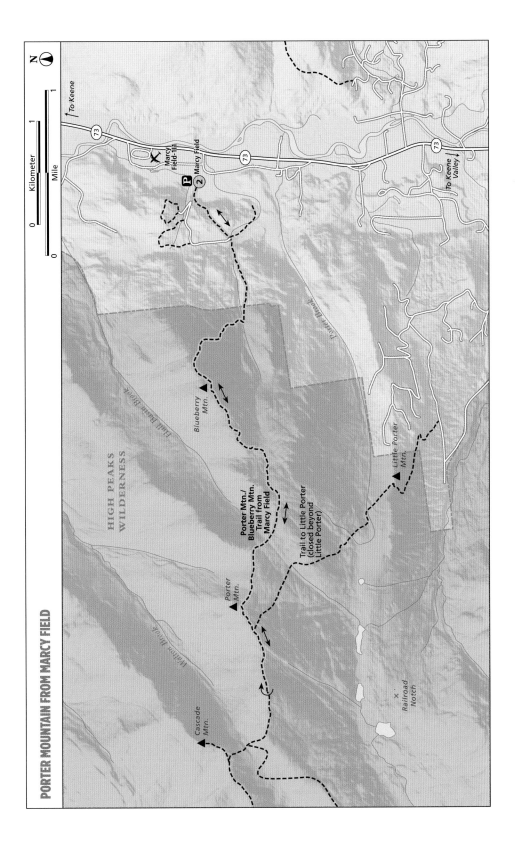

N

To Keene

Kilometer

Mile

73

To Keene

Marcy Field-HR

P

Marcy Field

2

73

Porter Brook

To Keene Valley

Hull Brook

Blueberry Mtn.

HIGH PEAKS WILDERNESS

Porter Mtn./ Blueberry Mtn. Trail from Marcy Field

Trail to Little Porter (closed beyond Little Porter)

Little Porter Mtn.

Porter Mtn.

Walton Brook

Cascade Mtn.

X Railroad Notch

73

A cloud inversion from Porter Mountain with Giant Mountain in the distance.

anymore. If one wishes to hike Little Porter, this will be the only way to legally access this peak. From this point, Porter is just another 0.4 miles ahead. This is a very windblown area, so definitely be careful of blowdown because this trail is not maintained very often. Upon arriving at the summit of Porter, you will be met with incredible 360-degree views and more than likely other hikers. The only way off this summit is to either continue straight toward Cascade or to backtrack the way you came up. Returning to your car will be done the exact same way as hiking up. (See the Bonus Hikes section if you want to add Cascade to this trip.)

MILES AND DIRECTIONS

- **0.0** Start at the Marcy Field trailhead walking on the gravel path for 100 yards.
- **0.05** Soon after the trailhead, turn left off the gravel path following the sign.
- **0.5** Continue straight as you approach another trail crossing, heading past a small stream to start the first ascent.
- **1.0** Trail turns sharp right, over a small stream. Begin first steep climb up to Blueberry.
- **1.6** Reach the top of Blueberry where the large glacial erratic lies.
- **2.5** Reach bottom of next crux ascent of trail up to Porter's East Peak. Hardest ascent of the day.
- **3.0** Reach high point of Porter's East Peak.
- **3.3** Great viewpoint to the north.
- **3.8** Reach "Trail Closed" intersection to the right for Little Porter. Continue straight.
- **4.4** Reach the summit of Porter Mountain. Return the way you came back to the trailhead.
- **8.9** Arrive back to Marcy Field trailhead.

GIANT MOUNTAIN WILDERNESS

Sunrise from Giant Mountain looking east toward Rocky Peak Ridge.

3 GIANT AND ROCKY PEAK RIDGE

Giant Mountain or historically Giant of the Valley is one of the more popular hikes of the forty-six. It is generally paired with Rocky Peak Ridge, however people commonly overlook that mountain, thinking that it is not one of the forty-six. This route to Giant is also the quickest and easiest way to tackle Rocky Peak Ridge. Alternatively, one can hike up to Giant via the Roaring Brook Trail to the west or the North Side Trail. The Ridge Trail is the most popular and offers the shortest, yet more exposed route up Giant.

Start: Giant Mountain Zander Scott Trailhead at Chapel Pond
Elevation gain: 4,400 feet
Summit elevation: Giant Mountain, 4,627 feet; Rocky Peak Ridge, 4,420 feet
Distance: 7.8 miles
Difficulty: 4 out of 7, moderate
Hiking time: 6–7 hours
Seasons/schedule: This hike is generally hiked in summer/fall.
Fees and permits: None
Canine compatibility: Dogs must be on leash. This trail may be challenging for dogs due to its steepness, exposure, and lack of water.
Trail surface: This trail is mostly exposed rock with some dirt sections.
Land status: Giant Mountain Wilderness
Nearest town: Keene Valley, NY
Water availability: There is little to no water, with one possible source near the beginning. Bring plenty of water (2.5 liters recommended).
Amenities available: Tent and privy sites at Wash Bowl with privy 1 mile from top.
Maximum grade: 1,000 feet/0.7 miles: ascent back up Giant
Special considerations: Make sure you have good footwear because this is very steep and rocky. There are also not many places to refill water, so bring lots of water on especially hot days. Trekking poles and sunglasses are highly recommended here. Be prepared for a difficult but rewarding outing.
Sunrise or sunset: The Giant Ridge Trail is great for first light. There is a good sunrise view from Rocky Peak Ridge intersection near Giant's summit.
Route type: Out-and-back
Views: The Ridge Trail has many views along the way. Giant's summit is 180°, and RPR is 270°.

FINDING THE TRAILHEAD

Zander Scott Trailhead is found across from Chapel Pond, 5 miles off I-87 exit 30 on NY 73. Limited parking available due to its popularity. **GPS:** 44.13864°N / 73.74400°W

THE HIKE

It's June 2, 1797. Charles C. Brodhead and his team of surveyors arrive near the summit of Giant Mountain with 2 feet of snow surrounding them. Yes . . . in June. This has been dubbed the first recorded ascent of any high peak, although there is speculation that there may have been unofficial ascents circa 1750. Brodhead approached this mountain from the east side. His duties were to mark the southern line of the Old Military Tract and would eventually bring him near present day Tabletop, over the MacIntyre Range, and ending toward Tupper Lake.

Autumn sunrise from Giant's Nubble looking up toward Giant with the direct Ridge Trail in view.

Unlike most trailheads, the start of this hike begins immediately from the road. Soon after passing the "Giant Mountain Wilderness" sign, you will be met with the sign-in box. Please make sure to sign in, as it protects you and keeps an accurate log of trail usage. After passing the sign-in, you'll quickly jaunt over a wooden walkway crossing a little stream. For the next 0.5 miles, it is nothing but trail markers and the winding path up and through the hardwood forest. During this half-mile section, it will gradually get steeper and steeper, so steep that you will come across an Adirondack rarity—something people out west call "switchbacks." After about eight turns or so, the trail will start straightening out and eventually cross two of the only water sources on your hike. Sometimes they are barren, and sometimes they are flowing with clean water.

After passing these two streams, the trail will continue upward and slowly start to top out at the Ridge Outlook above the Washbowl Cliffs. It is here you will get your first view of the surrounding valley, Chapel Pond, and other distant high peaks. After taking in the view, continue on the path for about 0.3 miles. This section will be relatively flat compared to the rest of the mountain. Soon after this viewpoint, you will be met with one of Giant's prized points of interest, Giant Washbowl. At this point you will find a trail sign pointing left to Roaring Brook Falls, or right, taking you toward Giant. You will continue to follow the path to the right as you cross a wooden bridge next to the Washbowl (a beautiful pond that offers great camping just off to the left). Eventually you'll be met with another sign 0.25 miles later. This sign will point left to Giant's Nubble, or right to Giant Mountain. The Nubble is an awesome viewpoint if you're looking to cut your trip short. This is a fantastic plan B. It's only about 0.3 miles following this turn. This sign also represents approximately the 1-mile point.

As you turn right to continue up the trail, you will be met with a very steep rocky and rooty section. Be very careful here, especially if there is ice. After scrambling past this section, you will be met with your first exposed part of the trail. There are discs on the trees, as well as yellow lines on the rock to keep hikers from walking off course. Over the next 0.5 miles, you will be weaving in and out of the trees and over exposed rock.

As you carefully follow the trail over the 0.5 miles, eventually you'll come to a turn. This quick turn used to be titled "Over the bump or around the bump." You will notice that there is debris covering the trail leading over the bump. It will force you left around the bump. You'll make your way around the bump and eventually continue on the trail for the next 0.25 miles. You will be met with another sign, which signifies 1 mile to the summit of Giant. This is also where the Roaring Brook Trail intersects with the main trail. A privy is located at this point. This is the last realistic bathroom spot. After this, you will briefly go up a steep section of trail to which will eventually start to flatten out.

Half a mile after this sign, you will eventually get your first view of the summit. Through the trees, you can make out the multiple eroded slides such as Eagle Slide and the Diagonal Slide. As you gaze at the summit above, continue moving forward. This is the last 0.3 miles to the summit. It will slowly start to get steeper and steeper and eventually turn into some scrambling. After this 0.3-mile section, just before you think you're at the top, you will be met with the last sign. This sign indicates Rocky Peak Ridge to the right, or the summit straight ahead. Make your way straight for 0.1 miles where you will be met with the summit of Giant Mountain.

As you gaze out to the mountains with the same view that Brodhead had, you can see Vermont and Schroon Lake to the left with the Dix Range prominently in front. Panning to the right, a majority of Central High Peaks Wilderness can be seen with Whiteface Mountain being to the far right and the Ausable Club In the valley below. After taking in the views, make your way back to the previous intersection sign. From here, this is where the real fun begins. Turn left making your way toward Rocky Peak Ridge. This sign indicates 1.2 miles. After heading down this trail for 2 minutes, you will be greeted with an incredible view of Rocky Peak Ridge and Vermont to the east. This is also an incredible spot to watch the sunrise. Here you will start to make your steep descent down into the col between. After 0.2 miles, you'll be met with a short 10-foot cliff. Descend this cliff looking to the right side where there are plenty of stiff branches to assist your way down. (At this point there is also a neat spur trail to view Giant's East Slide, which is considered the largest slide in the eastern United States.)

The trail descending between these two mountains is very, very steep. Be very careful in wet conditions. You will descend approximately 700 feet over 0.5 miles during this time. Once you reach the bottom, it will flatten out for approximately 100 feet before ascending up toward RPR. This side going up is much easier than the section you just hiked. You will make your way up for 0.5 miles. After this final push, you will be met with the exposed and beautiful 360-degree summit of Rocky Peak Ridge. The summit

An incredible panoramic view from the summit of Giant.

elevation is 4,420 feet. After this, you will turn back around and make your way toward Giant, carefully descending between the two. Keep in mind that going back up toward Giant will be the hardest part of the day. Take your time going up this section. After making it out and back successfully, be very careful on the descent back to the car.

MILES AND DIRECTIONS

0.0 Start at Zander Scott Trailhead.

0.4 Reach first sign of river. Follow and eventually cross over.

0.5 Arrive at the first viewpoint looking over Chapel Pond.

0.6 Reach Giant's Washbowl and intersection, turning right over the wood walkway.

1.0 Next sign indicating Giant's Nubble. Turn right up to the steep rocks and roots.

1.1 Reach first point of hike on exposed ridge rock. Continue following the yellow lines and trail markers for 0.7 miles.

1.7 Reach "The Bump," turning left at the debris around the bump.

1.9 Roaring Brook Trail intersects with Ridge Trail. Continue straight. Also the location of only privy on route.

2.7 Reach turning point for Rocky Peak Ridge. Pass this heading straight toward Giant's Summit.

2.8 Reach Giant's Summit.

2.9 Return to previous sign, turning left toward Rocky Peak Ridge.

3.0 Great viewpoint of Rocky Peak Ridge.

3.2 Reach small vertical drop down. Location of spur trail to Giant's East Slide.

3.4 Reach bottom of trail to RPR.

4.0 Reach summit of Rocky Peak Ridge. Return toward Giant.

4.6 Start hardest ascent back up to Giant.

5.1 Reach Giant's Ridge Trail. Return down the Ridge Trail to the trailhead the way you came.

7.8 Arrive back at the trailhead.

GIANT AND ROCKY PEAK RIDGE

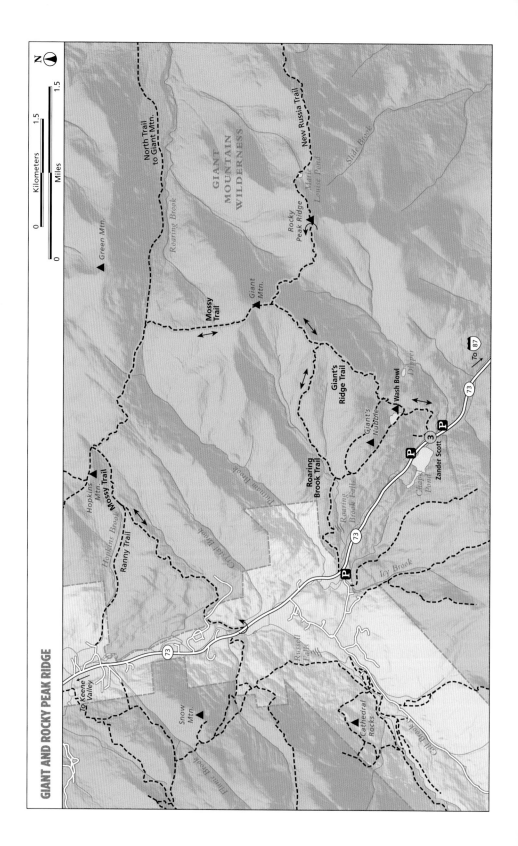

N

0   Kilometers   1.5

0   Miles   1.5

North Trail
to Giant Mtn.

Green Mtn.

Roaring Brook

GIANT
MOUNTAIN
WILDERNESS

New Russia Trail

Slide Brook

Mane
Louise Pond

Rocky
Peak Ridge

Mossy
Trail

Giant
Mtn.

Giant's
Ridge Trail

Dipper

Giant's
Nubble

Wash Bowl

87
To

73

3

P

P

Zander Scott

Hopkins
Mtn.

Mossy Trail

Ranny Trail

Hopkins Brook

Roaring
Brook Trail

Putnam Brook

Crystal Brook

Roaring
Brook Falls

Chapel
Pond

73

Icy Brook

73

To Keene
Valley

Snow
Mtn.

Russell
Falls

Cathedral
Rocks

Gill Brook

Fillun Brook

P

OTHER ROUTES

ROARING BROOK FALLS—7.7 MILES, 3,350 FEET

The Roaring Brook Falls Trail is a fantastic alternative to the Ridge Trail if there is not enough parking or you're seeking a different option. It's about 0.5 miles longer and offers many different environmental features as well. Go check out the awesome waterfall! The trailhead is right across the street from the AMR.

MOSSY CASCADE/HOPKINS MOUNTAIN LOOP—13 MILES, 5,000 FEET

This is the least recommended way to approach this mountain as it is the longest and most rugged. This trail takes you up to Hopkins Mountain, but eventually breaks right just before Hopkins to head toward the back side of Giant. This northside approach brings you in between Green Mountain (3,957 feet) and Giant Mountain. Out-and-back RPR, and then descend via the Roaring Brook Falls Trail, back down to NY 73, walking the road back to your car.

A bluebird winter day from the summit of Giant Mountain.

4 ROCKY PEAK RIDGE FROM NEW RUSSIA

One of the most unique traverses in Adirondack Park, the East Trail from New Russia to Rocky Peak Ridge offers a wide range of biodiversity and geographical features. Everything from exposed ridgelines and glacial erratics to a plethora of wild blueberries and lush alpine vegetation can be found along this route. This trail will take hikers on a tour that is worthy of being called an iconic Adirondack hike. This route certainly falls into the category of historical. Being the closest High Peaks trail to Elizabethtown might make it the historical gateway to the High Peaks.

Start: East Trail to Giant Mountain–Blueberry Cobbles
Elevation gain: 4,800 feet
Summit elevation: 4,420 feet
Distance: 12.8 miles
Difficulty: 5 out of 7, difficult
Hiking time: 8–10 hours
Seasons/schedule: This hike is generally hiked in summer/fall and is not recommended for winter.
Fees and permits: None
Canine compatibility: Dogs must be on leash. This trail is long but dog friendly.
Trail surface: This trail is mainly well-traveled dirt. More exposed rock up higher. A very nice trail.
Land status: Giant Mountain Wilderness
Nearest town: New Russia, NY
Water availability: There is little to no water on the entire trail. Heat exhaustion and dehydration is something to take seriously when tackling this hike, so make sure to bring more water than you usually take.
Amenities available: One campsite at Marie Louise Pond.
Maximum grade: 1,200 feet/1.3 miles: ascent up to Bald Peak

Special considerations: Be prepared for a hard day due to the nature of the trail. If done in full, this is a route for more for experienced hikers. There are few to no water sources, so bring lots of water. Avoid this hike on hot days. Trekking poles and sunglasses are highly recommended. Consider Blueberry Cobbles or Bald Mountain as an alternative for younger kids and family outings. This route can also be done as a traverse car to car over Giant Mountain. Read the end of "The Hike" section for more information. This trail is not recommended during rain or thunderstorms because it is very exposed to the elements. In the wintertime, this trail is not used much at all and would be a serious trail break through the snow. This is a marked and moderately maintained trail.
Sunrise or sunset: Blueberry Cobbles or Bald Peak would be preferred for sunrise via this trail.
Route type: Out-and-back (or traverse over Giant)
Views: Multiple treeless viewpoints along the way. Views galore!

FINDING THE TRAILHEAD

Giant Mountain East is located 5 miles south of Elizabethtown on US 9. Take exit 30 off the Northway (I-87), and head toward Elizabethtown. The trailhead is on your left after 5 miles. **GPS:** 44.14994°N / 73.62628°W

THE HIKE

The true origin of this mountain's name is still unknown. The toponym "Rocky Peak" was appearing on federal maps by 1894, well before the Great Fire of 1903. Charles Broadhead did not venture this route nor summit Rocky Peak Ridge during his 1797 endeavor (see Hike 3). The first trail cut circa 1880 was destroyed by the fire, and the trail we have today was not cut until 1968. The first ascent of this peak was done by two guides from New Russia in 1878.

With there being plenty of history behind this mountain, today it is well-known as one of the most unique and beautiful mountains of the forty-six despite its past.

There should be plenty of parking at the trailhead. The first 1.5 miles of trail is a very pleasant walk through hardwood and pine forests. You will start following a small stream about 0.6 miles in, only then to continue up the gradual path for another mile until you reach the first outlook just before Blueberry Cobbles. Once you reach the ridgeline of

Hiker standing on top of Rocky Peak Ridge.

Blueberry, you will be met with an intersection approximately 2.0 miles from the trailhead. Taking a left at this intersection will route you up to the summit of Blueberry adding on an extra 0.25 miles, or you bear to the right which keeps you from going up and over Blueberry, eliminating the extra elevation gain.

Either direction will eventually merge back onto the original East Trail route. Blueberry is one of two notable mountains you will hike over when getting to Rocky Peak Ridge, the other being Bald Peak. Once heading toward Bald Peak, this next 1.3-mile section will be rather steep, mixing in view spots and many S turns. There will be approximately 1,200 feet of climbing. Eventually you will reach the summit of Bald Peak. This will bring you just over 50 percent of your way to the summit of Rocky Peak Ridge. When looking to the west, you can see a large mountain in front of you which unfortunately is not Rocky Peak Ridge, but one of the leading ridgelines approximately 0.5 miles before the true summit.

As you leave Bald Peak, you will pass many beautiful features such as large glacial erratics. You will descend approximately 250 feet following this summit. After reaching the bottom of this descent (Dickerson Notch), you will start to climb your way up approximately a mile as you approach the East Peak ridgeline of Rocky Peak Ridge. This 1-mile section will take you approximately 1,100 feet of climbing. Eventually you will make it to the ridgeline which has beautiful flat trails in and out of exposed rock and forest. After 0.8 miles on this ridgeline, you will eventually come to Marie Louise Pond. This is one of the highest elevation alpine ponds in the park. It is a gorgeous spot and offers an incredible campsite as well at a very high elevation of 3,920 feet. This water is not potable and should be boiled for at least 10 minutes if needed for consumption.

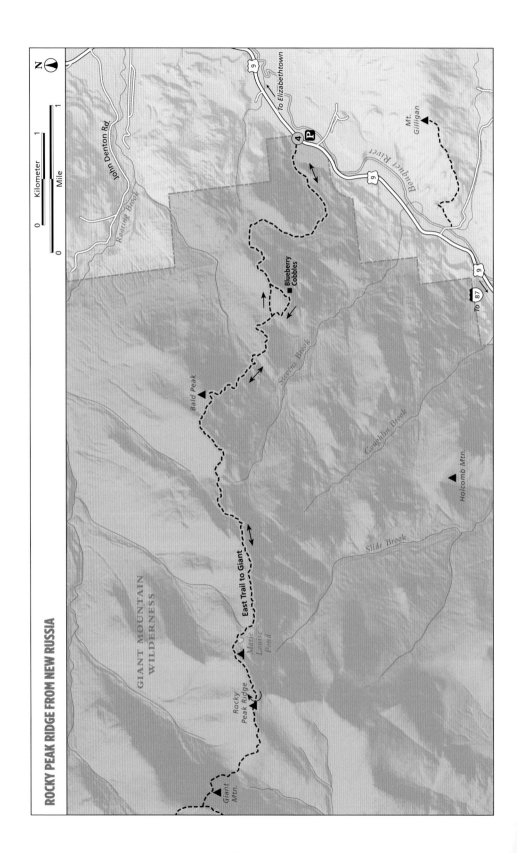

ROCKY PEAK RIDGE FROM NEW RUSSIA

N

Kilometer

0   1

Mile

0   1

John Denton Rd

Roaring Brook

To Elizabethtown

9

4 P

9

Bouquet River

Mt. Gilligan

9

To 87

Blueberry Cobbles

Stevens Brook

Coughlin Brook

Holcomb Mtn.

Slide Brook

Bald Peak

GIANT MOUNTAIN WILDERNESS

East Trail to Giant

Marie Louise Pond

Rocky Peak Ridge

Giant Mtn.

When passing this pond, you will walk over a wooden walkway circumnavigating the outside of the pond. The summit of Rocky Peak Ridge can be seen in the distance. With only 0.5 miles to go, you will continue up the beautiful exposed rocky ridge. The summit is indicated by a large stack of rocks. Arriving at the summit, you can clearly see Giant Mountain to the west, a majority of the High Peaks to the south, and Canada and Vermont to the north and east.

MILES AND DIRECTIONS

- **0.0** Start at trailhead for Giant via East Trail/Blueberry Mountain.
- **0.1** Start uphill travel.
- **0.6** Cross a small stream that parallels the trail.
- **1.6** Reach first viewpoint.
- **2.0** Reach trail split for Blueberry or to avoid Blueberry.
- **2.6** Reach Mason Mountain bump. Head downhill to only then go up steeply toward Bald Peak.
- **3.8** Reach Bald Peak Summit.
- **4.2** Reach Dickerson Notch at the base of hardest ascent to RPR East Peak shoulder.
- **5.6** Reach Marie Louise Pond.
- **6.4** Rocky Peak Ridge Summit. From here, either return the 6.4 miles back the same way, or continue the traverse to Giant Mountain, 4 miles to trailhead.
- **12.8** Arrive back at the Giant via East Trail/Blueberry Mountain Trailhead.

OTHER ROUTES

NEW RUSSIA TRAVERSE—9.4 MILES, 4,500 FEET

This hike can also be done as a traverse, car to car, from New Russia to Giant's main trailhead going up and over Giant Mountain. It is common for people to do this option and leave a car at both ends of the trailhead. This is also a time-saver and may be recommended instead of doing Rocky Peak Ridge as an out-and-back of the entire New Russia Trail. This will save approximately 2.4 miles of hiking.

BIG SLIDE

View from a near summit
vantage point on Big Slide.

5 BIG SLIDE MOUNTAIN

This mountain is one of three mountains in the High Peaks that stands by itself, with no immediate neighboring peaks. It is recommended that it be hiked by itself. Big Slide is certainly a fan favorite for its ease of accessibility and its famous "Brothers" route. This is a much easier high peak than most and is certainly high up there in beauty. Big Slide is great for a first-time High Peak hike and has multiple approaches.

Start: The Garden Trailhead
Elevation gain: 3,200 feet
Summit elevation: 4,240 feet
Distance: 9.6 miles
Difficulty: 3 out of 7, moderate. Vertical feet over this shorter distance and exposed ridges make this a moderately challenging hike.
Hiking time: 6–7 hours
Seasons/schedule: All seasons. This hike is generally hiked in summer/fall, but depending on conditions it can also be a great winter hiking experience with proper gear.
Fees and permits: $10 parking fee at parking lot for town of Keene Valley
Canine compatibility: Dogs must be on leash.
Trail surface: This trail is well trafficked. Mixed rock and dirt surfaces.
Land status: Central High Peaks Wilderness
Nearest town: Keene Valley, NY
Water availability: There are no water sources while on the Brothers Trail. Water can be accessed on Big Slide Brook and at Johns Brook Lodge.
Amenities available: Johns Brook Lodge (for guests) and public privies.
Maximum grade: 1,100 feet/0.9 miles: the approach to the First Brother
Special considerations: It is recommended to hike this route counterclockwise. Due to the exposed rock of The Brothers, it is highly recommended to consider good footwear and to avoid this route if it is raining. This trail is moderately technical with hands-on spots around the First and Second Brother. Parking can be very limited at this parking location. This hike is also exceptionally beautiful when done on a clear day, so bring a camera!
Sunrise or sunset: The Brothers Trail makes this mountain great for sunrise.
Route type: Loop or out-and-back
Views: Multiple 270-degree panoramic views along the way

FINDING THE TRAILHEAD

Follow Adirondack Street next to Ausable Inn for about a mile, turning right onto Johns Brook Lane. Parking limited; additional parking available on the street in Keene Valley. Weekdays are generally not full prior to 9 a.m. but can be full before 6 a.m. on weekends. **GPS:** 44.18911°N / 73.81561°W

THE HIKE

While standing upon the summits of these mountains, you may have noticed many bare rock landslides blanketing the surrounding peaks. These are known as "slides." These "slides" are a common sight throughout the region, and it's from one such event that Big Slide derives its name. In contrast to earlier assumptions, this mountain wasn't named for its pointed shape or the rock crown at its summit. Instead, it was named after a significant

Hiker ascending on the "Brothers" route on Big Slide.

landslide in September 1856. Otis Estes, a resident of Keene Valley at the time, observed the aftermath of this dramatic geological event and named the mountain accordingly. Big Slide's first summit was in 1812 by John Richards, making this the third oldest recorded high peak first ascent.

Upon reaching the trailhead, you'll locate the trailhead registry at the parking lot's end. After signing in, you're met with a trail fork. Head right to take the "Brothers" route toward Big Slide. The initial trail, around 0.5 miles, is strewn with small rocks and roots, proceeding uphill. You'll then veer left, crossing a small stream, before confronting a significantly steeper incline, leading to some large rocks with minor scrambles.

The first viewpoint is roughly 1 mile in, a half mile from the First Brother. More steep sections and rock scrambles follow. At 1.5 miles, you reach the First Brother, with the Second and Third Brother visible in the distance. You'll carefully descend and ascend between the Brothers, navigating minor scrambles and choosing your path around rocky sections wisely, guided by yellow lines. Another 0.25 miles bring you to the Second Brother, offering views of the entire Ausable Valley. After another 0.5 miles, you'll start the steep 0.25-mile climb, around 300 feet, up the Third Brother. The summit of the Third Brother, reached after about 2.5 miles, is at 3,700 feet. Beyond the Third Brother, the trail descends for 0.6 miles, presenting muddy spots and wooden planks before arriving at Slide Brook. The trail then heads uphill toward the summit, 0.5 miles away. At the trail intersection, turn right toward Big Slide. The steep, technical final 0.25-mile ascent includes a ladder that you can either climb or bypass by hugging the right side of the rock. This leads to a ledge offering a remarkable view of the Great Range and the face of Big Slide, which is a perfect photo spot. The summit is reached by continuing past the viewpoint and scrambling a short distance. From the summit, you'll marvel at the panoramic view of the Great Range, extending from Giant to Marcy and parts of Colden, with Nippletop and the Dix Range in the distance. You then carefully backtrack for 0.25 miles to the previous trail intersection, where you can either return the way you came or continue the loop. If continuing, follow the red markers straight down for a steep, rocky 2.4-mile descent into Johns Brook Valley, which is a more rugged route than the ascent.

After the first of many river crossings 1.2 miles in, the trail becomes less steep. Carefully navigate these crossings, checking for trail markers or rock cairns on the other side. Eventually, you reach the bottom to meet the Phelps Trail. You have the option to turn right to the Johns Brook Lodge for a brief visit and water refill, or left to return to the

BIG SLIDE MOUNTAIN

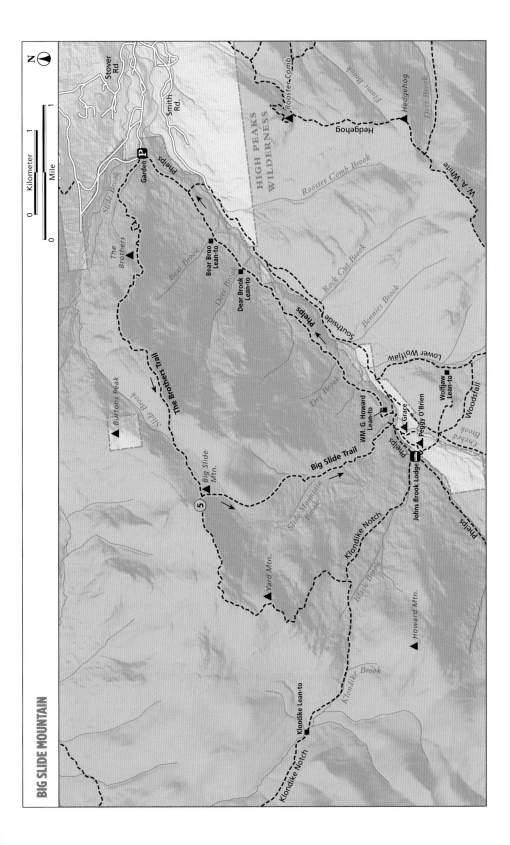

car, 3.1 miles away. At the next sign-in box, continue uphill without signing in, passing Howard lean-to, and bear right.

From here, the trail is quite straightforward with more river crossings, wooden bridges, and hemlock forests. About 0.5 miles from the car, you'll see a sign pointing toward the Garden Trailhead or the closed South Side Trail. Head left for the final 0.5 miles back to the Garden Trailhead.

MILES AND DIRECTIONS

0.0   Start at the Garden Trailhead for The Brothers up Big Slide.

0.5   Cross small river, starting steeper ascent.

1.0   Reach first viewpoint.

1.5   Top of First Brother.

1.8   Reach Second Brother.

2.5   Top of Third Brother.

3.1   Cross Slide Brook.

3.5   Trail intersection for Big Slide or valley descent.

3.8   Top out on the summit of Big Slide.

4.1   Intersection of Brothers trail or descent into Johns Brook Valley.

5.2   First river crossing on the way down.

6.5   Bottom out onto Phelps Trail, turning left.

9.1   Reach half-mile sign to the Garden Trailhead.

9.6   Arrive at Garden Trailhead.

OTHER ROUTES

BIG SLIDE VIA THE KLONDIKE—12.5 MILES, 2,800 FEET

This trail to Big Slide is certainly the least traveled and most rugged approach to this mountain. In fact, many people are unaware of this route. This route starts at the South Meadows Trailhead on Adirondack Loj Road. Take South Meadows dirt road all the way to the end as if you were hiking the Marcy Dam Truck Trail. The very end of this road is the Klondike/South Meadows parking area. From here, you can take the Klondike Notch Trail 4 miles until you reach the Yard Mountain Trail up Big Slide. This is a great way to experience the road less traveled or to go on some lesser-hiked trails. The Klondike Notch Lean-to is also a great spot to take a trip to.

LOWER GREAT RANGE

Lower Great Range from descending Basin Mountain.

6 UPPER AND LOWER WOLFJAW MOUNTAINS

People will generally pair these two mountains with the rest of the Lower Great Range. However, for an easier day, one may consider hiking these two peaks together as one hike. These two mountains are not the most spectacular peaks, and they are not among the most hiked or recommended. They are generally reserved for those hiking the whole range or for the whole forty-six. They also offer unique forest ridgelines and diverse technical features. These two peaks are great for those looking to break away from the typical alpine summit peak but still get some views.

Start: Adirondack Mountain Reserve (AMR)/Ausable Club/St. Huberts
Elevation gain: 3,900 feet
Summit elevation: Upper Wolfjaw, 4,185 feet; Lower Wolfjaw, 4,175 feet
Distance: 11.2 miles
Difficulty: 4 out of 7, moderate. Terrain overall is very steep and has many challenges.
Hiking time: 7–9 hours
Seasons/schedule: All seasons. This hike is generally hiked in summer/fall, but depending on conditions it can also be a great winter hiking experience with proper gear. This would be a more challenging winter climb.
Fees and permits: Free reservation required for parking at the AMR May–Oct.
Canine compatibility: Dogs are not allowed, but they can be taken if this is hiked from the Garden Trailhead.
Trail surface: This trail is well trafficked. Mixed rock and dirt surfaces with scrambling up high.
Land status: AMR property/Central High Peaks Wilderness
Nearest town: Keene Valley, NY
Water availability: There are rivers down low but no water sources higher up.

Amenities available: Wedge Brook campsite at 2,700 feet.
Maximum grade: 500 feet/0.3 miles: going up Upper Wolfjaw
Special considerations: Trekking poles are recommended here and on every hike in this book. If you do not own any, I highly suggest buying a pair. This trail has some very steep sections. This route is certainly for the more seasoned hiker. Do Upper Wolfjaw first. Lower Wolfjaw is much easier to hike, and I always recommend getting the hard one out of the way first. The trail between the two mountains is rugged, windblown, and steep. There are plenty of roots and rocks to grab. This is a marked and moderately maintained trail.
Sunrise or sunset: Neither of these peaks should be done at night, but Upper Wolfjaw would have an incredible sunrise if you're up for the challenge. (Hike responsibly!)
Route type: Out-and-back
Views: Multiple 180-degree panoramic views on Upper Wolfjaw, but few views on Lower Wolfjaw

FINDING THE TRAILHEAD

The AMR/St. Huberts Trailhead is right across the street from Roaring Brook Falls Trailhead for Giant, labeled as St. Huberts Parking Area or the Adirondack Mountain Reserve. Approximately 7.5 miles from I-87. Reservations are needed May–October. **GPS:** 44.14970°N / 73.76806°W

THE HIKE

These two not very distinct peaks are nestled at the end of the Lower Great Range. It's not uncommon for people to hike either one of these mountains separately or together as a day hike. They're more commonly paired with Armstrong and Gothics. This entire hike would be known as the Lower Great Range Loop. However, some may find that combination too challenging and seek to separate these two mountains from the others. If you're a strong hiker, I would suggest doing the complete Lower Great Range Loop, but for those seeking an easier trip, this is a good option.

According to topographic history, these two mountains were once regarded as one. Verplanck Colvin is credited with calling them the Wolfjaws. It wasn't until 1895 that the USGS listed these peaks as two separate mountains. The Wolfjaws can be hiked from the Garden, Rooster Comb, or the AMR. When arriving at the AMR parking lot, you'll start walking up the gravel road connected to it, taking you uphill past the golf course, eventually turning left at the tennis courts. This will take you down a short, paved road to the sign-in and a big AMR gate. If this is your first time arriving at this spot, you will eventually become well acquainted with this property over the journey of your forty-six. This gravel road leads to many other incredible locations such as Indian Head, Rainbow Falls, Nippletop, and the Colvin Range. As you walk past the wooden gate, the road extends 3.5 miles, but you will only be on it for a mile. After a short, roughly 20-minute walk, you will be met with a wooden bridge on your right. This wooden bridge will have a sign indicating the Wolfjaws. Turn right at this bridge. For 0.1 miles, this path will eventually lead you deeper into the forest, crossing over the East Trail intersection. Continue straight at this intersection. This trail will start to slowly bear left and after 0.25 miles will bring you down to the Ausable River. This beautiful bridge will lead you across to a short but steep embankment on the other side.

This next section of trail will have you travel 0.7 miles and climb around 300 feet. At the end of the 0.7 miles, you will be met with another trail intersection at Wedge Brook

A partial view through the trees from the summit of Lower Wolfjaw.

Falls. This is a nice, beautiful little waterfall. I suggest taking a second to go check it out. Turn right at this intersection, following the cascading river uphill. Over the course of the next 1 mile, you will ascend roughly 1,000 feet, with the first half mile being steeper than the second. Eventually, you will bear left away from this river and the trail becomes surrounded by wide-open, steep hardwood forest for the next mile. After this mile, you will arrive at the Wedge Brook campsite. This campsite is at the 2,800-foot elevation mark. This is where you'll set up camp if you want to do an overnight. It's the only campsite along the way. As you look through the tops of the trees, you can see towering cliffs around you. These massive walls make up the distinct features of the Wolfjaws when viewed from a distance.

As you make your way past the campsites, you will start curving left. The trail will become steeper and steeper and the hardwood forest will disappear. After traveling past the campsites for 0.4 miles, you will be met with a fork. To the right is a shortcut to Lower Wolfjaw but left is the direction this route follows, taking you in between the two mountains (you will eventually return by the trail on the right after Lower Wolfjaw). You'll come across the trail to Lower Wolfjaw 0.2 miles past the fork. It is another 100 yards past this point that you will meet another sign. This next sign will point down toward Johns Brook Lodge or left to Upper Wolfjaw. Turn left following the Range Trail. It is 0.7 miles to Upper Wolfjaw from here. Continuing to Upper Wolfjaw, the trail will gradually start to incline. After 0.1 miles, the trail becomes extremely steep. It will remain this grade for 0.3 miles. There are multiple switchbacks in this section because of the steepness.

You will experience many scrambles and sections with root and tree limb grabbing. After climbing approximately 500 feet, you will approach the summit of Upper Wolfjaw Notch. This is a sub summit 0.3 miles away from the true summit. As you make your way up and over the Notch, you will pass some very interesting blowdown forest on your left and a large mud pit with debris. This will mark the midpoint between these two peaks before ascending another short and steep 0.2 miles to the summit. Once you reach the top, keep a lookout for the trail hidden to the right where the summit outlook is. Don't miss it! If you start going down, you went too far. This little spur trail will spit you out on top of a rock summit. This summit view is absolutely gorgeous. To the left, the Notch and Lower Wolfjaw can be seen with Giant and RPR in the background. Center stage is Dix and Nippletop, while Armstrong can be seen to the right blocking Gothics.

As you get ready to depart, you will return down the way you came to the summit. There is no other way off the rock. Head back to the trail, turning left, and start making the 0.7-mile journey back toward the Notch, up and over, carefully descending all the way back to the intersection of Lower Wolfjaw. This 0.5-mile ascent to the summit is nothing spectacular. This roughly has the same grade and trail surface the whole way. You'll climb around 500 feet, while experiencing plenty of rocky scrambles and tree limb grabbing. About one-third of the way up (0.2 miles), you will be met with the spur trail/shortcut that will eventually take you back down the way you came up. However, you will continue, staying to the left. At this point there is a short but funky rock scramble. Continue up the trail for another 0.3 miles before finally reaching the summit. The summit will be marked by a large protruding rock, a couple of trees, and an intersection sign. Stand on the rock to bag the summit. A small view can be seen through the trees. If you look carefully into the valley, you will be able to see the roof of Johns Brook Lodge. You

UPPER AND LOWER WOLFJAW MOUNTAINS

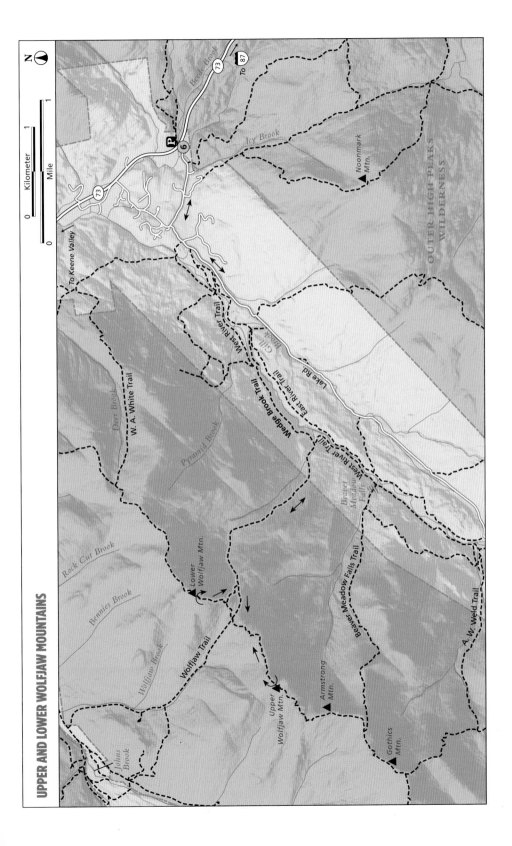

can also make out Big Slide at center, with Cascade, Porter, Whiteface, and Esther just poking up in the background.

Make your way back the way you came. Eventually you will meet back up with that spur trail you saw on the way up. I recommend turning left at this spur trail to save time. This is a steep 0.2-mile section back to the Wedge Brook Trail. Eventually bear left, taking the Wedge Brook Trail all the way back down following the same directions you came from your car.

MILES AND DIRECTIONS

0.0   Start at AMR parking lot trailhead.

0.5   Reach AMR gate for Lake Road.

1.5   Turn right over Wolfjaw's wooden bridge.

2.0   Cross Ausable River.

2.7   Reach Wedge Brook Falls and intersection.

3.8   Wedge Brook campsite.

4.5   Range Trail intersects; Upper Wolfjaw ascent.

4.9   UWJ Notch.

5.2   Upper Wolfjaw summit; backtrack to LWJ Trail.

6.0   Start ascending LWJ.

6.5   LWJ summit; backtrack down.

6.7   Turn left at Wedge Brook cutoff trail.

7.0   Intersect with Wedge Brook Trail; return to the car the same way you came.

11.2   Arrive back at the AMR parking lot.

OTHER ROUTES

THE GARDEN—11.5 MILES, 3,800 FEET

This way is highly recommended as an alternative. It's similar to the AMR approach but without the reservation system. It's less traveled and a little more rugged but a fantastic alternate option. This route will take you to Johns Brook Lodge, and out-and-back Upper and Lower Wolfjaws. It's essentially the same as AMR but from the other side of the valley.

ROOSTER COMB TRAILHEAD—12.1 MILES, 5,000 FEET

This way up the Wolfjaws is the more difficult approach. Personally, I'm not sure why people hike these mountains from this direction, unless you are specifically looking for a different and more challenging way. This approach has you going up toward Rooster Comb, over Hedgehog, and up to LWJ, down and up to UWJ. Then you have to go down and then back up LWJ again, back over Hedgehog, and back to the trailhead.

7 GOTHICS AND ARMSTRONG MOUNTAINS

Gothics is certainly among many hikers' favorite mountains and has a neighboring peak, Armstrong Mountain. The two peaks are commonly hiked together and are also frequently included as part of the Lower Great Range Loop. Gothics is considered one of the most attractive high peaks, both to look at from below and up high. Armstrong, however, is a stepping stone along the way with only 161 feet of vertical gain. Although the mountain has great views and is considered one of the forty-six high peaks, it does not meet the modern-day qualifications when determining a high peak for height or distance from a neighboring peak. However, by historical measures, it still stands to this day as a high peak.

Start: Adirondack Mountain Reserve (AMR)/Ausable Club/St. Huberts
Elevation gain: 4,100 feet
Summit elevation: Gothics, 4736 feet; Armstrong Mountain, 4,400 feet
Distance: 13.3 miles
Difficulty: 4 out of 7, moderate. Terrain overall is very steep and has many challenges.
Hiking time: 9–11 hours
Seasons/schedule: This hike is generally hiked in summer/fall, but depending on conditions it can also be a great winter hiking experience with proper gear. This would be a more challenging winter climb.
Fees and permits: Free reservation required for parking at the AMR May–Oct.
Canine compatibility: Dogs are not allowed, but they can be taken if this is hiked from the Garden Trailhead (Gothics, Armstrong, and Upper Wolfjaw).
Trail surface: This trail is well trafficked. Mixed rock and dirt surfaces with scrambling up high. Lots of steep and rocky scrambles.
Land status: AMR property/Central High Peaks Wilderness

Nearest town: Keene Valley, NY
Water availability: There are plenty of rivers down low but no water sources higher up.
Amenities available: None; no privy or campsites.
Maximum grade: 600 feet/0.4 miles: going up Pyramid Peak
Special considerations: There is no easy way to get up to Gothics. Be prepared for a steep and long approach. There are plenty of "intense" sections when approaching this range that demand caution and trekking poles. This route is certainly for the more advanced hiker.
Sunrise or sunset: If one is up for the challenge, your author would rather be on Gothics for sunrise or more specifically, Pyramid Peak right before it. Sunset would also be very good here.
Route type: Lollipop loop
Views: Gothics has some of the best views of any high peak. Pyramid Peak along the way is also many hikers' favorite view in all the High Peaks. Armstrong also has a really great 180-degree theater view of the north side of Gothics.

FINDING THE TRAILHEAD

AMR/St. Huberts is right across the street from Roaring Brook Falls Trailhead for Giant, labeled as St. Huberts Parking Area or the Adirondack Mountain

Reserve. Approximately 7.5 miles from I-87. Reservations are needed May–October.
GPS: 44.14970°N / 73.76806°W

THE HIKE

Gothics is probably the coolest of High Peaks toponyms. You may have asked yourself where this name stems from. This unusual mountain is named after its Gothic appearance with its sheer rock face as seen from the north side. History tells that this peak may have been named by Orson Phelps as he sat on Mount Marcy in 1857. However, this is likely not true due to two factors. First being that the name "Gothics" was used in locally written literature in 1850, and second, the gothic-like features on this mountain are barely even visible from Marcy's summit, being nearly covered up by Basin Mountain. But aside from where the name came from, this mountain hits the top of the bar when it comes to the things that make a high peak special.

Armstrong Mountain is named after a lumberman from Plattsburgh, New York, Thomas Armstrong. This peak once was called Mountain Brook Hump but officially named after Armstrong in 1869 by Almon Thomas. For all the love that this high peak deserves, unfortunately it does not meet the 46ers criteria, but traditionally has stood as one regardless. The rule is 300 feet of rise or more from a neighboring peak, and Armstrong only rises a mere 161 feet from Gothics.

Upon your arrival at the AMR parking lot, you will commence your journey by walking up the gravel road that connects to it. This uphill path will guide you past the golf course and, after a while, you will turn left at the tennis courts. Shortly thereafter, you will arrive at a sign-in area and a large wooden AMR gate via Lake Road. If this is your first visit to this location, you will inevitably establish a strong bond with the property during your 46er journey. The gravel road that you are on leads to numerous other remarkable sites, including Indian Head, Rainbow Falls, Nippletop, and the Colvin Range.

As you walk past the wooden gate, this road continues for 3.5 miles. You'll take this road all the way to the very end. Once you reach the very end, the road will fade and turn toward the reservoir at the end of Lower Ausable Lake. Here, you will cross the bridge, go over gravel and eventually sharply turn left back into the woods. Soon after this, you will come across your first green sign reading "Gothics via Weld Trail" and left for "Sawteeth via Scenic Route." Continue toward Gothics. Shortly after this, you will be met with your second green sign. This sign has the spur trail to Rainbow Falls. This is an incredible 100-foot waterfall. Feel free to go check it out before continuing your hike. At the sign, continue following the directions toward Gothics, bearing left/straight. After 0.1 miles upward, you'll come up to an overlook at the top of Rainbow Falls.

Following this overlook is where the real hike will begin. From here, you will continue for 1.5 miles, ascending 1,500 feet. This trail is all around rocky and rooty, a very stereotypical climb in the High Peaks. At the end of 1.5 miles, you will be met with an intersection sign: left for Sawteeth in 0.5 miles (yellow trail markers) and right for Gothics in 1 mile/Pyramid Peak in 0.5 miles (blue trail markers). Turn right, heading toward Gothics. This next 0.5-mile ascent up Pyramid Peak will be the hardest climb of the day. Here, you will climb nearly 900 feet in this half mile. It will have some steep scrambles and plenty of tree limb grabbing. Upon cresting the summit, you will find a short trail to the left with an incredible panoramic view of the Upper Great Range. This is possibly the best view of your trip. Take it in!

There are many waterfalls that can be hiked to from Lake Road. Beaver Meadow Falls during the autumn.

The panoramic views from Armstrong looking toward Gothics.

From here, you can see Gothics rising up like a monolith in front of you, about 0.4 miles from here. After leaving Pyramid, you will descend about 150 feet into the col before rapidly climbing 200 feet up the other side. There will be more scrambles and steep rocky parts here. After 0.1 miles of climbing, you will see a trail to the left and a sign pointing back toward Sawteeth. Do not turn left but continue straight. The trail will eventually bring you out onto Gothic's ridge above tree line. Continue to follow this path looking for trail markers and rock indicators, staying along the ridgeline. Eventually you will crest the highest point. Welcome to the summit of Gothics, where you can see 360 degrees of the glorious High Peaks. Once you continue, you will head north (continuing the same direction) immediately back into the trees. The trail will be moderately difficult descending for the next 0.4 miles before reaching the intersection for Beaver Meadow Trail or to Armstrong. Turn left following the sign for the ADK Range Trail. Armstrong is another 0.4 miles away.

During this short section, you will notice that you do not climb too much on your way to Armstrong. Along this section, you will go up, then briefly down, then back up. Right before the summit, you will turn sharply left up a small scramble. You will then pop out on the theater stage like rock overlooking the north side of Gothics. There is nothing here to mark the true summit. After taking in the views, you will return the way you came, back to the trail intersection for Beaver Meadow Falls. The descent back down into the valley is a long 2.2 miles and will have you drop about 2,300 feet. Over the course of this descent, you will encounter many moderate scrambles, ladders, and other variable conditions making it rather challenging. Definitely take it slowly. About 0.25 miles from the bottom, you'll come across a trail on the right indicating Lost Lookout. Keep straight.

This final 0.25-mile descent will be steep. Eventually it will spit you out right next to Beaver Meadow Falls. This is a beautiful waterfall. Continue on while carefully looking for trail markers on the trees indicating the path continuing past the falls. Be careful not to accidentally take the West River Trail (which heads left). Walk away from the waterfall,

GOTHICS AND ARMSTRONG MOUNTAINS

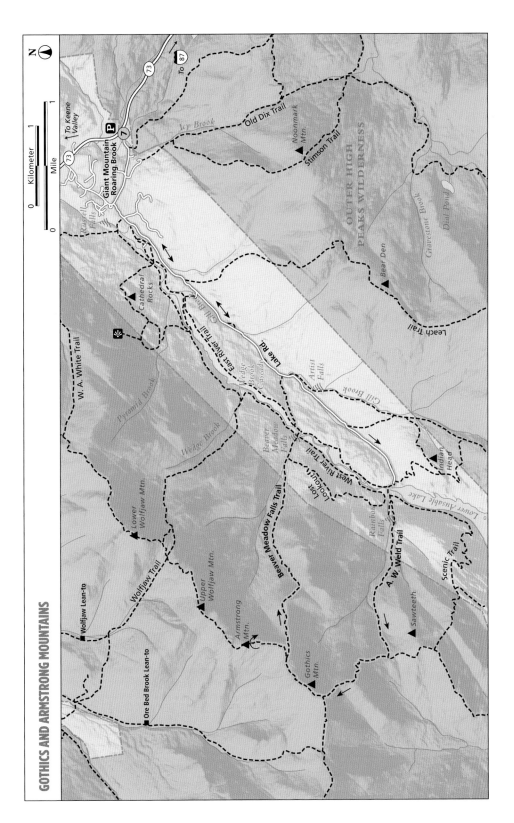

N

0 Kilometer 1

0 Mile 1

To Keene Valley

73

P

Giant Mountain Roaring Brook

7

73

87

To

Russell Falls

Icy Brook

Old Dix Trail

Noonmark Mtn.

Stimson Trail

Cathedral Rocks

Gill Brook

OUTER HIGH PEAKS WILDERNESS

Bear Den

Gravestone Brook

Dial Pond

W. A. White Trail

East River Trail

Lake Rd.

Leach Trail

Wedge Brook Cascade

Artist Falls

Pyramid Brook

Wedge Brook

Beaver Meadow Falls

Gill Brook

Lower Wolfjaw Mtn.

West River Trail

Lookout

Indian Head

Wolfjaw Trail

Upper Wolfjaw Mtn.

Beaver Meadow Falls Trail

Rainbow Falls

Lower Ausable Lake

Wolfjaw Lean-to

Armstrong Mtn.

A. W. Weld Trail

Ore Bed Brook Lean-to

Gothics Mtn.

Sawteeth

Scenic Trail

and not to the left. You'll briefly shoot uphill before intersecting the East River Trail. Turn left onto the East River Trail. Soon after this, you will turn right to continue on the Beaver Meadows Trail following signs to Lake Road. After 0.5 miles, it will spit you out onto Lake Road where then you will be 2 miles from the gate. Continue down the road and back to your car. Lake Road is a curse and a blessing at the end of every hike out of the AMR.

MILES AND DIRECTIONS

0.0   Start at the AMR Trailhead parking lot.

0.5   Reach AMR gate for Lake Road.

4.0   End of Lake Road, crossing the reservoir bridge.

4.1   Pass the Rainbow Falls sign heading up to Gothics.

5.6   Reach intersection for Sawteeth/Pyramid, turning left.

6.1   Summit of Pyramid Peak.

6.6   Summit of Gothics Mountain.

7.0   Intersection for Beaver Meadow Falls (BMF) and Armstrong via Range Trail.

7.4   Armstrong's summit; turn around.

7.8   Intersection down Beaver Meadow Falls Trail.

10.0 Reach Beaver Meadow Falls.

10.1 East River Trail intersection.

10.2 Turn right onto BMF Trail to Lake Road.

10.7 Reach Lake Road, going back to the gate.

12.7 AMR gate.

13.3 Arrive back at the AMR Trailhead parking lot.

8 SAWTEETH VIA THE SCENIC ROUTE

Sawteeth's name was given as a descriptive toponym in the same way that Gothics was. Due to its "saw"-like features when looking at it from nearly every angle, it is certainly understandable how it got this name (especially when hiking this mountain via the Scenic Route). Although Sawteeth is geographically another connecting peak to the Lower Great Range, it can be inconvenient to take on when not added to the Lower Great Range Loop. Regardless, this guide will take you up Sawteeth via the Scenic Route as a day hike by itself.

Start: Adirondack Mountain Reserve (AMR)/Ausable Club/St. Huberts
Elevation gain: 3,250 feet
Summit elevation: 4,100 feet
Distance: 13.2 miles
Difficulty: 4 out of 7, moderate
Hiking time: 7–9 hours
Seasons/schedule: This hike is generally hiked in summer/fall and is not recommended for winter due its lack of foot traffic.
Fees and permits: Free reservation required for parking at the AMR May–Oct.
Canine compatibility: Dogs are not allowed on this hike unless you enter and leave from the Garden Trailhead (which is much more difficult).
Trail surface: This trail is old and rugged. It progressively gets steeper and will have many scrambles. This is a marked and infrequently maintained trail. Mixed rock and dirt surfaces with many steep ledges and rocky scrambles most of the way up. Steep!
Land status: AMR property/Central High Peaks Wilderness
Nearest town: Keene Valley, NY
Water availability: There is little to no water except near the bottom of the Weld Trail. Bring plenty of water.
Amenities available: None; no privy or campsites.
Maximum grade: 1,000 feet/0.7 miles: going up bottom of the Scenic Route

Special considerations: If you have the experience and ability and are planning on doing the Lower Great Range Loop, I suggest adding this 4,100-foot peak to your list as a short out-and-back at the Pyramid Peak intersection along the Weld Trail. Otherwise, it will make for an inconvenient, but very fun day hike. The Scenic Route is exceptionally steep and rugged. It is always better to tackle the steepest parts on the way up and not down (in your author's opinion). Therefore, it is recommended to do this loop going up the Scenic Route and not down. There are plenty of great vantage points. I recommend stopping at every single one of them for the fullest experience. If brutally steep and rocky isn't your taste, then I would suggest doing this out-and-back via the A. W. Weld Trail.
Sunrise or sunset: Neither. This route should certainly be done while there is daylight. However, the morning light going up the Scenic Route is quite spectacular.
Route type: Lollipop loop
Views: The Scenic Route is quite scenic. Take advantage of all the outlooks. There are good views scattered along this route. The true summit does not have views.

FINDING THE TRAILHEAD

AMR/St. Hubert Trailhead is right across the street from Roaring Brook Falls Trailhead for Giant, labeled as St. Huberts Parking Area or the Adirondack Mountain Reserve. Approximately 7.5 miles from I-87. Reservations are needed May–October. **GPS:** 44.14970°N / 73.76806°W

THE HIKE

Sawteeth is a very unique mountain. It is one of only two peaks that has one word as its name, the other being Gothics. Even though this peak was named Sawteeth in the 1850s, USGS maps depicted this mountain as "Resigonia," which is supposedly an Italian translation for "Big Saw." When hiking the Scenic Route, there will be plenty of distinct geographical features to experience. There are many outlooks and viewpoints along the way. I recommended going up the Scenic Route, despite its difficulty, because of how unique this approach is. After all, the Scenic Route is the original route cut up this mountain.

When you reach the AMR parking lot, you'll begin your ascent up the gravel road that connects to it. As you walk uphill, you'll pass the golf course and eventually turn left at the tennis courts. Following a short, paved road, you'll come to the sign-in area and a large gate marking the entrance to the AMR property. If this is your first time visiting this spot, you'll form a strong connection with the location over the course of your 46er journey. The gravel road you're on leads to several other amazing destinations, such as Indian Head, Rainbow Falls, Nippletop, and the Colvin Range. As you walk past the wooden gate, the road extends 3.5 miles. You'll take this road all the way to the very end. Once you reach the very end, the road will fade and turn toward the reservoir at the end of Lower Ausable Lake. Here, you will cross the bridge, go over gravel, and eventually sharply turn left back into the woods. Soon after this, you will come across your first green sign reading "Gothics via Weld Trail" and left for "Sawteeth via Scenic Route." Turn left, following the directions for the Scenic Route.

This lightly used section of trail will follow the lake for 0.9 miles. As you parallel Lower Ausable Lake, look for an opening looking out at Indian Head. You can look up to the rock and see the shape of a Native American's head in the rock. This is the feature that gives "Indian Head" its name. This trail will

There are nearly half a dozen different views while ascending the scenic route up Sawteeth. Looking back down toward Indian Head.

have you maneuver past downed trees and debris. Be vigilant for trail markers. After the halfway point, you will start heading slightly away from the lake. After the full 0.9 miles, the trail will abruptly stop and veer right, going straight up. Some people miss this turn, which has created a slight herd path beyond this point. Be careful to not miss the trail markers when this path turns to the right. There will be many signs indicating outlooks along this path going up. At this point, the trail becomes clearer to follow and should not be difficult to navigate. You will climb about 1,000 feet over the course of the next 0.7 miles. There will be many switchbacks, ladders, and rock scrambles. After 0.7 miles, you will reach a sign indicating Outlook #4.

The trail will taper and gradually incline over the next 0.3 miles before approaching a sign pointing left to Marble Point. (This is a 0.6-mile out-and-back to a fantastic ledge view of the Ausable Lakes Valley. Feel free to add this to your trip.) About 0.1 miles past this sign, the trail will become very steep again. This next section is about 0.4 miles in length. Eventually you will pass Outlook #5 before ultimately cresting the top of Saw-teeth Southeast Peak. Crest over the top of this mountain, down into Rifle Notch. This col is very distinct when viewing Sawteeth from any angle. You'll descend approximately 150 feet down into Rifle Notch, before immediately going back up to your final ascent. About 0.1 miles past this col, you will pass the sign pointing left to the Warden Camps at the Upper Lake. Do not follow this sign with the red trail markers but continue on the trail (yellow markers) in the direction you were going. Shortly after this, you will come out to a "summit" viewpoint with another trail sign. This is considered the unofficial summit. It's not the true summit, but it is the highest point with a view. Here, you can briefly see the rest of the Upper Great Range, with Pyramid and Gothics to the right, with Haystack and Marcy to the left.

After taking in the views, continue on the trail in the same direction. After you leave this point, you will maneuver through the trees with a slight downhill, then back uphill. This slight uphill is the true summit, approximately 150 yards from the viewpoint you just came from (there might be a slight herd path into the trees on your left where the true summit is). The descent down from this point is steep, technical, but beautiful. You will pass a couple of viewpoints looking out over the Great Range while maneuvering down steep ledges. Don't be afraid to use tree limbs and roots to assist your way down. It's pretty steep here. It is 0.4 miles to the next intersection before descending into the valley. Eventually it will flatten out, and you will reach the next intersection. A sign to the left will indicate Pyramid and Gothics straight ahead, and another sign will point down to Lake Road via the Weld Trail. Turn right, following the path down the Weld Trail.

Despite what the sign says, it is a 1.6-mile descent to the reservoir that you crossed at the beginning of your trip. You will know you are close to the bottom once you finally cross a river. You will also pass the outlook to Rainbow Falls right before the bottom. At the bottom, continue following the signs toward Lake Road, walking back to the car the way you came in.

MILES AND DIRECTIONS

0.0 Start at AMR Trailhead parking lot.

0.5 Reach AMR gate for Lake Road.

4.0 End of Lake Road, crossing the reservoir bridge.

SAWTEETH VIA THE SCENIC ROUTE

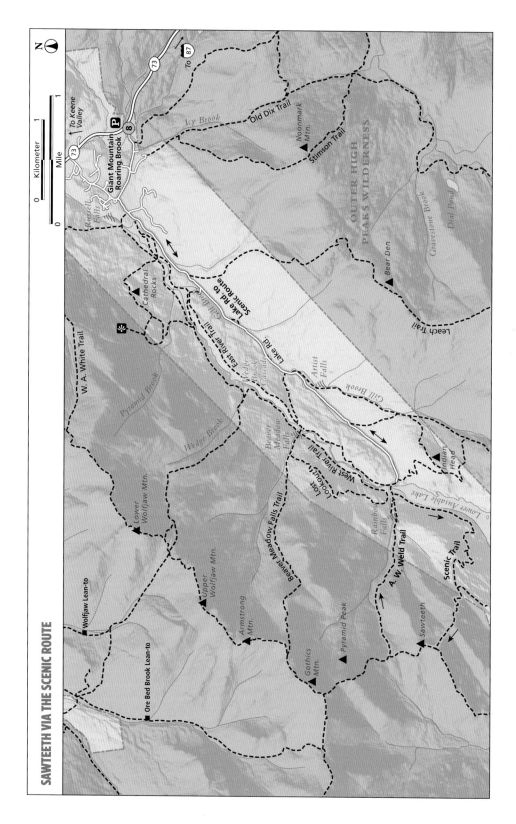

N

0   Kilometer   1
0   Mile   1

To Keene Valley

73

87

To 73

8

P Giant Mountain Roaring Brook

Russell Falls

Icy Brook

Old Dix Trail

Noonmark Mtn.

Stimson Trail

OUTER HIGH PEAKS WILDERNESS

Bear Den

Leach Trail

Gravestone Brook

Dial Pond

Cathedral Rocks

W. A. White Trail

East River Trail

Gill Brook

Lake Rd. to Scenic Route

Lake Rd.

Artist Falls

Gill Brook

Pyramid Brook

Wedge Brook

Wedge Brook Cascade

Beaver Meadow Falls

West River Trail

Lookout

Indian Head

Lower Wolfjaw Mtn.

Wolfjaw Lean-to

Upper Wolfjaw Mtn.

Armstrong Mtn.

Beaver Meadow Falls Trail

Rainbow Falls

A. W. Weld Trail

Lower Ausable Lake

Ore Bed Brook Lean-to

Gothics Mtn.

Pyramid Peak

Sawteeth

Scenic Trail

The true summit of Sawteeth doesn't have views. However, there is a spot near the true summit that does. Looking north toward the Great Range.

4.1	Turn right at the green sign indicating the Scenic Route, following the lake.
5.0	Sharp turn right leading you straight up the mountain.
5.8	Reach top of the first steep climb with Outlook #4.
6.1	Sign indicating Marble Point (POI).
6.6	Crest top of Sawteeth Southeast Peak.
6.8	Enter Rifle Notch.
7.0	Reach unofficial summit of Sawteeth with view of the Great Range.
7.5	Reach intersection to Gothics and Weld Trail descent. Turn Left downhill.
9.1	Bottom of Weld Trail, crossing the reservoir.
9.2	Lake Road back to the car.
13.2	Arrive back at the AMR Trailhead parking lot.

OTHER ROUTES

SAWTEETH OUT-AND-BACK VIA THE WELD TRAIL—12.4 MILES, 3,100 FEET

This route up Sawteeth is easier. It's the only other way to climb this mountain. Instead of turning left up the Scenic Trail at the Lower Ausable Lake Reservoir, you will continue straight following the Weld Trail up toward Gothics, but following the signs to Sawteeth instead.

UPPER GREAT RANGE

Morning light on Mount Haystack looking back toward Little Haystack.

9 SADDLEBACK MOUNTAIN

This peak, one of many mountains named for its appearance, is not hard to picture as it looks very much like a saddleback. Atop this mountain lies adjacent humps with a slight dip in the middle creating a topographic saddle. This mountain is commonly paired with Basin and Haystack Mountains but can certainly be hiked "à la carte." (Note that this specific hike does not talk about the Saddleback Cliffs. See Haystack, Basin, and Saddleback Loop on page 91.)

Start: The Garden Trailhead
Elevation gain: 3,300 feet
Summit elevation: 4,515 feet
Distance: 14.2 miles
Difficulty: 4 out of 7, moderate
Hiking time: 8–10 hours
Seasons/schedule: All seasons. This hike is generally hiked in summer/fall, but depending on conditions it can also be a great winter hiking experience with proper gear.
Fees and permits: $10 parking fee at parking lot for town of Keene Valley
Canine compatibility: Dogs must be on leash.
Trail surface: This trail is well trafficked. Mixed rock and dirt surfaces with some scrambles up high.
Land status: Central High Peaks Wilderness
Nearest town: Keene Valley, NY
Water availability: There is plenty of water along most of this hike. There is a water station at Johns Brook Lodge and many rivers along the way.

Amenities available: Johns Brook Lodge (for guests only), many privies and tent sites.
Maximum grade: 1,050 feet/0.75 miles: from the slide ladder to the first saddle
Special considerations: Doing Saddleback by itself is something to consider if one wants to avoid the cliffs on the other side or wants to break up Haystack and Basin. Saddleback is not terribly technical when going up this route and makes for a much more mellow approach to the mountain.
Sunrise or sunset: Saddleback has a great west-facing summit making for a fantastic sunset view with the rest of the Great Range in focus. The morning light when coming up this trail is also very nice.
Route type: Out-and-back
Views: 180-degree views at the summit with some good viewpoints looking toward Gothics and Basin's east side when in the saddle.

FINDING THE TRAILHEAD

From Keene Valley, follow Adirondack Street next to Ausable Inn for about a mile, turning right onto Johns Brook Lane. Parking limited; additional parking available on the street in Keene Valley. Weekdays are generally not full prior to 9 a.m. but can be full before 6 a.m. on weekends. **GPS:** 44.18911°N / 73.81561°W

THE HIKE

Saddleback is an all-around moderate high peak with unique features. The approach is simple, yet beautiful. Saddleback is generally paired with Basin and Haystack but can certainly be hiked by itself. One might want to consider doing this "à la carte" if the Upper Great Range "HaBaSa" hike is too much, or if you are wanting to avoid the exposure and heights of the Saddleback Cliffs from the western side (see Hike 12). This hike starts at the Garden Trailhead in Keene Valley. Upon signing in, you will be taking the trail

These long wooden steps are climbed parallel to the Lower Orebed Slide.

straight to Johns Brook Lodge (JBL). You will be met with an intersection sign 0.5 miles in pointing left to the South Side Trail or right continuing to JBL. Turn right. Over the next 3 miles, you will literally go "over the rivers and through the woods to Grandma's house," except "Grandma's house" is Johns Brook Lodge. Half a mile from JBL, you'll be met with a quick descent down to a second sign-in. It is highly recommended to also sign in at this registry. From here, you can get to the Orebed Brook Trail by either turning left or right, but for this route, we will be turning right to end up at JBL. The lodge is a good place to refill water or even to spend the night if you made a reservation. You will find the next trail sign located right in front of the lodge porch. It's a very tall, six-layered sign with many different directions. You will follow the blue trail marker indicating left toward Saddleback Mountain. Despite the sign saying 4.3 miles, it's really only 3.6 miles to the summit from this point. Turning here, the trail will bring you briefly over a nice wooden bridge, down and up an embankment. At the end of this bridge, you will briefly turn right, and then slowly turn left to continue on the same Woodsfall Trail. After about 5 minutes, you will briefly cross Orebed Brook and steeply up the other side.

Shortly after this, you will be met with a three-way intersection. One sign indicates the Short Job Lookout and Wolfjaw Mountains, while the other is for the Orebed Brook Trail (OBT). Take the rightmost path to follow the OBT.

You will follow this path for the next 2.2 miles, eventually crossing two streams. One is 0.7 miles in at the Orebed Brook Lean-to and the other is 1.3 miles in. The second one following the lean-to is a nameless stream that runs off the Gothics North Face. From here, you'll be 1 mile from the slide entrance. This next mile will be more rugged, eventually leading to multiple trail diversions from washouts in years past. Be vigilant of the trail markers. After correctly following the path, you will be at the bottom of the Lower Orebed Slide. Here at the entrance, there will be rock spray-painted with yellow markings to indicate where the trail goes, feeding you onto a set of very long wooden steps on the left side of the slide.

Once you reach the steps, follow them all the way to the top, where the trail will eventually enter back into the woods. At this point, you will be 0.25 miles from the Range Trail intersection. Be careful with this section when it is wet. There are many slick and mossy spots along this push. You will eventually crest the Range Trail where there will be an alpine zone sign and two trail signs. One will point left to Gothics (yellow) and

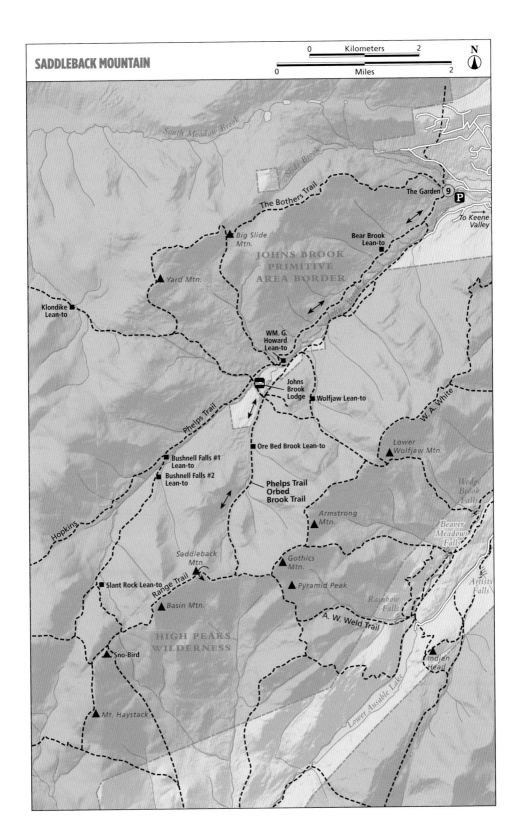

SADDLEBACK MOUNTAIN

0   Kilometers   2

0   Miles   2

N

South Meadow Brook

Slide Brook

The Bothers Trail

The Garden 9 P

To Keene Valley

Big Slide Mtn.

Bear Brook Lean-to

JOHNS BROOK PRIMITIVE AREA BORDER

Yard Mtn.

Klondike Lean-to

Johns Brook

WM. G. Howard Lean-to

Johns Brook Lodge

Wolfjaw Lean-to

W. A. White

Phelps Trail

Ore Bed Brook Lean-to

Lower Wolfjaw Mtn.

Wedge Brook Falls

Bushnell Falls #1 Lean-to

Bushnell Falls #2 Lean-to

Phelps Trail Orbed Brook Trail

Beaver Meadows Falls

Hopkins

Armstrong Mtn.

Artists Falls

Saddleback Mtn.

Gothics Mtn.

Slant Rock Lean-to

Range Trail

Basin Mtn.

Pyramid Peak

Rainbow Falls

A. W. Weld Trail

HIGH PEAKS WILDERNESS

Sno-Bird

Indian Head

Mt. Haystack

Lower Ausable Lake

Halfway up Saddleback, you are greeted with this breathtaking view of Gothics.

the other to Saddleback (blue). This sign is also at exactly 4,000 feet of elevation. Turn following the signs to Saddleback.

You are 0.5 miles from Saddleback. The first 0.3 miles of this final ascent will have you climb 450 feet. There will be many steep scrambling spots with rocks, slabs, and tree limbs. This final push is certainly the hardest part of the day. While climbing up, there will be many viewpoints looking back toward Gothics. The "cable route" is very distinctly visible from this angle. Eventually you will crest the first saddle of the mountain, but it is not over yet. The summit is 0.2 miles from the first saddle. You will have to dip down in between the two saddles first. You may see Saddleback's summit, the second saddle, in the distance. Halfway between the two saddles, there will be a spur trail to the left that will take you to an incredible viewpoint overlooking Basin and the Ausable Lake Valley.

Continuing past this point, you will briefly climb back up, arriving at the true summit of Saddleback Mountain. Basin Mountain takes up most of your view from here with Marcy poking up in the background. You may also notice the summit of Haystack barely protruding to the left of Basin, Colden, and the MacIntyre Range to the right. This drop-off is also where the "Cliffs" are. The trail continues to the right off the summit following the yellow spray-painted rocks, but we can save that for another day. Continue back to the trailhead the same way you came to Saddleback.

MILES AND DIRECTIONS

0.0   Start at the Garden Trailhead.

0.5   Turn right at the trail sign to Johns Brook Lodge (JBL).

3.1   Reach second sign-in, turning right to JBL.

3.6   Reach JBL, turning left after the porch.

3.7   Cross bridge, heading to Orebed Brook Trail intersection.

4.0   Turn right onto the Orebed Brook Trail following the blue trail markers.

6.2   Walk up the stairs on the Orebed Slide.

6.6   Range Trail intersects. Turn right.

7.1   Summit of Saddleback. Turn back the same way you came.

14.2   Arrive back at the Garden Trailhead.

10 BASIN MOUNTAIN

Basin Mountain is up there on the list as one of your author's favorite mountains. This peak certainly qualifies as an all-around beast. In 1857 Orson Phelps named Basin after its basin-like appearance from Mount Marcy. This mountain can be hiked by itself but is commonly paired with Haystack and (or) Saddleback as well. It is very challenging and offers some of the best views of any high peak with spectacular 360-degree views in the middle of the Great Range.

Start: The Garden Trailhead
Elevation gain: 4,100 feet
Summit elevation: 4,827 feet
Distance: 17.8 miles
Difficulty: 5 out of 7, difficult
Hiking time: 10–12 hours
Seasons/schedule: All seasons. This hike is generally hiked in summer/fall, but depending on conditions it can also be a great winter hiking experience with proper gear.
Fees and permits: $10 parking fee at parking lot for town of Keene Valley
Canine compatibility: Leashed dogs are permitted, but high waters could prove to be challenging. The trail has very steep and exposed rock sections that could be difficult as well.
Trail surface: This trail is well trafficked. Mixed rock and dirt surfaces on approach with many with some scrambles and slab up high. The trail overall is maintained and well-marked with plenty of diverse sections.
Land status: Central High Peaks Wilderness
Nearest town: Keene Valley, NY
Water availability: There is plenty of water along most of this hike. There is a water station at Johns Brook Lodge and many rivers along the way.

Amenities available: Johns Brook Lodge (for guests only), many privies and tent sites.
Maximum grade: 700 feet/0.5 miles: majority of the final Basin ascent
Special considerations: This peak should NOT be considered in bad weather. This mountain is especially remote, technical, and exposed. It should be done on a day with sun and little wind. The main ascent up this face is very steep, slablike, and has some sketchy spots. If you have a very challenging time going up, you'll have an even more difficult time descending it. The only other way off is the opposite side over the Saddleback Cliffs.
Sunrise or sunset: Basin has the most underrated sunset in the High Peaks. Although hiking off a high peak after sunset is no fun, this mountain just might be worth it.
Route type: Out-and-back
Views: The summit of this mountain is certainly one to inspire. It truly defines the meaning of *Heaven Up-h'isted-ness* with its 360-degree views of every quadrant of the High Peaks. It boasts a panoramic view of Haystack's Johanssen Face, Skylight, Marcy, Colden, and the Macintyre Range.

FINDING THE TRAILHEAD

Follow Adirondack Street next to Ausable Inn for about a mile, turning right onto Johns Brook Lane. Parking limited; additional parking available on the street in Keene Valley. Weekdays are generally not full prior to 9 a.m. but can be full before 6 a.m. on weekends. **GPS:** 44.18911°N / 73.81561°W

THE HIKE

Bob Marshall (#3) could not have described his opinion of Basin any better. He wrote, "No words can describe a person's feeling as he looks over this enormous hollow and gets perhaps the finest view now possible of the type of forest which once covered all of the North woods region" when standing on this mountain's summit. It is your author's hope that you too can experience the spectacular elements of this mountain. Basin Mountain is generally paired with Haystack and (or) Saddleback. However, the Upper Great Range may be split into two or three different hikes depending on hiking ability.

This hike starts at the Garden Trailhead in Keene Valley. Upon signing in, you will be taking the trail straight into Johns Brook Lodge (JBL). You will be met with an intersection sign 0.5 miles in pointing left to the South Side Trail or right continuing to JBL. Turn right. Over the next 3 miles, you will continue to Johns Brook Lodge. 0.5 miles from JBL, you'll be met with a quick descent down to a second sign in. It is highly recommended to also sign in at this registry. From here, you can get to the Orebed trail by either turning left or right, but for this route, turn right to end up at JBL. Half a mile later, you will arrive at JBL. This lodge is a good place to refill water or even to spend the night if you made reservations. You will find the next trail sign located right in front of this porch. It's a very tall, six-layered sign with many different directions. You will follow the bottom yellow trail marker sign pointing toward Bushnell Falls (1.8 miles) and Mount Marcy (5.5 miles).

Continuing on, you'll enter back into the woods on your way toward Bushnell Falls. After approximately 1.6 miles, you'll come up to another trail sign pointing right for the Hopkins Trail. This is a transfer route that would take you to the Van Hoevenberg Trail toward Marcy from the Loj side. Continue straight on the current trail. Here, you will dip down toward Johns Brook. Cross the river to the other side, following the yellow

The trail up Basin is steep and very slablike.

trail markers. Shortly after crossing, you will pass a privy on your right and the Bushnell Falls lean-to on your left. After crossing this river, it is another 1.6 miles to your next destination; Slant Rock. This next 1.6-mile section will have you climb about 600 feet of elevation, eventually crossing through some beautiful new-growth forest (this section of forest used to have well over 30 downed trees along the trail, but in recent years, the blowdown has been cleared). During this 1.6-mile section, you will cross two notable rivers, one being Basin Brook about 1 mile from Bushnell Falls, and the second being Johns Brook again right before Slant Rock.

After 3.3 miles from Johns Brook Lodge, you will finally arrive at Slant Rock and campsite. You'll notice that this is Slant Rock because of the massive, slanted rock at the site (a great spot to take a break if needed). Once you depart, you will continue heading past the rock following the trail markers. 0.1-mile past Slant Rock, you will come to another trail sign. This trail sign points to the Range Trail, back to Slant Rock, or toward Marcy. This is where you will turn left onto Shorey's Shortcut Trail. Follow the sign to the Range Trail (1.1 miles). This section of Shorey's Shortcut is in fact 1.1 miles. The first 0.5 miles will have you climb 650 feet. Shorey's Shortcut is steep, rocky, mossy and hands-on. This section of the trail is more rugged than most. Please take this section cautiously. The difficulty of this section outweighs the extra distance and vertical feet one would have to climb to avoid it. It is highly suggested to take this route rather than going up Little Haystack first, and then down. An alternate route to where Shorey's would take you is 1.5 miles longer and still very challenging. Just take it slowly!

The trail will eventually flatten out halfway up Shorey's. You'll start to get great views of Basin and the surrounding valley. Eventually you'll crest the shortcut where you will be able to look in between Haystack and Basin. The end of the shortcut will have you drop approximately 300 feet, exiting you onto the Range Trail. When arriving at the Range Trail, you will be met with a three-layered trail sign. Turn left following the

The view from the summit of Basin is like none other.

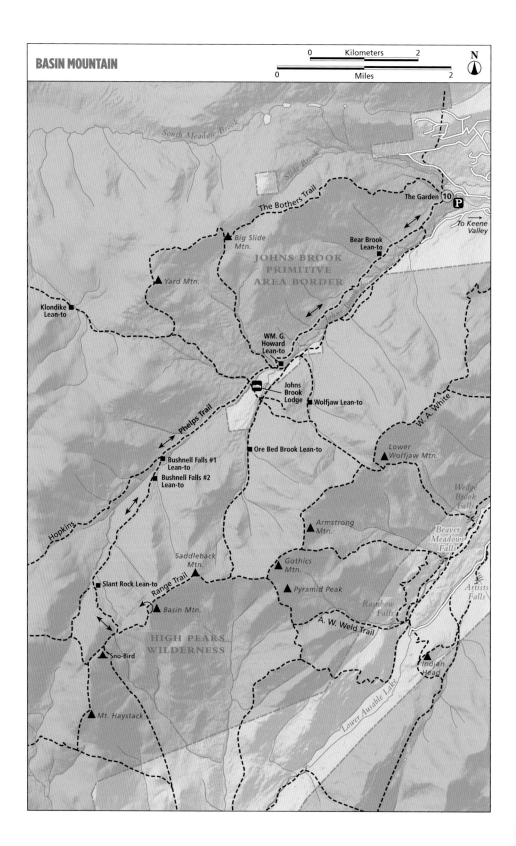

BASIN MOUNTAIN

0   Kilometers   2

0   Miles   2

N

The Garden (10) P

To Keene Valley

The Bothers Trail

Big Slide Mtn.

Bear Brook Lean-to

JOHNS BROOK PRIMITIVE AREA BORDER

Yard Mtn.

Slide Brook

South Meadow Brook

Klondike Lean-to

Johns Brook

WM. G. Howard Lean-to

Johns Brook Lodge

Wolfjaw Lean-to

Phelps Trail

W. A. White

Ore Bed Brook Lean-to

Lower Wolfjaw Mtn.

Wedge Brook Falls

Bushnell Falls #1 Lean-to

Bushnell Falls #2 Lean-to

Beaver Meadows Falls

Hopkins

Armstrong Mtn.

Saddleback Mtn.

Artists Falls

Slant Rock Lean-to

Range Trail

Gothics Mtn.

Pyramid Peak

Basin Mtn.

Rainbow Falls

A. W. Weld Trail

HIGH PEAKS WILDERNESS

Sno-Bird

Indian Head

Mt. Haystack

Lower Ausable Lake

directions toward Basin (0.7 miles). This 0.7-mile climb up Basin will be the most challenging part of your day. The first 0.4 miles will have you climb 700 feet. During this first half of the ascent, you will climb ladders and many scrambles. There are many spots that will require you to think about how to maneuver. Take it slow! Eventually you will make it past all the technical parts of the ascent and the trail will gradually start to taper. Right before the summit, you will climb up a notable rock ledge, bringing you up above the tree line. After you climb this last big rock ledge, you are near the top.

Carefully follow the rock cairns, making sure to not step on any alpine vegetation. Welcome to the summit of Basin. From here, you can see everything. Simply the best view on any high peak in my opinion. When ready to leave, carefully return the way you came.

The trail up Basin with Marcy in view. The red plant is a form of bog bilberry with lots of anthocyanin.

MILES AND DIRECTIONS

0.0 Start at the Garden.

0.5 Turn right at the trail sign to Johns Brook Lodge (JBL).

3.1 Reach second sign-in, turning right to JBL.

3.6 Reach Johns Brook Lodge, continuing straight toward Bushnell Falls.

5.4 Reach Bushnell Falls area, crossing Johns Brook after passing the Hopkins Trail.

7.0 Reach Slant Rock.

7.1 Turn at Shorey's Shortcut intersection. Sign indication for Range Trail (1.1).

8.2 Exit the shortcut onto the Range Trail intersection. Turn left up Basin.

8.9 Reach Summit of Basin. Turn back the way you came.

17.8 Arrive back at the Garden Trailhead.

11 MOUNT HAYSTACK

If you ask any 46er what their favorite mountain is, you will commonly hear the answer "Oh, definitely Haystack." This mountain will leave a lasting impression on any hiker, even in bad weather. It is home to many great stories of adventures from pioneers to modern-day trekkers. This mountain is beautiful to look at from all angles and has one of the most unique summits of any Northeast 115 peak. It is highly recommended to hike this when the timing is just right.

Start: The Garden Trailhead
Elevation gain: 4,050 feet
Summit elevation: 4,960 feet
Distance: 18.0 miles
Difficulty: 5 out of 7, difficult
Hiking time: 10–12 hours
Seasons/schedule: All seasons. This hike is generally hiked in summer/fall, but depending on conditions it can also be a great winter hiking experience with proper gear and experience.
Fees and permits: $10 parking fee at parking lot for town of Keene Valley
Canine compatibility: Leashed dogs are permitted, but high waters could prove to be challenging. The trail has very steep and exposed rock sections that could be difficult as well.
Trail surface: This trail is well trafficked. Mixed rock and dirt surfaces on approach with many scrambles and slab up high with the last 0.5 miles being entirely exposed.
Land status: Central High Peaks Wilderness
Nearest town: Keene Valley, NY
Water availability: There is plenty of water along most of this hike. There is a water station at Johns Brook Lodge and many rivers along the way.

Amenities available: Johns Brook Lodge (for guests only), many privies and tent sites.
Maximum grade: 1,250 feet/1 mile: Slant Rock to first view of Haystack. Included in this section is a 350-foot/0.2-mile section starting at the Range/Phelps Trail intersection.
Special considerations: Just like Basin, this peak should *not* be considered in bad weather. This mountain is very remote, technical, and exposed. It should be done on a day with sun and little wind. The main ascent up this face is very steep, slablike, and has some sketchy spots. Bring sunglasses if it is sunny as Haystack's summit ridge is all above the tree line.
Sunrise or sunset: Are you up for a challenge? Haystack has one of the best sunrises of any high peak. One can consider camping at Sno-Bird 0.5 miles from Little Haystack for an easier attempt. Sunset on Haystack is also great, but I would not recommend being on this summit after dark.
Route type: Out-and-back
Views: Haystack has views galore. You will find yourself above the tree line for at least an hour. It has exceptional views of Panther Gorge, Basin, and Upper Ausable Lake.

FINDING THE TRAILHEAD

Follow Adirondack Street next to Ausable Inn for about a mile, turning right onto Johns Brook Lane. Parking limited; additional parking available on the street in Keene Valley. Weekdays are generally not full prior to 9 a.m. but can be full before 6 a.m. on weekends. **GPS:** 44.18911°N / 73.81561°W

Haystack as viewed from the high point (Horse Hill) just before the 0.5-mile out-and-back for Haystack.

THE HIKE

In August 1849, Old Mountain Phelps led a team from Elk Lake to Marcy passing over Haystack along the way. After he and his team reached Marcy, they looked back at Haystack, describing it as a "a great stack of rock resembling a stack of hay." Verplanck Colvin even called this mountain the "Matterhorn of the Adirondacks." From Bob Marshall to the newest 46er, this mountain remains the majority of people's favorite high peak. This mountain can be paired with Basin and Saddleback, but also can be hiked by itself. Hiking Haystack by itself is smart for those who are not as strong.

This hike starts at the Garden Trailhead in Keene Valley. Upon signing in, take the trail straight into Johns Brook Lodge (JBL). You will be met with an intersection sign 0.5 miles in pointing left to the South Side Trail or right continuing to JBL. Turn right. Over the next 3 miles, continue toward Johns Brook Lodge; 0.5 miles from JBL, you'll be met with a quick descent down to a second sign in. It is highly recommended to also sign in at this registry. Turn right, and 0.5 miles later, you will arrive at JBL. This lodge is a good place to refill water or even to spend the night if you made reservations. You will find your next trail sign located right in front of this porch. It's a very tall, six-layered sign with many different directions. One of the signs points to Haystack indicating 7.4 miles. This is simply a misleading distance. Turning this direction would have you go over Saddleback and Basin, however this approach is only 6.1 miles to Haystack. You will follow the bottom yellow trail marker sign pointing toward Bushnell Falls (1.8 miles) and Mount Marcy (5.5 miles).

Continuing on, you'll enter back into the woods on your way toward Bushnell Falls. After approximately 1.6 miles, you'll come up to another trail sign pointing right for the Hopkins Trail. This is a transfer route that would take you to the Van Hoevenberg Trail toward Marcy from the Loj side. Continue straight on the current trail. Here, you will dip down toward Johns Brook. Cross the river to the other side, following the yellow trail markers. Shortly after crossing, you will pass a privy on your right and the Bushnell Falls lean-to on your left. After crossing this river, it is another 1.6 miles to your next destination, Slant Rock. This next 1.6-mile section will have you climb about 600 feet, crossing through some beautiful new-growth forest. This section of forest used to have well over thirty downed trees along the trail, but in recent years, the blowdown has been cleared. During this 1.6-mile section, you will cross two notable rivers, one being Basin Brook about 1 mile from Bushnell Falls, and the second being Johns Brook, right before Slant Rock.

After 3.4 miles from Johns Brook Lodge, you will finally arrive at Slant Rock and campsite. You'll notice that this is Slant Rock because of the massive, slanted rock at the site (this is a great spot to take a break if needed). Once you depart, you will continue heading past the rock following the trail markers. A tenth of a mile past Slant Rock, you will come to another trail sign. This trail sign points to the Range Trail, back to Slant Rock, or toward Marcy. Continue following the path toward Marcy (2.1 miles). From here, it will get steeper and rockier for 0.8 miles up to the Range Trail intersection. It will also parallel Johns Brook. After 0.8 miles, you'll make it to the Range Trail intersection. You will see a sign indicating the Phelps/Range Trail intersection for Marcy and Haystack (1 mile). Continue left at this sign toward Haystack.

Hikers climbing to the summit of Haystack for sunrise.

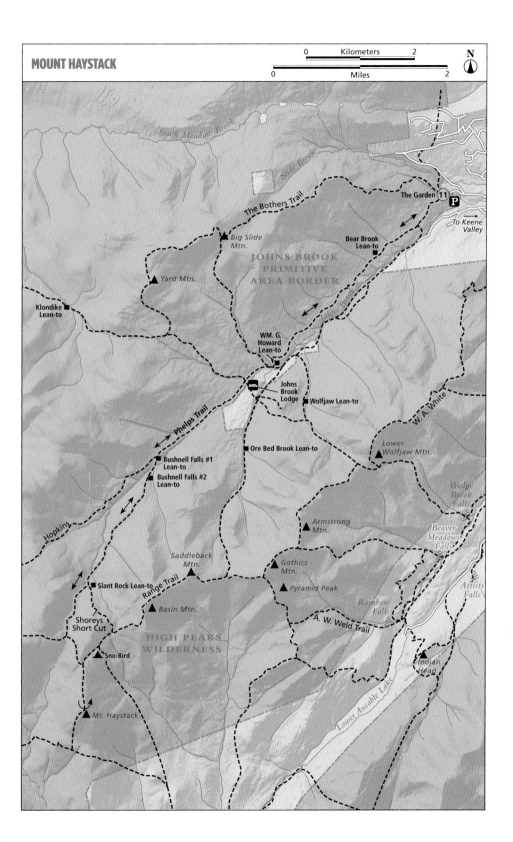

Kilometers

0   2

Miles

0   2

N

South Meadow Brook

Slide Brook

The Bothers Trail

The Garden 11 P

To Keene Valley

Big Slide Mtn.

Bear Brook Lean-to

Yard Mtn.

JOHNS BROOK PRIMITIVE AREA BORDER

Klondike Lean-to

Johns Brook

WM. G. Howard Lean-to

Phelps Trail

Johns Brook Lodge

Wolfjaw Lean-to

W. A. White

Ore Bed Brook Lean-to

Lower Wolfjaw Mtn.

Bushnell Falls #1 Lean-to

Bushnell Falls #2 Lean-to

Wedge Brook Falls

Beaver Meadows Falls

Hopkins

Armstrong Mtn.

Saddleback Mtn.

Artists Falls

Slant Rock Lean-to

Range Trail

Gothics Mtn.

Pyramid Peak

Rainbow Falls

Shoreys Short Cut

Basin Mtn.

A. W. Weld Trail

HIGH PEAKS WILDERNESS

Sno-Bird

Indian Head

Lower Ausable Lake

Mt. Haystack

This next section is 0.5 miles long. This will be very steep and technical, requiring your hands to maneuver certain areas. Take it slowly for this half mile. Eventually you will crest this sub-mountain. As you crest, you will come up to a rock perched on top where you can see everything around you, including Haystack directly in front. Continue on the trail, eventually dipping down 150 feet, intersecting with the Range Trail. Here you will meet an intersection sign pointing you 0.5 miles to the summit of Haystack. It is important to note this section. From here to the summit is entirely exposed. Make sure you're dressed accordingly and take everything with you. It will be 1 mile of technical exposed ridgeline out-and-back to the summit.

Upon starting your climb up to Little Haystack, there will be yellow paint on the rocks and stacks of rocks directing you the whole way to the summit. Be very vigilant and follow these indicators. They are for your safety and the preservation of the surrounding area. Eventually you will reach the summit of Little Haystack. From here, the trail will bring you downward to the left and eventually to the right. Continue following the paint and stacks of rock. This is a very technical area that will require your hands to maneuver down. Getting down Little Haystack can be somewhat challenging if you go the wrong way. Make sure to follow the yellow paint. Carefully maneuver yourself down, connecting back with the trail at the bottom. The trail at the bottom will weave into the forest, then back up more rock. The path will continue as it has, bringing you up and around rock, slowly approaching the summit. Continue following the rock stacks. Eventually you will reach the summit of this gorgeous 4,960-foot peak. Take it in! From here, you can

PANTHER GORGE: THE HIDDEN CHASM BY KEVIN MACKENZIE

Panther Gorge is a 2,000-foot-deep, north-northeast trending glacial valley located between Mts. Marcy and Haystack. Its rugged location, diverse cliffs, and remote rock/ice climbs set it apart from other High Peak areas. Most Adirondack hikers pursuing the forty-six high peaks rub shoulders with Panther Gorge en route to Mount Marcy, Mount Skylight, or Mount Haystack. The latter arguably offers the most dramatic overlook of the chasm where a person can witness nature's power by peering at the sheer slabs, curving slides, shadowy crags, and Marcy's summit—a landscape of constant change. Few people, however, enter the gorge. There is no easy access. It is unpathed and requires navigation over densely forested slopes, talus, streams, blowdown fields, and beaver ponds. Hikers generally keep to the marked trails or camp at Panther Gorge Lean-to in the south end of the gorge. Panther Gorge is also host to a surprisingly rich history. The footsteps of present-day backcountry enthusiasts tramp atop of those of several notable Adirondack pioneers. The author Alfred Billings Street trekked through the area in 1865. He named the gorge during his sojourn and described "enormous crags, green with moss and crowned with trees." Orson "Old Mountain" Phelps, one of the most famous Adirondack guides, once led clients up Marcy via the gorge during the 1850–1870s. Phelps was also a principal guide to Verplanck Colvin, superintendent of the Adirondack Survey. Colvin ascertained the true height of Mount Marcy during the 1870s and set up a basecamp in Panther Gorge for his survey work. Even the philosopher William James pondered the deeper meanings of life from within the chasm during a trip in 1898.

To many modern wilderness aficionados, Panther Gorge is a symbol of nature in the raw—free of motorized noise, cell phones, and people. Only the whispers of wind through the pines, rush of water, birdsong, or during winter, popping ice accompany one's thoughts. It is forever wild.

see all the way down into Panther Gorge, Marcy, Boreas Ponds to the south and the rest of the Great Range. Return the 9 miles back to the Garden Trailhead.

Upon returning the 0.5 miles back to the Range Trail intersection, an alternate way back would be to turn right at the sign going down toward Basin, taking Shorey's Shortcut back out to Slant Rock instead. Shorey's Shortcut Trail is right before you climb the 0.7 miles up to Basin (see Hike 10).

MILES AND DIRECTIONS

0.0 Start at the Garden Trailhead.

0.5 Turn right at the trail sign to Johns Brook Lodge (JBL).

3.1 Reach second sign-in, turning right to JBL.

3.6 Reach Johns Brook Lodge, continuing straight toward Bushnell Falls.

5.4 Reach Bushnell Falls area, crossing Johns Brook after passing the Hopkins Trail.

7.0 Reach Slant Rock.

7.1 Reach next sign following directions toward Marcy.

8.0 Reach Range Trail intersection, turning left toward Haystack.

8.5 Reach intersection of Range Trail, 0.5 miles to Haystack.

8.6 Summit of Little Haystack.

9.0 Summit of Mount Haystack; return the way you came.

18.0 Arrive back at Garden Trailhead.

OTHER ROUTES

ADIRONDACK LOJ—18.6 MILES, 4,600 FEET

Not a terrible choice for an alternate route, but certainly one to consider. A little more distance and elevation, but shoots you right back out to the Loj in Lake Placid. This direction has you going nearly all the way up to Mount Marcy via the Van Hoevenberg Trail. About half a mile from Marcy, you will turn left on the Range Trail, bringing you down and then back up to Haystack.

ELK LAKE TO HAYSTACK VIA PANTHER GORGE—24.1 MILES, 5,100 FEET

This is the least traveled and most rugged way to Haystack for sure. This is a very long day and might want to be considered as an overnight in Panther Gorge. It will bring you to a very remote part of the forest, but an excellent part. This is a fantastic alternative to those who want to experience even more ruggedness of the High Peaks Wilderness with a challenge.

12 HAYSTACK, BASIN, AND SADDLEBACK LOOP

If I could only hike one loop for the rest of my life, this would be it. This route, also known as "HaBaSa," is by far the best overall hiking experience in the High Peaks Wilderness (assuming you are physically capable). Of course, this is my opinion, but I think many people who have tackled this loop would say the same. You will experience all that the High Peaks has to offer, and this loop is a must for anyone looking to have the best first impression of the High Peaks. But be warned, this is not for the beginner or even moderate hiker by any means. This is a briefer guide to these three peaks. More details can be found on each one individually (see Hikes 9, 10, and 11).

Start: The Garden Trailhead
Elevation gain: 5,100 feet
Summit elevation: Mount Haystack, 4,960 feet; Basin Mountain, 4,827 feet; Saddleback Mountain, 4,515 feet
Distance: 18.8 miles
Difficulty: 6 out of 7, very difficult
Hiking time: 12–14 hours
Seasons/schedule: All seasons. This hike is generally hiked in summer/fall, but it can be challenging in the winter. Having larger groups should be considered if tackling it in winter.
Fees and permits: $10 parking fee at parking lot for town of Keene Valley
Canine compatibility: Leashed dogs are permitted, but technical trails and high waters could prove to be challenging.
Trail surface: This trail is well trafficked. There are mixed rock and dirt surfaces on approach with many scrambles and slab up high over the three peaks.
Land status: Central High Peaks Wilderness
Nearest town: Keene Valley, NY
Water availability: There is plenty of water along most of this hike. There is a water station at Johns Brook Lodge and many rivers along the way. There is little water up high but some possible refilling at Sno-Bird Campsite.
Amenities available: Johns Brook Lodge (for guests only), many privies and tent sites.

Maximum grade: Haystack: 1,250 feet/1 mile (Slant Rock to first view of Haystack). Included in this section is a 350-foot/0.2-mile section starting at the Range/Phelps Trail intersection. Basin: 700 feet/0.5 miles (majority of the final Basin ascent). Saddleback: 220 feet/0.10 miles up the "Cliffs."
Special considerations: I would not approach this hike without trekking poles and gaiters. With the amount of mud and technical uphill and downhill challenges, trekking poles will come in handy in many places. It is recommended to start with Haystack and end on Saddleback. Be sure to pack plenty of water as that water is few and far between once you are at elevation. I would also recommend starting this hike very early so that you have plenty of daylight while up high. Assess yourself on every summit before going to the next. You can get yourself into some very poor situations on this loop if you do not plan accordingly.
Sunrise or sunset: Neither. Start this hike around 5 or 6 a.m. depending on the time of year. You can also take my Haystack sunrise advice from the previous hike (see Hike 11).
Route type: Lollipop loop
Views: The views are excellent on every peak.

FINDING THE TRAILHEAD

Follow Adirondack Street next to Ausable Inn for about a mile, turning right onto Johns Brook Lane. Parking limited; additional parking available on the street in Keene Valley. Weekdays are generally not full prior to 9 a.m. but can be full before 6 a.m. on weekends. **GPS:** 44.18911°N / 73.81561°W

THE HIKE

The Haystack, Basin, and Saddleback loop (HaBaSa) is one of the most challenging hikes under 20 miles in the High Peaks. Let's get straight to the hike.

The approach to Haystack is described in greater detail in the previous chapter, so this chapter provides abridged directions to Haystack. See the three previous chapters for more detailed information on each of these three mountains.

Your hike begins at the Garden Trailhead in Keene Valley. Upon signing in, head straight onto the trail leading to Johns Brook Lodge (JBL). After half a mile, an intersection sign appears, pointing left to the South Side Trail and right toward JBL. Continue right. After another 2.5 miles, you'll pass a second register. Proceed right toward JBL. This lodge serves as a great pit stop for water refills or even an overnight stay, if prebooked.

Leaving JBL, you enter back into the forest, heading toward Bushnell Falls. Bypassing the Hopkins Trail, you dip down to cross Johns Brook. The next 1.6 miles will take you through a beautiful new-growth forest as you ascend about 600 feet of elevation. Reaching Slant Rock campsite, continue to follow the trail markers and aim for Mount Marcy. The trail now steepens and becomes rocky leading up to the Phelps/Range Trail intersection. At this intersection, a sign indicates a mile to Haystack. Turning left here, be prepared for a steep and technical trail for the next half mile. On cresting this sub-mountain, the trail drops down, leading to the Range Trail intersection. From here, the last 0.5 miles to Haystack's summit is exposed, so ensure you're dressed appropriately. The climb to Little Haystack is clearly marked by yellow paint on rocks and stacks of rocks that guide you all the way to the summit. On reaching Little Haystack, follow the trail as it zigzags downward and then upward again, approaching Haystack's summit. This area is technical and will require your hands to navigate.

Once you've savored the views from Haystack, return to the Range Trail intersection. Turn right, following the Range Trail toward Basin. On this stretch, you'll pass the Sno-Bird Campsite, a great spot for an overnight stay if you're extending your hike. Near this site is a good spot to get water in a side stream. The ascent to Basin is possibly the most challenging part of your day. In the first 0.4 miles, you climb 700 feet via ladders and scrambles, demanding careful navigation. As you progress, the trail gradually tapers off, with a large rock ledge marking your entry above the tree line and near Basin's summit. Be cautious not to step on any alpine vegetation and enjoy the stunning view from Basin's summit.

On descending Basin, you'll be met with a clear view of Saddleback and the Lower Great Range. The descent is marked but tricky, featuring technical dropdowns and areas where you might need to grab tree limbs for support. This leads to Basin's shoulder, which you'll cross to catch sight of the infamous Saddleback Cliffs. Between Saddleback and Basin, there is no exit. At the base of the cliffs, the trail ascends a few hundred feet. It's marked by yellow blazes on the rocks, guiding you up the cliffs and eventually to the

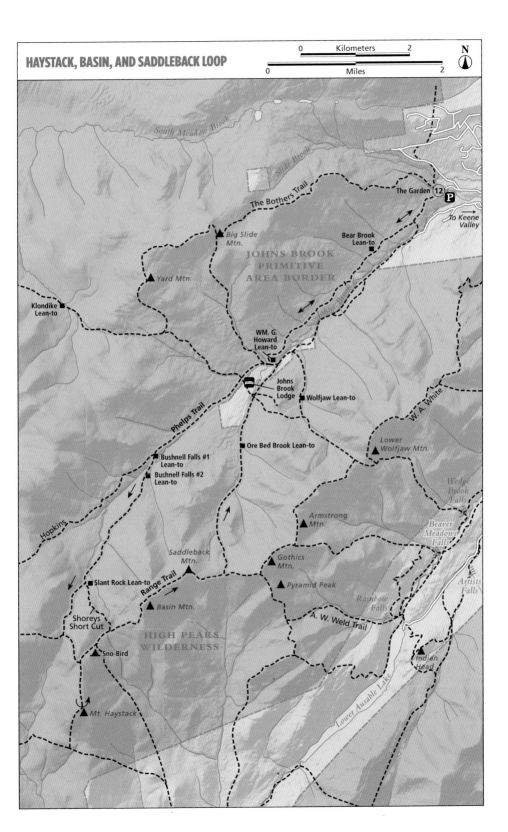

Kilometers

0 — 2

Miles

0 — 2

N

South Meadow Brook

Slide Brook

The Bothers Trail

The Garden 12

P

To Keene Valley

Big Slide Mtn.

Bear Brook Lean-to

Yard Mtn.

JOHNS BROOK PRIMITIVE AREA BORDER

Johns Brook

Klondike Lean-to

WM. G. Howard Lean-to

Johns Brook Lodge

Wolfjaw Lean-to

Phelps Trail

W. A. White

Ore Bed Brook Lean-to

Lower Wolfjaw Mtn.

Bushnell Falls #1 Lean-to

Wedge Brook Falls

Bushnell Falls #2 Lean-to

Armstrong Mtn.

Beaver Meadows Falls

Hopkins

Saddleback Mtn.

Gothics Mtn.

Artists Falls

Slant Rock Lean-to

Range Trail

Pyramid Peak

Basin Mtn.

Rainbow Falls

A. W. Weld Trail

Shoreys Short Cut

HIGH PEAKS WILDERNESS

Sno-Bird

Indian Head

Mt. Haystack

Lower Ausable Lake

summit of Saddleback Mountain. This achievement is certainly one to celebrate. Take this section cautiously.

To wrap up the hike, follow the Range Trail over Saddleback's ridgeline until you reach the Orebed Brook Trail intersection. Take the Orebed Brook Trail, which will lead you back all the way to JBL. From there, follow your initial path back to the Garden Trailhead, concluding your unforgettable HaBaSa adventure.

MILES AND DIRECTIONS

0.0   Start at the Garden Trailhead.

0.5   Turn right at the trail sign to JBL.

3.1   Reach second sign-in, turning right to JBL.

3.6   Reach Johns Brook Lodge, continuing straight toward Bushnell Falls.

5.4   Reach Bushnell Falls area, crossing Johns Brook after passing the Hopkins Trail.

7.0   Reach Slant Rock.

7.1   Reach next sign following directions toward Marcy.

8.0   Reach Range Trail intersection, turning left toward Haystack.

8.5   Reach intersection of Range Trail, 0.5 miles to Haystack.

8.6   Summit of Little Haystack.

9.0   Summit of Mount Haystack. Return to Range Trail.

9.5   Return to the Range Trail, heading right toward Basin.

9.9   Pass Sno-Bird Campsite.

10.0   Reach Range Trail sign pointing 0.7 miles to Basin.

10.7   Reach Basin's summit. Continue off the back side.

11.2   Reach base of Saddleback Cliffs.

11.3   Summit of Saddleback.

11.8   Orebed Brook Trail/Range Trail intersection. Turn left following the OBT all the way back to JBL. Follow signs to JBL.

15.0   Reach JBL.

18.8   Arrive back at the Garden Trailhead.

Haystack, Basin, and Saddleback from the sky.

MOUNT MARCY

Crisp July morning from the highest point in New York, Mount Marcy.

13 MOUNT MARCY

The tallest peak in New York State should certainly not be overlooked. Although Mount Marcy cleaves the sky, it was never actually named Tahawas ("Cloud Splitter") like some people believe. Charles Hoffman, an editor of a New York journal in the 1830s, created this name in an article about his endeavors in the Adirondacks, thus birthing this alleged Native American toponym. From the summit of Mount Marcy, one can see every single high peak except for Couchsachraga, the shortest high peak. (Yes, your author has stood on Marcy and counted every single peak, including East Dix, to make sure this is accurate, as well as having seen Marcy from the forty-four other peaks.) Some say you can't see Nye Mountain or Grace Peak from Marcy, but this is not true. You can in fact see them.

Start: Adirondack Loj
Elevation gain: 3,500 feet
Summit elevation: 5,344 feet
Distance: 14.8 miles
Difficulty: 4 out of 7, moderate
Hiking time: 8–10 hours
Seasons/schedule: This hike is best in June–Oct. This is a good winter hiking challenge, but it is very inclement and remote. For advanced winter hikers only.
Fees and permits: $15 to park at Adirondack Loj
Canine compatibility: Dogs must be on leash.
Trail surface: Due to its popularity, this route is well eroded from foot traffic. This route is not short of large rocks. Overall, it is rocky and muddy.
Land status: Central High Peaks Wilderness
Nearest town: Lake Placid, NY
Water availability: There is some water on the route, but not much, so bring plenty of water (2.5 liters recommended).

Amenities available: The Adirondack Loj, Info Center, and the Hungry Hiker. Many tent sites and privies along the route.
Maximum grade: 650 feet/0.6 miles: two sections this steep. Halfway point and final push.
Special considerations: This is a long walk, so be prepared. Do not wear sneakers or cotton. Make sure to pack a headlamp and extra batteries. It is recommended to bring a windbreaker on any day because it is a very windy summit. Because of how rocky this route is, I would highly suggest bringing trekking poles.
Sunrise or sunset: If you are a bold enough night hiker, sunrise on this mountain is quite the spectacle. Bring a group of friends for the company.
Route type: Out-and-back
Views: The views are excellent, but only the last 0.5 miles has views.

FINDING THE TRAILHEAD

Adirondack Loj is located 1.5 miles southeast of Lake Placid on NY 73; turn down Adirondack Loj Road and drive for 5 miles. Popular and often packed; arrive early. Weekdays are generally not full prior to 9 a.m. but can be full before 6 a.m. on weekends. Marcy Dam Truck Trail at the end of South Meadows can be used if parking is full. **GPS:** 44.18313°N / 73.96445°W

Hiker stands on top of Mount Marcy for sunrise.

THE HIKE

There are many ways to tackle New York's tallest peak, but the most popular is from the famous Adirondack Loj via the Van Hoevenberg Trail. Mount Marcy is not just tall, but it is a lengthy out-and-back hike and should not be taken lightly. On the way up this mountain, you will venture deep into the wilderness in the footsteps of many who first explored the High Peaks. This chapter describes a route that takes you only up Marcy and not any other peak for those who want to climb this as a day hike. This trail starts out at the end of Parking Lot Number 1, right in front of the High Peaks Info Center (this is a great place for information on hiking conditions). You will find the start with a large sign-in area. Please sign in as this keeps accurate logs of trail usage and is for your safety as well. From this point, there will be a large map next to the booth that depicts the surrounding trails in the Central High Peaks region.

Upon starting your hike, you will have a nice, casual walk all the way to Marcy Dam. Along the first mile, you will pass over some hills, spruce forest, and mixed terrain. You will come to the first trail sign 1 mile in. This is the intersection for the MacIntyre Range (straight) and Marcy Dam (left). Turn left. Marcy Dam is 1.3 miles from this point. The trail will continue for the next 1.3 miles. Eventually you will arrive at Marcy Dam. Upon arrival, you will be met with the collapsed dam (center), your main trail to the left, and a spur trail to the right of the dam, leading out to the dam opening. When you arrive at Marcy Dam, continue to the left. Soon after, you will turn onto the crossover bridge, bringing you to the other side. Turn right after this bridge. After a short walk from the bridge, you will arrive at the other side of the dam. Here, you will eventually see a second sign-in. I recommend signing in at this register as well. Continue past the sign-in.

You should be looking for your next turn sign right after the sign-in. It will specifically point to Marcy. At this turn, there are two directions. Turning right will take you toward Avalanche Lake and Colden. Turning left will take you to the Van Hoevenberg Trail toward Marcy. Turn left following the signs for Marcy. From here the trail will slowly start to gain incline. The trail conditions will also become rockier. One mile from

Two hikers enjoying their time at Indian Falls. MacIntyre Range is in the background.

Marcy Dam, you will pass the Phelps Mountain turn sign. Continue past this. There is only really one direction to Marcy at this point. A quarter of a mile past the Phelps turn, you will cross a bridge. The trail will get fairly steep at this point. After about 0.15 miles of climbing, you will pass the cutoff for the Mount Marcy Ski Trail. Please do not take the ski trail. Even though on the map it shows this way to be slightly shorter, it is very overgrown and mossy. It will slow you down (and it is for ski usage only). Turn right, continuing to follow the Van Hoevenberg Trail.

The trail will progressively get rockier. After 0.7 miles, you will reach the top of this current section. The ski trail will meet back up with the Van Hoevenberg Trail, and you will also pass the turn for Tabletop Mountain. Shortly after this turn, you arrive at Indian Falls.

To get a view of the falls, briefly turn right at this point. You will come out onto the top of the waterfall overlooking the MacIntyre Range. Make sure to backtrack properly and to not follow the yellow trail markers (which would take you down the falls). After returning to the trail, continue to follow the blue trail markers. Right after returning to the trail, you will come to your next turn. Turn left (turning you right would be the same yellow trail as previously stated, taking you down the falls). The trail will continue in its mixed fashion, slowly gaining elevation for the next 1.4 miles. The Hopkins Trail cutoff to Johns Brook Valley will be after 1.4 miles. At this sign, turn right, continuing to follow the blue trail markers toward Marcy. The trail will continue, gradually getting steeper.

Over the next 0.6 miles, you will pass two vegetation openings. These are the lower and upper plateaus. Lean-tos used to be at these spots. These 0.6 miles from the Hopkins sign will bring you to the shoulder of Marcy. This is the Range Trail intersection. Turning left will bring you down and over toward Haystack and the rest of the Great Range. Turn right, following the trail to Marcy. You are at 4,800 feet above sea level at this point and have about 550 feet of vertical climbing left. The trail will bring you between a plethora of alpine vegetation. It is very vital to stay on the exact trail for the remainder of the hike to avoid damaging this unique ecosystem. This final 0.5 miles push up Marcy is gorgeous. You will cross over some boardwalks, followed by a couple of scrambles. The trail will have many irregular sections. Continue to follow the yellow painted rock and the cairns carefully the rest of the way up. Do not divert off the trail. If there is white string on the ground with signs, please be mindful of it. After this final push, you will have made it to the top of New York. You will be met by a large summit plaque that was brought in 1937 to commemorate the centennial of the first ascent.

If it's a clear day, take in the views. From here you can see upward of 131 miles away to Mount Washington (weather permitting), as well as forty-five of the forty-six high peaks (some debate the visibility of East Dix, but it is *microscopically* visible just to the left of Hough). Return the 7.4 miles to the car the same way you came.

Boardwalks on the last 0.5-mile stretch to the summit of Mount Marcy.

MOUNT MARCY: A SHORT SYNOPSIS
BY JAMES APPLETON

The tallest mountain in the state of New York comes with a rich history all on its own. The first documented ascent was made on August 5, 1837, by a New York state survey party of eight men including William Redfield and Ebenezer Emmons. The survey party was led by Dr. Emmons who was leading the Geological Survey of New York State and was tasked with finding new resources within the state's Great Northern Wilderness. Mount Marcy was named by Ebenezer Emmons in 1837 after the state governor William Marcy. Emmons also selected the name "Adirondack" as reference to that specific group of high peaks around Marcy, not the entire region. However, now the Mount Marcy area is referred to as the High Peaks and the park as a whole is known as the Adirondacks.

During the ascent William Redfield (who also has a high peak named after him) referred to the mountain as "the High Peak of Essex" before Dr. Emmons's renaming. In 1849 local guide Orson Phelps (of Phelps Mountain fame) cut the first trail to Marcy's summit from the east and in 1878 cut the trail designed by Henry Van Hoevenberg to Marcy from the north. A year later in 1850, Phelps guided the first women to the summit of Marcy. On August 5, 1937, exactly 100 years after Emmons's historic first ascent a group of 200 hikers gathered on the Marcy summit to celebrate the centennial. Among those celebrating was the first female Adirondack 46er (#9) of all time, the beloved Grace Hudowalski. The Mount Marcy centennial celebration included a live radio broadcast, which involved 500 pounds of equipment to be brutally hauled up. In return it failed to broadcast.

Today the popular Van Hoevenberg Trail is the preferred route among hikers year after year to summit the highest peak in the state despite many different available routes to the top. One thing is for sure, however, no matter which way you travel up this mountain, the views at the top will never disappoint.

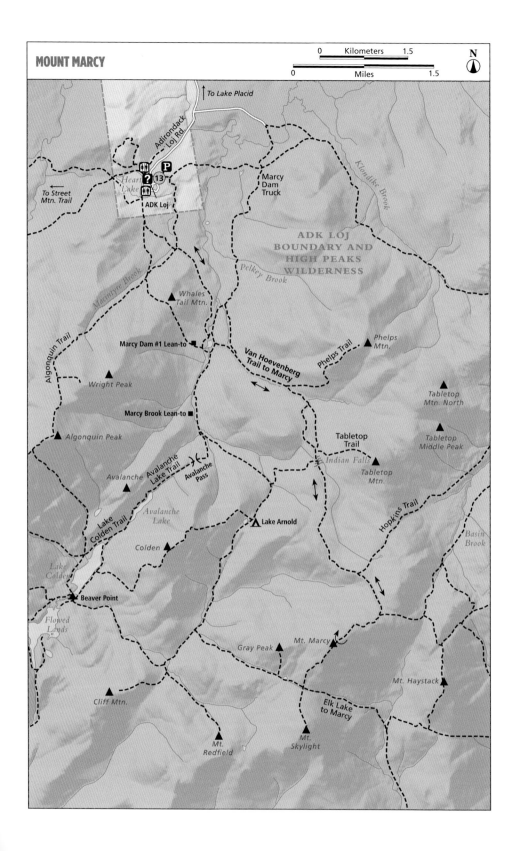

MILES AND DIRECTIONS

0.0 Start at Adirondack Loj

1.0 Turn left at Marcy Dam sign.

2.3 Arrive at Marcy Dam, turning left to go around to the other side.

2.4 Turn left toward Marcy at Van Hoevenberg Trail/Avalanche Pass sign.

3.6 Pass Phelps Mountain sign.

3.8 Cross bridge.

4.7 Arrive at Indian Falls. Follow blue trail markers.

6.4 Pass Hopkins Trail sign, turning right, continuing to follow the blue markers.

6.9 Reach Phelps Trail intersection, turning right to Marcy.

7.4 Summit of Mount Marcy, 5,344 feet.

14.8 Arrive back at Adirondack Loj.

OTHER ROUTES

MARCY VIA UPPER WORKS (TAHAWAS)—19.8 MILES, 4,100 FEET

This more challenging approach may be considered for multiple reasons. This is a good approach if you want to save time having to drive all the way to Lake Placid, as well as if you plan on doing an overnight. This would be the Lake Colden approach. This is also a good route if you want to include Gray, Skylight, Redfield, or Cliff on your hike.

MARCY FROM THE GARDEN (KEENE VALLEY) —18.2 MILES, 4,100 FEET

This alternate approach is a good median. To see a detailed guide on this approach, see the "Mount Haystack" chapter on page 84.

MARCY FROM ELK LAKE—24.3 MILES, 5,200 FEET

This is the least traveled and most rugged way to Marcy for sure. This is a very long day and might want to be considered as an overnight in Panther Gorge. It will bring you to a very remote part of the forest, but an excellent part. This is a fantastic alternative for those who want to experience even more ruggedness of the High Peaks Wilderness with a challenge.

MACINTYRE RANGE

Morning light hitting the MacIntyre Range with Boundary and Algonquin Peak in the distance from Iroquois.

14 WRIGHT PEAK

Wright Peak is one of the easier high peaks on the list, if not second to Cascade and Porter. This is a great mountain for those looking to have the full High Peaks experience without venturing too deep into the woods. It is under 10 miles yet offers some of the best short-and-sweet views in the Central High Peaks region. Wright Peak is part of six other peaks in this full range.

Start: Adirondack Loj
Elevation gain: 2,600 feet
Summit elevation: 4,587 feet
Distance: 7.6 miles
Difficulty: 3 out of 7, moderate. (All 3 peaks would be 5 out of 7.)
Hiking time: 5–6 hours
Seasons/schedule: This hike is best in June–Mar. It is good for winter hiking without the remoteness.
Fees and permits: $15 to park at Adirondack Loj
Canine compatibility: Dogs must be on leash.
Trail surface: Due to its popularity, this route is well eroded from foot traffic. This route has many rocky sections, but is very well maintained. As short as this hike is, it's pretty brutal on the knees because of its steepness. This is the definition of short and steep for sure.
Land status: Central High Peaks Wilderness
Nearest town: Lake Placid, NY
Water availability: There is some water on the route, but not much,
so bring plenty of water (2.5 liters recommended).
Amenities available: The Adirondack Loj, Info Center, and the Hungry Hiker. One tent site and privy along the way.
Maximum grade: 550 feet/0.4 miles: final summit push
Special considerations: This peak is sometimes paired with Algonquin and Iroquois. If you are going for your 46 and have good weather and stamina, it is recommended to go for all three high peaks as a day hike. However, don't be fooled by how short of a hike this is. It's still a beast of a peak! There is also plane wreckage and a memorial plaque near the summit. This summit is also incredibly windy.
Sunrise or sunset: Both but especially for sunrise. Highly recommended for sunrise training.
Route type: Out-and-back
Views: There are excellent 360-degree views.

FINDING THE TRAILHEAD
Adirondack Loj is located 1.5 miles southeast of Lake Placid on NY 73; turn down Adirondack Loj Road and drive for 5 miles. Popular and often packed; arrive early. Weekdays are generally not full prior to 9 a.m. but can be full before 6 a.m. on weekends. **GPS:** 44.18313°N / 73.96445°W

THE HIKE
One of the most popular hikes out of the Loj, Wright Peak is perfect for a first-time High Peaks hike. It is shorter in distance than most and offers incredible views. It is also noted to be one of the windiest summits in the region, if not the Northeast. This peak is positioned in such a way that the wind is funneled right to it by the valley. You can expect this summit to be breezy or windy nearly every day of the year.

A telephoto view of Wright Peak from Gray Peak. If you look closely, you can also see the trail on Colden's Northeast Peak.

This trail starts out at the end of Parking Lot Number 1, right in front of the High Peaks Info Center. (This is a great place for information on hiking conditions.) You will find the start with a large sign-in area. (Please sign in as this maintains accurate logs of trail usage and for your safety as well.) From this point, there will be a large map next to the booth that depicts the surrounding trails in the Central High Peaks region.

Upon starting your hike you will have a nice, casual walk all the way to Marcy Dam. The first mile will pass over some hills, spruce forest and mixed terrain. You will come to the first trail sign 1 mile in. This is the intersection for the MacIntyre Range (straight) and Marcy Dam (left). Go straight following the signs to Algonquin. From here, it is a direct shot all the way up, while only passing a few notable points of interest. After moving past this 1-mile sign, you will continue for another 2.3 miles until the Wright Peak turn sign. The trail following this first 1-mile sign is easy to follow. The trail will have mixed conditions beyond this point, slowly becoming rockier. You will pass over a few streams, large scrambles, and ski trails. About 1.6 miles from the 1-mile sign (2.6 miles total), you will approach McIntyre falls. Just before the falls will be the Wright Peak Ski Trail and the MacIntyre Falls Campsite. Please do not hike up the ski trail. This waterfall, if running, will be your only water source.

Pass the waterfall, following the trail markers for another 0.7 miles. You'll eventually crest and come to the turn sign to Wright Peak and a privy sign. This is the 4,000-foot mark. Turn right to Wright Peak. This 0.4-mile ascent is very dramatic. This path will be the steepest part, climbing 550 feet. The dirt will disappear, and wet slab rock will remain. Be careful here. Eventually, you will pass the alpine zone sign right before you arrive at the tree line, halfway up. There is a steep, hands-on rock climb right here. You will see yellow blazes painted on the rock. There should be plenty of spots to grab onto to help yourself up this short technical spot.

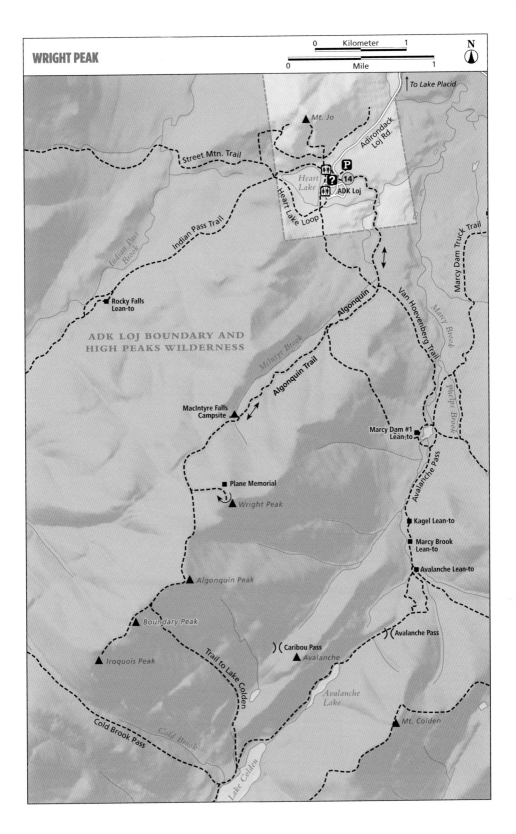

0   Kilometer   1

0   Mile   1

N

To Lake Placid

Mt. Jo

Adirondack Loj Rd.

Street Mtn. Trail

P

Heart Lake

?

14

ADK Loj

Heart Lake Loop

Indian Pass Trail

Indian Pass Brook

Marcy Dam Truck Trail

Rocky Falls Lean-to

ADK LOJ BOUNDARY AND HIGH PEAKS WILDERNESS

McIntyre Brook

Algonquin

Van Hoevenberg Trail

Marcy Brook

Phelps Brook

Algonquin Trail

MacIntyre Falls Campsite

Marcy Dam #1 Lean-to

Avalanche Pass

Plane Memorial

Wright Peak

Kagel Lean-to

Marcy Brook Lean-to

Avalanche Lean-to

Algonquin Peak

Boundary Peak

Trail to Lake Colden

Caribou Pass

Avalanche Pass

Iroquois Peak

Avalanche

Avalanche Lake

Cold Brook Pass

Cold Brook

Mt. Colden

Lake Colden

After this, you will be on the final exposed part of the climb. The rest of the way up will be hard, so take your time. The path can clearly be seen by yellow blazes and cairns. Follow them carefully. They will prevent you from stepping off the path and potentially stepping on delicate alpine plants. Eventually you will see the final summit ledge. Hop up, and welcome to the summit! From here, you can see Algonquin's Northeast Bowl (right), Mount Colden (center) with Mount Marcy behind it, and Heart Lake (left). There is no trail off the other side. Return to your car the way you came. If you would like to see the plane wreckage, you will find a spur trail right before the summit leading you to a memorial plaque. This is about a 5-minute walk away from the trail. Be careful not to step on any alpine plants. You will find the memorial plaque down to your right when walking this ridge. Return to the trail the way you came and walk back to the Loj.

MILES AND DIRECTIONS

0.0   Start at Adirondack Loj.

1.0   Reach sign pointing toward Algonquin, following the trail straight.

2.6   Pass MacIntyre Falls.

3.3   Reach Wright Peak turn.

3.8   Summit Wright Peak; turn around to head back the way you came.

7.6   Return to Loj.

Trail runner looking out toward Marcy from Wright Peak above the clouds.

15 ALGONQUIN AND IROQUOIS PEAKS

Named in 1837 after Archibald MacIntrye, leader of the McIntyre Iron Works, the MacIntyre Range stands prominent and visible from every corridor in the High Peaks. These two neighboring mountains are the two highest points within this range, Algonquin being the second highest in the state. They also boast some of the most breathtaking views of any mountain in the Northeast. This range is shorter in distance than most but packs in a lot of elevation gain and sometimes very dangerous weather.

Start: Adirondack Loj
Elevation gain: 3,800 feet
Summit elevation: Algonquin Peak, 5,114 feet; Iroquois Peak, 4,840 feet
Distance: 10.2 miles
Difficulty: 4 out of 7, moderate. Very steep and exposed.
Hiking time: 6–8 hours
Seasons/schedule: This hike is best in June–Oct.
Fees and permits: $15 to park at Adirondack Loj
Canine compatibility: There is not a lot of water, but the shorter distance makes this easier. Dogs must be on leash.
Trail surface: Due to its popularity, this route is well eroded from foot traffic. This route is rocky but very well maintained. Bring trekking poles.
Land status: Central High Peaks Wilderness
Nearest town: Lake Placid, NY
Water availability: There is some water on the route, but not much, so bring plenty of water (2.5 liters recommended).

Amenities available: The Adirondack Loj, Info Center, and the Hungry Hiker. One tent site and privy along the way.
Maximum grade: 1,100 feet/0.7 miles: last 0.7 miles up Algonquin
Special considerations: If you are going for your 46 and have good weather and stamina, it is recommended to go for all three high peaks as a day hike, but if anything, Iroquois is more important than Wright Peak. Iroquois has a history of being difficult to complete due to poor visibility and weather on the range. It is a pain to go back and get to later, so plan accordingly. It is not recommended to turn this into a loop via Lake Colden. It makes it twice as hard and will certainly not save any time.
Sunrise or sunset: Algonquin is great for either.
Route type: Out-and-back
Views: There are excellent 360-degree views.

FINDING THE TRAILHEAD

Adirondack Loj is located 1.5 miles southeast of Lake Placid on NY 73; turn down Adirondack Loj Road and drive for 5 miles. Popular and often packed; arrive early. Weekdays are generally not full prior to 9 a.m. but can be full before 6 a.m. on weekends. **GPS:** 44.18313°N / 73.96445°W

THE HIKE

Algonquin, formerly known as Mount MacIntyre until it was changed in 1837, is commonly confused with Marcy by uneducated tourists. This is because of how prominent it

The sunrise from Algonquin Peak with Mount Colden in the background.

looks from the roadside. This range towers over the surrounding area as you drive down Adirondack Loj Road. This peak was also first summited only three days after Mount Marcy by the same group. What a week for firsts!

This trail starts out at the end of Parking Lot Number 1, right in front of the High Peaks Info Center (this is a great place for information on hiking conditions). You will find the start with a large sign-in area. Please sign in as this ensures accurate logs of trail usage and is for your safety as well. From this point, there will be a large map next to the booth that depicts the surrounding trails in the Central High Peaks region.

Upon starting your hike, you will have a nice, casual walk all the way to Marcy Dam. The first mile will pass over some hills, spruce forest, and mixed terrain. You will come to the first trail sign 1 mile in. This is the intersection for the MacIntyre Range (straight) and Marcy Dam (left). Go straight following the signs to Algonquin. From here, it is a direct shot all the way up, while only passing a few notable points of interest. After moving past this 1-mile sign, you will continue for another 2.3 miles until the Wright Peak turn sign. The trail is easy to follow and will have mixed conditions beyond this point, slowly becoming rockier. You will pass over a couple streams, large scrambles, and ski trails. About 1.6 miles from the 1-mile sign (2.6 miles total), you will approach MacIntyre Falls. Just before the falls will be the Wright Peak Ski Trail and the MacIntyre Falls Campsite. Please do not hike up the ski trail. This waterfall, if running, will be your only water source.

Pass the waterfall, following the trail markers for another 0.7 miles. You'll eventually crest and come to the turn sign to Wright Peak and a privy sign. This is the 4,000-foot mark. There isn't a direct sign pointing to Algonquin here, just to Wright Peak. Continue straight at this sign. Algonquin is another 0.7 miles away. During this section, you will climb 1,100 feet. About 0.1 miles past this point, you will come to a very steep, open slab section. It can be very wet. Stick to the right side of this slab for an easier climb. From here on, the trail will not let up much. After another 0.5 miles (3.8 miles total) you will reach the alpine zone sign indicating the tree line. Move past this sign to the right and look for the yellow paint on the rock. You will briefly climb up this rock, entering the

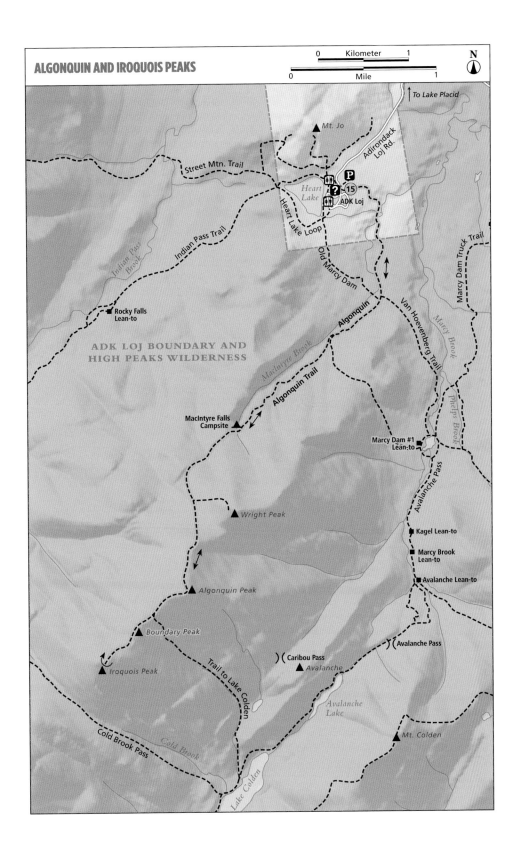

ALGONQUIN AND IROQUOIS PEAKS

0 Kilometer 1

0 Mile 1

N

To Lake Placid

Mt. Jo

Adirondack Loj Rd.

Street Mtn. Trail

P

15

ADK Loj

Heart Lake

Heart Lake Loop

Indian Pass Trail

Indian Pass Brook

Old Marcy Dam

Rocky Falls Lean-to

ADK LOJ BOUNDARY AND HIGH PEAKS WILDERNESS

Algonquin

Van Hoevenberg Trail

Marcy Dam Truck Trail

Marcy Brook

MacIntyre Brook

Algonquin Trail

Phelps Brook

MacIntyre Falls Campsite

Marcy Dam #1 Lean-to

Wright Peak

Avalanche Pass

Kagel Lean-to

Marcy Brook Lean-to

Avalanche Lean-to

Algonquin Peak

Boundary Peak

Caribou Pass

Avalanche Pass

Iroquois Peak

Trail to Lake Colden

Avalanche

Avalanche Lake

Mt. Colden

Cold Brook Pass

Cold Brook

Lake Colden

final push. It is at this point where you should consider turning around if you are struggling or in poor weather.

This is a gnarly summit approach. It will be marked by many rock cairns and yellow lines but can be incredibly hard to follow in poor visibility. Follow them carefully, making sure to stay away from alpine plants and grass. This final push will be about a quarter mile of travel. Eventually you will crest the summit of Algonquin Peak. There is a disk on the rock indicating the summit. Moving toward Iroquois can be confusing at first. The trail will continue slightly to the right past the summit. Look for the rock cairns and smaller rocks laid out as a directional path. You should be able to see the rock cairns guiding you all the way down the other side as you head toward Boundary Peak. Upon reaching the bottom, you will be met with a trail arrow on a sign pointing left. This is the trail down to Lake Colden. Do NOT turn left here. The Iroquois Trail will be to your right, taking you into the trees.

Iroquois is about 0.6 miles from this point and is not maintained or marked. However, it is still easy to navigate. The path will weave you through small spruce forest, eventually up toward Boundary Peak. Boundary Peak is a sub-peak between Algonquin and Iroquois. Continue following the yellow paint and rock cairns when hiking over it. The trail can be a little confusing here, so be vigilant. The trail will drop you back down in between the trees, over wooden boards and around boulders, eventually leading you to the base of Iroquois. This final push has some technicalities to it, so be careful which path you choose to take. Near the top, there will be freshly implanted wooden steps on a boulder. Do not take the blocked herd path navigating around this boulder to the right. Climbing up the steps will bring you to the summit of Iroquois. This is where the trail stops. Return to your car the way you came. It is highly recommended to travel back over Algonquin when returning.

Any attempt to continue toward Shepherd's Tooth or Mount Marshall is illegal. The trail has been destroyed and is not navigable anymore. It used to be a very popular herd path but is now in the process of regeneration.

MILES AND DIRECTIONS

- **0.0** Start at Adirondack Loj.
- **1.0** Reach the 1-mile sign, following the sign toward Algonquin.
- **2.6** Pass MacIntyre Falls.
- **3.3** Reach Wright Peak turn.
- **3.7** Reach tree line.
- **4.0** Summit of Algonquin.
- **4.3** Reach the junction to Lake Colden. Turn right.
- **4.6** Crest Boundary Peak.
- **5.1** Summit of Iroquois. Return the way you came.
- **10.2** Arrive back at the Adirondack Loj.

OTHER ROUTES

LAKE COLDEN LOOP—15.3 MILES, 4,400 FEET

This alternate route definitely makes this range more challenging. It is not my favorite nor many others', but is certainly another viable option. This route up or down between Boundary Peak and Lake Colden is 2.3 miles of sheer boulders and regret. It is slow going and grueling. Are you up for the challenge?

BOUNDARY PEAK HISTORY

Upon examining a map, one might wonder if Boundary Peak qualifies as a high peak. The simple answer is no. Nestled between Iroquois and Algonquin, this sub-peak has a fascinating history that belies its relatively inconspicuous position. Contrary to popular belief, Boundary Peak wasn't named for a border between Native American tribes and their traditional hunting grounds. Instead, the name traces back to surveyor Verplanck Colvin circa 1880. The first ascent of Boundary was made by another surveyor, Charles Broadhead, and his team in June 1797. Tasked by the state of New York to survey the Old Military Tract, Broadhead and his crew blazed a 40-mile straight line, encompassing nearly 17,000 vertical feet of climbing, from Elizabethtown to Tupper Lake. Their journey took them over Giant Mountain—achieving its first ascent—near the summit of Tabletop Mountain, and eventually over present-day Boundary Peak. Interestingly, although Broadhead was less than half a mile from Algonquin Peak's summit, he did not venture over to it. It took another 40 years before someone would explore the MacIntyre Range again, and nearly a century before Iroquois Peak was summited. Thus, the name Boundary Peak was born. To this day, you can observe the boundary line traversing this mountain on any general Adirondack High Peaks regional map. If you look closely, you'll notice a dotted black line running through Boundary, signifying its unique historical significance.

A still winter scene at the base of Iroquois looking up toward the summit. This range holds a great deal of snow in the winter.

STREET AND NYE

A soaked trail can be seen on the way to Street Mountain.

16 STREET AND NYE MOUNTAINS

Street and Nye are two neighboring peaks just to the west of Heart Lake, with one of them being well under the qualifications of a true high peak. However, by tradition, Nye remains to this day. This hike is generally accomplished in the first ten peaks of most people's 46er journey. Even though it's relatively easy compared to many hikes in this region, the infamous Indian Pass Brook has given this journey quite the reputation.

Start: Adirondack Loj
Elevation gain: 2,670 feet
Summit elevation: Street Mountain, 4,166 feet; Nye Mountain, 3,895 feet
Distance: 9.6 miles
Difficulty: 3 out of 7, moderate
Hiking time: 6–8 hours
Seasons/schedule: This hike is best in June–Oct.
Fees and permits: $15 to park at Adirondack Loj
Canine compatibility: Dogs must be on leash.
Trail surface: Due to the nature of these two mountains, the trail is mostly dirt and mud with some rocks scattered throughout.
Land status: Central High Peaks Wilderness
Nearest town: Lake Placid, NY
Water availability: There is some water on route via streams.

Amenities available: The Adirondack Loj, Info Center, and the Hungry Hiker. No camping or privy.
Maximum grade: 500 feet/0.4 miles: last 0.4 miles to intersection
Special considerations: The only real obstacle on this hike is the river crossing at Indian Pass Brook. Sometimes it's an easy rock hop and sometimes it's impassable due to water levels. Please check recent weather, forums, and the High Peaks Info Center upon arrival for conditions. Other than the brook, this is a fairly nice trail to hike with a moderate incline.
Sunrise or sunset: Neither. Just a day hike.
Route type: Out-and-back
Views: There are no views on either summit, but there are side trails near both summits with good views.

FINDING THE TRAILHEAD

Adirondack Loj is located 1.5 miles southeast of Lake Placid on NY 73; turn down Adirondack Loj Road and drive for 5 miles. Popular and often packed; arrive early. Weekdays are generally not full prior to 9 a.m. but can be full before 6 a.m. on weekends. **GPS:** 44.18313°N / 73.96445°W

THE HIKE

If you ask any 46er who hiked in the 1950s, you will hear many individuals claim that Street and Nye were their hardest mountain. This is because the blowdown on the east side of this range made the trip nearly impossible due to the "Big Blow" of 1950. Through prudent land management and trail restoration, this is not the case anymore. Today, you will find Street and Nye to be a joy; rather a "good day in the woods." This hike starts out at the Adirondack Loj.

The beginning of this trail is located right next to the toll booth at the entrance. This trail sign will also indicate Mount Jo and Indian Pass. Start at this point. You will start out on a small gravel path, eventually taking you to the lake. It will have you turn right after a couple minutes. As you come to the lake, you will pass the ADK Mountain Club Flora and Fauna building on your left, with the Mount Jo Trail on your right. Continue walking straight, going around the lake. Continue on this trail for about 0.25 miles. Eventually you will come to the official sign-in registry. After signing in, continue walking the path. The ADK Mountain Club recently put new trail signs up to indicate the correct paths.

After about 5 minutes from the sign-in, you will see the first trail sign pointing you toward Street and Nye. Take this trail. Be vigilant, as it is easy to miss this sign. From here, you will walk 1 mile to Indian Pass Brook. This mile is flat and easy. **Note:** Right before the river, there will be what looks like a trail going down to the left. This is *not* the river crossing. This is an alternate crossing point. You will see this spot when you first see the river. Walk past this point, continuing right on the trail. After another 0.1 miles, you will

A 1950 DEC image taken of the insurmountable amount of blowdown.

find the true crossing point, which is best if the weather permits. The trail is right on the other side. If the water is too high, a good spot to cross is back at the alternate point. Choose how you cross wisely. It could make or break your hike.

Once you get to the other side, continue to follow the trail, leading into a small meadow. The trail will turn sharply left. From here, it is easy going for the next 0.5 miles.

About 0.3 miles after crossing the river, you will come to a small stagnant water crossing with a large downed tree. Use this tree to cross over. Eventually you will start to gradually climb up the mountain. This change in incline is about 0.5 miles from the river. You will cross a few small streams as you approach this mountain. There will be small rock cairns indicating where to cross the trail. Be vigilant not to take a wrong herd path. If you lose the trail briefly, backtrack until you find it again. The trail will get steeper and steeper with mild trail conditions. You will follow what seems to be like a small drainage most of the way up this trail.

Your first view will be about 3.3 miles in (total) from the start. This will be indicated by a rock that you can walk out on that overlooks Algonquin and Wright. About 300 feet of elevation is left to climb until the intersection. The trail will become more rugged after this point. As you make your way up, eventually the trail will taper off and you will walk through a distinctly different part of the forest. There are a ton of stripped pines and downed trees in this spot. Soon after this is the intersection for the two peaks. The trail will abruptly stop, and you will be met with two directions. Turn right for Nye and left for Street (I generally hike Street first). The out-and-back for Street is about 1.2 miles. The trail to Street will have you maneuver some blowdown and briefly dip down before pushing up to the summit. After 0.6 miles, you will come up to the Street Mountain summit sign. Great views, right? To see a view, bear sharp right after the sign. You will find multiple herd paths taking you to viewpoints. One of them has a great 180-degree view of the Santanoni Range, Lost Pond, and the MacIntyre Range. Return to the intersection.

The trail to Nye is the definition of anticlimactic. It will take maybe 10 minutes or so to hit the summit. It is only a quarter of a mile to the top with very little elevation gain—most of the gain to Nye starts from the Street side. This trail will have you briefly dip down, then sharply back up. It will weave you through the dense spruce forest, eventually ending up at the 6-foot-tall Nye Mountain summit sign. To see a view from Nye, walk back about 30 seconds and you'll see a walk out view on the right. This will give a view of the surrounding area. Return to the car the way you came.

MILES AND DIRECTIONS

0.0 Start at Adirondack Loj toll booth, walking to and around the lake.

0.3 Reach the Indian Pass Brook sign-in registry.

0.5 Turn right onto the Street and Nye Trail.

1.6 Cross Indian Pass Brook.

2.2 Cross a small stream, indicating the base of the mountain.

3.6 First view of the MacIntyre Range.

3.9 Reach intersection for both mountains; turn left to go toward Street.

4.5 Reach summit of Street; turn around.

STREET AND NYE MOUNTAINS

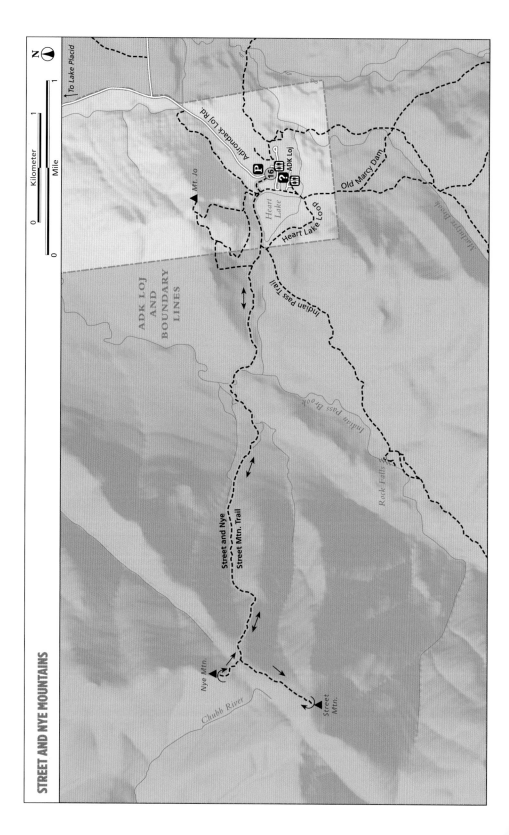

N

To Lake Placid

Kilometer
Mile

ADK LOJ
AND
BOUNDARY
LINES

Mt. Jo

P

16

ADK Loj

Heart
Lake

Heart Lake Loop

Old Marcy Dam

Madison Brook

Indian Pass Trail

Indian Pass Brook

Rock Falls

Street and Nye
Street Mtn. Trail

Chubb River

Nye Mtn.

Street Mtn.

5.1   Return to intersection.

5.4   Reach Nye summit.

5.7   Return to intersection; turn left to head back to the trailhead.

9.6   Arrive back at the Adirondack Loj.

WHAT IS A "LOJ" ANYWAY?

The Adirondack Loj, with its unique name, has a fascinating history involving its founder, Henry Van Hoevenberg, and Dr. Melvil Dewey, the creator of the Dewey Decimal System and founder of the Lake Placid Club (LPC). Henry Van Hoevenberg built the original Adirondack Lodge in 1880, which unfortunately succumbed to a devastating wildfire in 1903. In the aftermath, Van Hoevenberg crossed paths with Mr. Dewey, a visionary with a keen interest in the Adirondack region and an advocate for simplified, phonetic spelling. Dr. Dewey, recognizing the potential of the lodge, offered financial support to Van Hoevenberg to rebuild it. However, he made it clear that this support came with a condition: The lodge's name had to be changed phonetically to reflect his linguistic beliefs. Thus, the Adirondack Lodge became the Adirondack Loj. The partnership between Van Hoevenberg and Dewey played a critical role in the Loj's revival. Under the ownership of Dewey's Lake Placid Club, the property continued to be managed by Van Hoevenberg, ensuring that the Loj remained a central gathering point for outdoor enthusiasts.

Today, as the Heart Lake Program Center, the Adirondak Loj stands as a testament to the enduring bond between these two visionaries. The name Loj serves as a reminder of their shared passion for the Adirondacks, the importance of collaboration, and the innovative spirit of Dr. Melvil Dewey, who left an indelible mark not only on the world of library classification but also on this iconic location in the heart of the Adirondacks.

The view from Nye Mountain's spur trail just before the true summit.

PHELPS AND TABLETOP

Near summit view from Phelps Mountain looking out toward Mount Colden (left) and the MacIntyre Range (right).

17 PHELPS MOUNTAIN

This mountain is a great intro to the forty-six. It is relatively one of the easiest high peaks to hike and is recommended to those starting out. It is generally paired with Tabletop Mountain but can be hiked separately. This is a very good hike if someone just wants to get out onto a summit during a sunny day.

Start: Adirondack Loj
Elevation gain: 2,200 feet
Summit elevation: 4,161 feet
Distance: 9.2 miles
Difficulty: 3 out of 7, moderate (Phelps and Tabletop combined is 4 out of 7)
Hiking time: 5–6 hours
Seasons/schedule: Recommended every month except Apr. A good summer and winter hiking challenge.
Fees and permits: $15 to park at Adirondack Loj
Canine compatibility: Dogs must be on leash.
Trail surface: Due to its popularity, this route is well eroded from foot traffic. This route has many large rocks. Overall it is rocky and muddy.
Land status: Central High Peaks Wilderness

Nearest town: Lake Placid, NY
Water availability: There is not much water on route except for Marcy Dam.
Amenities available: The Adirondack Loj, Info Center, and the Hungry Hiker. Many tent sites and privies at Marcy Dam.
Maximum grade: 1,200 feet/1 miles: Phelps ascent
Special considerations: This hike is a good start for your 46er journey. It is short and packs an all-around good feel for hiking a high peak. Aside from that, there is not much technical data for this one. Just enjoy it!
Sunrise or sunset: Great for both.
Route type: Out-and-back
Views: There are good 180-degree panoramic views of the Great Range.

FINDING THE TRAILHEAD

Adirondack Loj is located 1.5 miles southeast of Lake Placid on NY 73; turn down Adirondack Loj Road and drive for 5 miles. Popular and often packed; arrive early. Weekdays are generally not full prior to 9 a.m. but can be full before 6 a.m. on weekends. Marcy Dam Truck Trail at the end of South Meadows can be used if parking is full. **GPS:** 44.18313°N / 73.96445°W

THE HIKE

Named after the great Adirondack guide Orson Schofield "Old Mountain" Phelps, this mountain is a fan favorite. However, Phelps himself never even summited this peak in his life. The first summit of this mountain wasn't until 1905, one year after Phelps's death. Verplanck Colvin originally named this mountain "Little Marcy" before the name was ultimately changed to Phelps Mountain. Upon starting your hike, you will have a nice, casual walk all the way to Marcy Dam. Along the first mile, you will pass over some hills, spruce forest, and mixed terrain. You will come to the first trail sign 1 mile in. This is the intersection for the MacIntyre Range (straight) and Marcy Dam (left). Turn left. The trail will continue as it has for the next 1.3 miles when you will arrive at Marcy Dam. Upon arrival, you will be met with the collapsed dam (center), your main trail to the left, and a spur trail to the right of the dam leading out to the dam opening; continue to the

Back side of Phelps as seen from Cascade Mountain. Mount Colden is visible just beyond.

left. Soon after, you will turn onto the crossover bridge, bringing you to the other side. Turn right after this bridge. After a short walk, you will arrive at the other side of the dam. Here, you will eventually see a second sign-in. I recommended signing in at this register as well. Continue past the sign-in.

Look for your next turn sign right after the sign-in. It will specifically point to Marcy. At this turn, there are two directions. Turning right will take you toward Avalanche Lake

Hiker hiking up Phelps in winter.

and Colden. Turning left will take you to the Van Hoevenberg Trail toward Marcy and Phelps. Turn left following the signs for Marcy. From here the trail will slowly start to gain incline. The trail conditions will also continue to be more mixed, becoming rockier. One mile from Marcy Dam, you will finally reach the Phelps Mountain turn sign. It will indicate 1 mile. This trail is very steep, climbing 1,200 feet, and will certainly feel longer than a mile. The terrain is very rocky here. During this mile, you will encounter many boulders, rock hops, and scrambles. As you near the halfway point, you will climb a decent rock scramble with a downed tree.

Continuing up, the trail will have less boulders and more flat rock surfaces. Near the top, the trees will slowly clear. Right before the

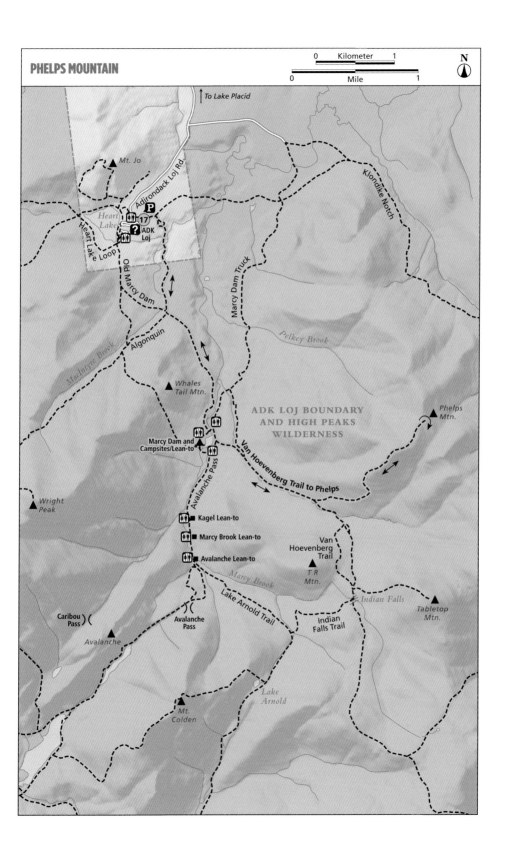

PHELPS MOUNTAIN

0 ——— Kilometer ——— 1
0 ——— Mile ——— 1

N

To Lake Placid

Mt. Jo

Heart Lake

Adirondack Loj Rd.

P
17
ADK Loj

Heart Lake Loop

Old Marcy Dam

Marcy Dam Truck

Klondike Notch

Pelkey Brook

Algonquin

MacIntyre Brook

Whales Tail Mtn.

ADK LOJ BOUNDARY
AND HIGH PEAKS
WILDERNESS

Phelps Mtn.

Marcy Dam and
Campsites/Lean-to

Avalanche Pass

Van Hoevenberg Trail to Phelps

Wright Peak

Kagel Lean-to

Marcy Brook Lean-to

Avalanche Lean-to

Van Hoevenberg Trail

T R Mtn.

Marcy Brook

Indian Falls

Tabletop Mtn.

Caribou Pass

Avalanche

Avalanche Pass

Lake Arnold Trail

Indian Falls Trail

Mt. Colden

Lake Arnold

Phelps summit is unique with its table-like rock top. Maybe this should have been named Tabletop?

top, you'll be met with what looks like a trail split. Look carefully for any trail maker or indication at this spot. The trail seems to go straight and right. Turn right, and you will briefly go down and around to the left coming out to another ledge view. Following this, you will walk on a narrow path right before the summit. You will hop up onto a ledge, welcoming you to the top. Looking out from here you can see Marcy, Tabletop, some of the Great Range, and the summit of Big Slide all the way to the left. There is also a great viewpoint just before the summit overlooking Avalanche Pass, Colden, and the MacIntyre Range. Return to the Loj the way you came.

MILES AND DIRECTIONS

0.0 Start at Adirondack Loj.

1.0 Turn left at Marcy Dam sign.

2.3 Arrive at Marcy Dam, turning left to go around to the other side.

2.4 Turn left toward Marcy at Van Hoevenberg Trail/Avalanche Pass sign.

3.6 Reach Phelps Mountain sign.

4.6 Reach summit of Phelps; turn around and head back the way you came.

9.2 Arrive back at the trailhead.

18 TABLETOP MOUNTAIN

Tabletop Mountain is generally paired with Phelps Mountain, and it is recommended to do so if doing your forty-six. The name of this mountain was given due to its flat top–like summit. This mountain is not too spectacular, but it is still quite unique in many ways. Tabletop is also a good peak to start out with before tackling other high peaks.

Start: Adirondack Loj
Elevation gain: 2,500 feet
Summit elevation: 4,427 feet
Distance: 10.6 miles
Difficulty: 3 out of 7, moderate (Phelps and Tabletop combined is 4 out of 7)
Hiking time: 6–7 hours
Seasons/schedule: Recommended every month except Apr. A good summer and winter hiking challenge.
Fees and permits: $15 to park at Adirondack Loj
Canine compatibility: Dogs must be on leash.
Trail surface: Due to its popularity, this route is well eroded from foot traffic. This route is worn, wet, and rugged.
Land status: Central High Peaks Wilderness

Nearest town: Lake Placid, NY
Water availability: There is not much water on route except for Marcy Dam and Phelps Brook.
Amenities available: The Adirondack Loj, Info Center, and the Hungry Hiker. Many tent sites and privies at Marcy Dam.
Maximum grade: 600 feet/0.4 miles: Tabletop ascent
Special considerations: This hike is a good ground break for your 46er journey. It's a little long but nice. Stop by Indian Falls shortly after the tabletop turnoff.
Sunrise or sunset: This is not recommended for either. Just a day hike.
Route type: Out-and-back
Views: The views are okay, with small panoramic views of the Great Range.

FINDING THE TRAILHEAD

Adirondack Loj is located 1.5 miles southeast of Lake Placid on NY 73; turn down Adirondack Loj Road and drive for 5 miles. Popular and often packed; arrive early. Weekdays are generally not full prior to 9 a.m. but can be full before 6 a.m. on weekends. Marcy Dam Truck Trail at the end of South Meadows can be used if parking is full. **GPS:** 44.18313°N / 73.96445°W

THE HIKE

It's always strange to hear about the surveying and summit history of the High Peaks. It was nearly 150 years between the first recorded high peak summit and the last. Tabletop, formally known as "Flat Top," has quite an interesting survey history. Even though the name of this mountain did not appear on maps until 1876, the first documented climb was in 1911 by Jim Suiter, who climbed Tabletop to contain a forest fire on the summit. Charles Broadhead came close to this summit in 1797 when surveying the Old Military Tract, describing it as a "very rough chief of timber fallen down by the wind." The summit of this mountain is not very spectacular. Even the ADK Mountain Club referred to the summit saying "One may as well climb a tree, for this 'table' is so well 'topped' that a good view from the summit is out of the question." Since then, there has been an effort to cut a view out on this dense forested peak.

The turn sign indicating the trail to Tabletop Mountain.

Upon starting your hike, you will have a nice, casual walk all the way to Marcy Dam. Along the first mile, you will pass over some hills, spruce forest, and mixed terrain. You will come to the first trail sign 1 mile in. This is the intersection for the MacIntyre Range (straight) and Marcy Dam (left). Turn left. Marcy dam is 1.3 miles from this point. The trail will continue as it has until you arrive at Marcy Dam. Upon arrival, you will be met with the collapsed dam (center), the main trail to the left, and a spur trail to the right of the dam, leading out to the dam opening. When you arrive at Marcy Dam, continue to the left. Soon after, you will turn onto the crossover bridge, bringing you to the other side. Turn right after this bridge. After a short walk, you will arrive at the other side of the dam. Here, you will eventually see a second sign-in. I recommend signing in at this register as well. Continue past the sign-in.

Look for your next turn sign right after the sign-in. It will specifically point to Marcy. At this turn, there are two directions. Turning right will take you toward Avalanche Lake and Colden. Turning left will take you to the Van Hoevenberg Trail toward Marcy. Turn left following the signs for Marcy. From here the trail will slowly start to gain incline. The trail conditions will also continue to be more mixed, slowly becoming rockier. One mile from Marcy Dam, you will pass the Phelps Mountain turn sign. Continue past this. There is only really one direction to Marcy at this point. A quarter-mile past the Phelps turn, you will cross a bridge. The trail will get fairly steep at this point. After about 0.15 mile of climbing, you will pass the cutoff for the Mount Marcy Ski Trail. Please do not take the ski trail. Even though the map shows this way to be slightly shorter, it is very overgrown and mossy. It will slow you down (and it is for ski use only). Turn right, continuing to follow the Van Hoevenberg Trail.

The trail will progressively get rockier. After 0.7 miles, you will reach the top of this section. The ski trail will meet back up, and you will come to the turn for Tabletop Mountain. (Briefly past this point is Indian Falls. Feel free to check it out.) Turn left, following the sign toward Tabletop Mountain. This trail is very rugged. It is not marked, nor really maintained. There are also many herd paths near the bottom because people in the past couldn't quite "figure out" the path. If you are vigilant enough, you may discern which path to correctly take when heading up. When you start out, the trail will briefly dip down. This trail is 0.6 miles up. Upon going up, the trail will appear to be dug into the earth and you'll be surrounded by thin, yet goofy looking trees. In wet conditions, this trail can be a small river. About halfway up, you will be met with a large rock scramble. Climbing this can be a tad dicey. After what feels like nearing the top, you will come to multiple mud pits. There will probably be many sticks and logs thrown down to help

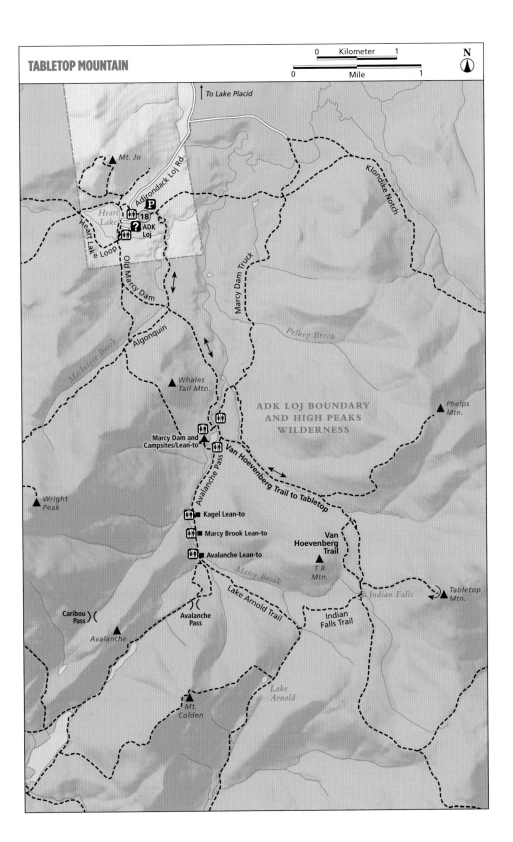

Kilometer

0   1

Mile

0   1

N

To Lake Placid

Mt. Jo

Adirondack Loj Rd.

P

Heart
Lake

18

ADK
Loj

Heart Lake Loop

Old Marcy Dam

Algonquin

McIntyre Brook

Marcy Dam Truck

Klondike Notch

Pelkey Brook

ADK LOJ BOUNDARY
AND HIGH PEAKS
WILDERNESS

Whales
Tail Mtn.

Phelps
Mtn.

Marcy Dam and
Campsites/Lean-to

Van Hoevenberg Trail to Tabletop

Avalanche Pass

Wright
Peak

Kagel Lean-to

Marcy Brook Lean-to

Avalanche Lean-to

Marcy Brook

Van
Hoevenberg
Trail

T R
Mtn.

Indian Falls

Tabletop
Mtn.

Caribou
Pass

Avalanche

Avalanche
Pass

Lake Arnold Trail

Indian
Falls Trail

Lake
Arnold

Mt.
Colden

assist hikers. After navigating over these two spots, you will be spat out onto the summit. You will be met with a brown and yellow Tabletop Mountain sign. Walk forward to get a view. From here, you can see the MacIntyre Range to the right, followed by Colden, Marcy, and Gray (center), Haystack (just barely poking up), and then Basin off to the left. From here, return to the Adirondack Loj from the way you came.

MILES AND DIRECTIONS

0.0   Start at Adirondack Loj.

1.0   Turn left at Marcy Dam sign.

2.3   Arrive at Marcy Dam, turning left to go around to the other side.

2.4   Turn left toward Marcy at Van Hoevenberg Trail/Avalanche Pass sign.

3.6   Pass Phelps Mountain sign.

3.8   Cross bridge.

4.7   Arrive at Tabletop Mountain turn sign.

5.3   Reach Tabletop Mountain summit. Return the way you came.

10.6   Arrive back at the Adirondack Loj.

A bright March day on the summit of Tabletop Mountain.

LAKE COLDEN REGION

Calm evening at Lake Colden Dam with Mount Colden in the distance.

19 **MOUNT COLDEN**

One of the few mountains that stands by itself, this indistinguishable peak is known as one of the most beautiful high peaks to look at. This is due to its intricate scarring from its natural slides covering all sides of the mountain. Nestled right in between Algonquin and Marcy, Mount Colden has a rich history behind it, making it a must for anyone looking for a good day hike.

Start: Adirondack Loj
Elevation gain: 3,150 feet
Summit elevation: 4,715 feet
Distance: 14.1-mile loop (12.8 out-and-back)
Difficulty: 4 out of 7, moderate
Hiking time: 8–10 hours
Seasons/schedule: Recommended every month except Apr and May. A good summer and winter hiking challenge.
Fees and permits: $15 to park at Adirondack Loj
Canine compatibility: Dogs must be on leash.
Trail surface: This trail is well-worn, having a variety of large rocks, latters, and rock slabs.
Land status: Central High Peaks Wilderness
Nearest town: Lake Placid, NY

Water availability: Water is available if you have a filter. There are such sources as Marcy Dam, Marcy Brook, Opalescent River, and Lake Colden.
Amenities available: The Adirondack Loj, Info Center, and the Hungry Hiker. Many tent sites and privies at Marcy Dam and Lake Colden.
Maximum grade: 1,200 feet/0.6 miles: Mount Colden Southwest Side
Special considerations: There is not much to complain about this peak. Bring a good sandwich for the top!
Sunrise or sunset: You could do either, but the sunset is much better (if you are willing to hike back in the dark).
Route type: Lollipop loop or out-and-back
Views: Colden has a large summit with plenty of incredibly unique perspectives on surrounding peaks.

FINDING THE TRAILHEAD

Adirondack Loj is located 1.5 miles southeast of Lake Placid on NY 73; turn down Adirondack Loj Road and drive for 5 miles. Popular and often packed; arrive early. Weekdays are generally not full prior to 9 a.m. but can be full before 6 a.m. on weekends. Marcy Dam Truck Trail at the end of South Meadows can be used if parking is full. **GPS:** 44.18313°N / 73.96445°W

THE HIKE

Mount Colden, once regarded by Alfred B. Street as "the most savage mountain, by far, of the Adirondacks,—the very wild-cat of mountains," now presents itself as an appealing and picturesque destination in the 21st century. The mountain captivates hikers with its accessibility, intriguing features, and distinct trails. Two main paths lead to Colden's summit: the Lake Colden Trail and the Lake Arnold Route. Established in 1923 by state forester Arthur S. Hopkins, the Lake Colden Trail offers a steep and challenging climb with continuous elevation gain. Modern-day hiker Jody Edwards (#1618) describes it as a demanding ascent that, while not as steep as the slides, remains one of the toughest "normal ascents." In contrast, the Lake Arnold Route, created in 1966, provides a shorter

Mount Colden from afar.

and more gradual climb, though not necessarily more accommodating. Named the "L. Morgan Porter Trail" in honor of the long-serving chairman of the Adirondack Mountain Club guidebook committee, this path approaches Colden from the northeast. This guide suggests taking the Lake Arnold Trail up the mountain and descending the back side to Lake Colden. However, for an easier hike, you can opt for an out-and-back route along the Lake Arnold Trail, cutting the hike down by nearly 2 miles.

As you embark on your hike, you'll enjoy a leisurely stroll toward Marcy Dam, passing through gentle hills, spruce forests, and varied terrain. After 1 mile, you'll reach the first trail sign, which indicates the intersection for the MacIntyre Range (straight) and Marcy Dam (left). Turn left here, with Marcy Dam just 1.3 miles away. The trail will maintain its character for the next stretch until you reach Marcy Dam. Upon arriving at Marcy Dam, you'll see the collapsed dam straight ahead, the main trail to the left, and a spur trail to the right, leading toward the dam opening. Keep left and cross the bridge, then turn right once you're on the other side. A short walk later, you'll find yourself at the opposite end of the dam, where you'll encounter a second sign-in register. It's a good idea to sign in here as well. Continue past the sign-in, and soon you'll come across another trail sign, directing you toward Marcy. At this junction, you have two options: turning right leads to Avalanche Lake and Colden, while turning left takes you along the Van Hoevenberg Trail toward Marcy. Continue along the trail to the right, enjoying the next 1.1-mile stretch leading to the Avalanche camps. As you approach the end of this section, you'll cross a wooden bridge. A mere 100 feet later, you'll find a campsite on the right and the next intersection on the left. At this junction, you can choose between two paths: straight ahead for Avalanche Lake (1 mile) or to the left for Lake Arnold (1.5 miles) and Mount Colden (2.9 miles). This is where you can decide whether to complete the rest of the loop clockwise or counterclockwise. I recommend taking the Lake Arnold Route first, as it provides an easier ascent to the summit, and allows you to descend the south side instead.

The trail heading up toward Avalanche Lake. This is a standard type of trail within the High Peaks.

Opting for the Lake Arnold Route, be prepared for an increased level of difficulty over the next 1.5 miles. The trail features increasingly rocky terrain that will challenge your footing. After completing the first mile of this section, you'll come across another trail sign located near a stream. This sign points toward Indian Falls. Be sure to continue past this sign in the direction of Lake Arnold, following the blue markers that guide your path. As you proceed, the following 0.5-mile stretch will become progressively more rugged, with the possibility of wet conditions depending on recent weather. Upon reaching the picturesque Lake Arnold, sitting at about 3,700 feet, your 1.5-mile climb will gradually come to an end. However, it's crucial not to miss the "high-up" Mount Colden turnoff sign near

The sunset from Colden's North East Peak.

the lake. This marker is easy to overlook, so be vigilant to avoid hiking beyond your intended turnoff point. The sign, which may be replaced in the coming years, currently indicates that Mount Colden is 1.4 miles away. Turn right at the sign and follow the yellow trail marker route that leads to the summit of Colden. Immediately, you'll encounter a brief muddy and rugged spot, as well as a quick viewpoint of the lake and a nearby tent site (marked by a sign). Once you pass through this muddy section, you'll quickly reconnect with the main trail, which will bring you across some helpful boardwalks.

The final 1.4-mile approach to Mount Colden isn't too demanding, though the trail will become increasingly steep and rugged as you get closer to the alpine level. Eventually, you'll enter the alpine zone, marked by a white sign. At this point, you're approaching Colden's smaller summit, Colden's Northeast Peak. Prepare for a steep scramble that leads to the top of this minor peak, which offers stunning views that rival those of the true summit. After taking in the scenery, continue along the trail to the left. From this vantage point, you can see the summit of Colden. Head toward it, finding the trail that brings you down a ladder and then some wooden stairs. This will lead you between the col of the two high points. The remainder of the trail up to Colden will be steep and rugged. As you near the top, you'll come across a very large rock. You have the option to either go underneath it or around it to the left. The trail will then guide you along the summit ridge. After a few minutes, you'll reach what appears to be the highest point. Here, you'll find a small spur trail that veers left. This slightly elevated spot is the true summit of Mount Colden and is marked by a drilled hole in the rock.

To enjoy even better views, continue past the summit toward the other side, where you'll discover the famous balanced rock overlooking the MacIntyre Range. As you walk further, grooved paths along the north side ridge emerge. Be mindful of the fragile alpine vegetation and stick to designated paths and trail blazes. A leisurely exploration of the summit rewards you with stunning 360-degree views. Begin your descent along the south side of the mountain. This trail will challenge your grip, as the initial steep descent is mostly bare, flat rock, which can be slippery when wet. After several drops and scrambles, you'll encounter the region's longest set of stairs. This 1.5-mile descent, with a 2,000-foot decline, will eventually lead you to the east side of Lake Colden. At the bottom, you'll reach a sign. Turn right for an incredible view of Algonquin and surrounding peaks across the lake. You're now 1 mile from Avalanche Lake. Continue to follow the signs for Avalanche Lake and the Loj. As you approach the lake, the trail will take you to its left side. The path across Avalanche Pass is a unique spectacle, featuring massive rocks, dropdown maneuvers, stairs, ladders, and boardwalks.

Parallel to Mount Colden, you'll see the impressive cliffs of the mountainside, the Trap Dike, and eventually Hitch-Up Matilda. These boards offer a one-of-a-kind experience and boast a century-long history, albeit with multiple wooden board interchanges. Once the lake ends, you'll be 1 mile from the Avalanche Camp intersection. The trail will guide you through the preface entrance of the pass, long switchbacks, and eventually back to Avalanche Camp.

From this point onward, the route back to the Adirondack Loj is the same as the way you came in. Follow the trail to Marcy Dam and complete your journey back to the Loj.

MILES AND DIRECTIONS

0.0 Start at Adirondack Loj.

1.0 Turn left at Marcy Dam sign.

2.3 Arrive at Marcy Dam, turning left to go around to the other side.

2.4 Turn right at intersection split for Van Hoe Trail to Marcy or Avalanche Lake/Colden.

3.5 Reach Avalanche Camp, turning left, following signs to Lake Arnold.

4.5 Pass Marcy Brook with turn sign toward Indian Falls; continue straight.

5.1 Reach Lake Arnold, turning right at the "1.4 miles" Mount Colden ascent sign.

5.9 Reach summit of Little Colden (Northeast Peak).

The summit view from Colden is amazing. The famous balanced rock and MacIntyre Range can be seen here.

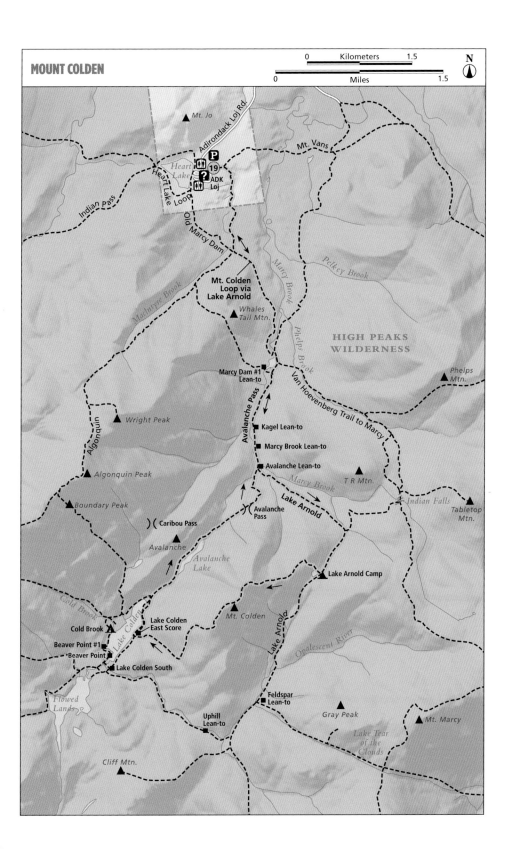

MOUNT COLDEN

Kilometers 0 1.5
Miles 0 1.5

N

Mt. Jo

Adirondack Loj Rd.

Mt. Vans

Heart Lake

P 19
ADK Loj

Indian Pass

Heart Lake Loop

Old Marcy Dam

Mt. Colden Loop via Lake Arnold

McIntyre Brook

Marcy Brook

Pelkey Brook

Whales Tail Mtn.

Phelps Brook

HIGH PEAKS WILDERNESS

Phelps Mtn.

Marcy Dam #1 Lean-to

Avalanche Pass

Van Hoevenberg Trail to Marcy

Algonquin

Wright Peak

Kagel Lean-to

Marcy Brook Lean-to

Avalanche Lean-to

Marcy Brook

T R Mtn.

Indian Falls

Algonquin Peak

Boundary Peak

Caribou Pass

Avalanche Pass

Lake Arnold

Tabletop Mtn.

Avalanche

Avalanche Lake

Lake Arnold Camp

Cold Brook

Lake Colden East Score

Mt. Colden

Lake Arnold

Opalescent River

Cold Brook

Beaver Point #1

Beaver Point

Lake Colden South

Flowed Lands

Feldspar Lean-to

Gray Peak

Mt. Marcy

Uphill Lean-to

Lake Tear of the Clouds

Cliff Mtn.

6.4 Summit of Mount Colden. Continue straight along the ridge, descending the other side.

7.9 Reach shore of Lake Colden, turning right at sign toward Avalanche Lake.

8.9 Reach Avalanche Pass/Lake.

9.4 Reach other side of Avalanche Lake, descending back to Avalanche Camp.

10.5 Return to Avalanche Camp, following the trail back to the Adirondack Loj.

14.1 Arrive back at Adirondcak Loj.

MOUNT COLDEN'S TRAP DIKE

If you've been around the High Peaks long enough, you're probably familiar with the infamous Mount Colden Trap Dike (sometimes spelled Dyke). What is it? How has it gotten its current reputation in recent years? This geologically unique feature has a rich history and presents a challenging climb for those who seek to attempt it. While early explorers of the region were naming peaks, they didn't take the time to climb Colden. In 1837, Professor Ebenezer Emmons climbed 1,500 feet up Colden's Trap Dike but didn't summit. This is probably due to his circumstances with entering the slide and only being left with trees toward the top of the dike. He described the dike as a "remarkable geological formation cutting through the mountain, consisting of sienite or hornblende and granular feldspar." The dike's formation is a result of magma intruding into existing rock fissures, which then solidified and eroded over time, creating a striking feature on the mountain, rather than the preassumed creation by a stream as mentioned in Emmons's initial observations. The first recorded ascent of Colden goes to Robert Clark and Alexander Ralph, employees of the McIntyre Iron Works. Their 1850 climb via the Trap Dike marked the first true high peak summit reached "for the sheer joy of climbing", setting a precedent for future climbers. Alfred B. Street described Colden as "the most savage mountain" of the Adirondacks, but today, it's accessible, interesting, and picturesque.

Trails approach Colden's summit from opposite sides. The Trap Dike, on the other hand, is not a trail and should not be considered by everyday hikers. However, it is nothing short of the greatest marvel, the most talked-about climb, and one of the most interesting features in all the Adirondacks. According to Jim Goodwin (#24), who made the first recorded winter ascent in 1935, the Trap Dike offers the most enjoyable alpine climbing in the Adirondacks. However, the dike has been the site of multiple deaths and accidents, in both winter and summer. The dike has also seen more rescues than any other Adirondack route, with climbers freezing in fear and requiring assistance. Some episodes are reminiscent of Verplanck Colvin's daring descent down the dike in 1872, which he chose not to detail in his report to the state legislature. Given the Trap Dike's history and reputation, it shouldn't be considered a standard route for climbing Mount Colden. Those who choose to attempt it should be well-prepared and understand the risks involved. Proper research, planning, and knowledge of one's own limits are crucial for a safe and successful climb. The Trap Dike is a testament to the power and beauty 'f the Adirondacks, but caution must be exercised when tackling this formidable feature. As the popularity of outdoor activities continues to grow, it's essential to remember the lessons of the past and respect the inherent dangers of such an endeavor.

The Irene Slide and Trap Dike as viewed from Algonquin Peak shortly after it was formed. KEVIN MACKENZIE

20 **MOUNT MARSHALL**

Nestled away at the end of the MacIntyre Range, Mount Marshall finds itself as one of the most iconic and unique peaks of the forty-six. Named after Bob Marshall, this mountain showcases a rich history and striking natural beauty. As you traverse its verdant, moss-covered trails, uncover the captivating stories behind its namesake. A perfect day hike for adventurers, Mount Marshall offers a compelling journey through the heart of the High Peaks.

Start: Upper Works
Elevation gain: 2,900 feet
Summit elevation: 4,360 feet
Distance: 14.5 miles
Difficulty: 4 out of 7, moderate
Hiking time: 7–9 hours
Seasons/schedule: Recommended every month except Apr and May. A good summer and winter hiking challenge.
Fees and permits: None
Canine compatibility: Dogs must be on leash.
Trail surface: The Calamity Trail toward Lake Colden is wide and rugged. Well worn with some trail management. You'll find stone stairs, boardwalks, and plenty of mud. The trail up Mount Marshall is unmarked, windy, muddy, and wet.
Land status: Central High Peaks Wilderness
Nearest town: Newcomb, NY/Lake Placid, NY

Water availability: Water is available if you have a filter. There are such sources as Calamity Brook and Herbert Brook.
Amenities available: Some porta potties at the trailhead. Three camping spots along the way with a privy at the base.
Maximum grade: 1,100 feet/1 mile up: Mount Marshall
Special considerations: This trail can be very wet. Definitely bring gaiters and Gore-Tex.
Sunrise or sunset: It would be a challenge, but the sunrise would be great from the ledge view near the summit.
Route type: Out-and-back
Views: This mountain has few to no views; however, there is an amazing outcropping near the top giving a panoramic view.

FINDING THE TRAILHEAD

From I-87 exit 29, head west on Blue Ridge Road for 17.4 miles to Tahawus Road. Turn right, proceed for 6.3 miles, and make a left at the High Peaks trails sign. Follow to the end. The trailhead is less than a mile past the old blast furnace. **GPS:** 44.08621°N / 74.05554°W

THE HIKE

Mount Marshall, standing at 4,360 feet, is named after wilderness activist Bob Marshall (#3). In 1918, Bob, his brother George, and their guide Herb Clark climbed the then-unnamed peak, naming it Herbert Peak. It was soon renamed Mount Clinton, honoring former New York Governor DeWitt Clinton. Although the Marshall brothers never wanted a mountain named after them, their fans petitioned to change the peak's name in Bob's honor in 1942. The first ascent took place on June 26, 1921. Mount Marshall's beauty captivated the trio, who marveled at its lush, rainforest-like vegetation. They were impressed by the mountain's wild, unspoiled nature, considering it "among the

A panoramic view from Mount Marshall from a spur trail just before the summit.

wildest in the Adirondacks." As they ascended, the dense woods at the summit gave way to surprisingly good views from ledges they discovered. Bob Marshall was a passionate hiker and wilderness advocate, often regarded as the father of "ultra-hiking." In 1935, he cofounded the Wilderness Society, and his guidebook, *The High Peaks of the Adirondacks*, is considered the first modern Adirondack guidebook. His untimely death in 1939 left an indelible mark on wilderness conservation and exploration. So whether hiking this as your first or last 46er, or simply looking to climb this peak in tribute, you will certainly find a special place for this peak.

Starting at the popular southern High Peaks trailhead Upper Works, this approach is one of four to the peak, preferred due to its hiking distance. At the new hikers' parking lot, you'll likely find space on a busy weekday. Near the parking spot is MacNaughton Cottage, where Teddy Roosevelt began his midnight ride. From there, follow the gravel road to the old parking lot, about a 5-minute walk, where you'll find the sign-in. After signing in, begin your trek. You'll soon cross the Hudson River and arrive at your first sign 0.4 miles in. Turning left offers a beautiful view of Henderson Lake, while turning right keeps you on the Calamity Brook Trail; keep right. In 0.2 miles, you'll encounter another trail sign; keep right, as turning left leads to Indian Pass. Over the next 1.2 miles, traverse varied terrain while following red trail markers. You'll reach another trail intersection 1.8 miles from the car. This is the Calamity Crossover Trail; don't turn left. Instead, keep right, crossing the bridge and following directions toward Lake Colden. The trail remains relatively flat for another 0.5 miles before steepening.

After hiking 1.1 miles past the last sign, you'll pass the Calamity Brook campsites, about 2.9 miles from the car. Continue on the trail for another 1.5 miles until you reach the David Henderson Memorial, a cool spot to check out and learn about. The memorial eulogizes Henderson's death from an accidental self-inflicted gunshot wound, giving Calamity Mountain, Lake, Brook, and Trail their names. The memorial is 4.4 miles from the start. In another 0.25 miles, you'll reach Flowed Lands and encounter another sign-in box. Just beyond it, a good spur trail offers a fantastic view of the Flowed Lands. At the sign-in box, bear left, dipping down and up, and follow the trail toward Lake Colden. For the next 0.7 miles, you'll make your way around the Flowed Lands, through the woods, over a small hill, and eventually arrive at the Mount Marshall turnoff, about 5.4 miles from the car. The turnoff is only marked by a large stack of rocks, so keep an eye out for it. Right after the turnoff, you'll find a lean-to if you want to repack, eat, rest, or drop an item.

Begin the 1.7-mile ascent at the rocks, climbing approximately 1,600 feet. This unmarked and unmaintained trail requires visual caution due to numerous misleading paths. Initially, you'll navigate narrow brush and steep embankments before reaching the main climb. As you ascend, you'll cross Herbert Brook several times, following it most of the way up, with small cairns marking the path. The trail will have you dodge many mud boggy areas. When the brook starts to fade, you are near the top. About 0.25 miles from the top, the trail bears left before a steep section leading to the summit. It then bears right just before the top, where you'll reach Mount Marshall's summit. Though the views are terrible, you can see Iroquois and Shepherds Tooth from a nearby outcropping. To find the best view, briefly head back down the trail, and look for a spur trail to your right. If you pass a trail on your left, you've gone too far. This spur trail offers impressive views of the southern High Peaks, Mount Colden, and Marcy. When ready, return to the main trail. At this point, choose to return the way you came or take Cold Brook Pass. In this guide, we'll retrace our steps. If opting for Cold Brook Pass, take that left after leaving the summit or just past this view spur. This path leads down, up and over Marshall's Northeast Peak, and down to the Cold Brook Trail, passing the Mount Marshall plane wreck. Whichever way you choose, follow trail logic on your descent.

Here are the coordinates to the plane wreck if you want to check it out: 44.131261°N / 74.000715°W. The wreck is 0.25 miles after turning right on the Cold Brook Pass Trail.

MILES AND DIRECTIONS

0.0 Start at the Upper Works Trailhead parking lot.

0.1 Sign-in box.

0.4 Turn right at the first sign.

0.5 Turn right at Indian Pass/Calamity Trail sign.

1.8 Keep right, crossing bridge at Crossover/Calamity Trail sign.

2.4 Steeper trail section starts.

2.9 Pass Calamity Brook Campsite.

4.4 David Henderson Memorial.

4.6 Reach Flowed Lands sign-in box.

MOUNT MARSHALL

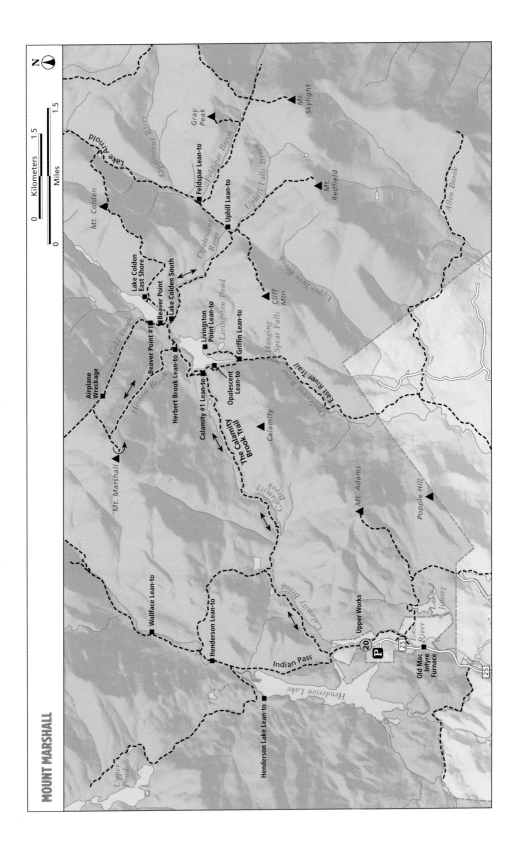

N

| 0 | Kilometers | 1.5 |
| 0 | Miles | 1.5 |

Upper Pond

Henderson Lake

Wallface Lean-to

Henderson Lean-to

Indian Pass

Henderson Lake Lean-to

Calamity Brook

Upper Works

Mt. Adams

Popple Hill

Old Mac Intyre Furnace

East River

Lake Jimmy

20

P

25

25

Calamity Brook

The Calamity Brook Trail

Calamity

East River Trail

Opalescent River

Hanging Spear Falls

Mt. Marshall

Airplane Wreckage

Herbert Brook

Cold Brook

Beaver Point #1

Beaver Point

Herbert Brook Lean-to

Calamity #1 Lean-to

Opalescent Lean-to

Griffin Lean-to

Livingston Point Lean-to

Livingston Pond

Lake Colden South

Lake Colden East Shore

Mt. Colden

Lake Arnold

Cliff Mtn.

Upper Twin Brook

Uphill Lean-to

Opalescent River

Uphill Falls Brook

Feldspar Lean-to

Feldspar Brook

Gray Peak

Mt. Redfield

Mt. Skylight

Allen Brook

5.4 Stack of rocks indicating Mount Marshall turn/ascent.

7.2 Reach Mount Marshall summit; return the way you came.

14.5 Arrive back at Upper Works Trailhead.

OTHER ROUTES

VIA ADIRONDACK LOJ—16.5 MILES, 3,100 FEET

This approach is preferred if you're staying in Lake Placid. It will save you 3 hours of driving to Upper Works. Begin your hike at the HPIC at Heart Lake/Adirondack Loj. Take the standard hikers' trail into Marcy Dam. Follow the trail as if you were hiking to Avalanche Lake. Keep following signs to Avalanche Lake. Navigate through Avalanche Lake, following signs toward Lake Colden, staying on the left side of the lake. You will reach a sign before Lake Colden giving you the left or right option. Navigating to the left side of Lake Colden is faster. Take this trail, passing Colden Trail, and eventually you will come to the Mount Marcy Trail. Turn right toward Lake Colden. You will then come to Lake Colden Dam. Cross the wooden dam, up the ladder, turning right onto the Lake Colden Trail. Follow the trail for about 0.3 miles until you come across the large stack of rocks indicating the start of Mount Marshall ascent. Follow the regular guide instructions from here to reach the top.

VIA INDIAN PASS BROOK FROM ADIRONDACK LOJ—16.1 MILES, 2,900 FEET

One lesser-known route to Mount Marshall might be the most underrated. Though it offers fewer visual highlights and sees fewer hikers, this path could be easier on the feet. Despite being 1.5 miles longer than the standard route, it might be just as fast, especially from the Adirondack Loj side. To follow this route, take the Indian Pass Trail for 5.5 miles, passing Scott's Clearing, which is 4.5 miles from the Loj. The turnoff to Mount Marshall is another mile ahead. This trail is well-marked and less eroded than other routes. While it requires more initial vertical climbing compared to the Upper Works route, the overall effort is comparable. After ascending 1.9 miles, take the right turn to the summit, first climbing over MacIntyre Mountain and then up to the top.

The turn for Mount Marshall, indicated by a stack of rocks. JAMES HOUGHTALING

21 MOUNT REDFIELD AND CLIFF MOUNTAIN

While not the most sought after duo of peaks, nor the most graceful, these two will certainly test your backcountry resilience. Typically tackled together, they are often reserved for the latter stages of an aspiring 46er's journey. Rugged and authentic, these peaks demand determination and grit.

Start: Upper Works
Elevation gain: 4,100 feet
Summit elevation: Mount Redfield, 4,606 feet; Cliff Mountain, 3,960 feet
Distance: 18.6 miles
Difficulty: 5 out of 7, difficult
Hiking time: 11–13 hours
Seasons/schedule: Recommended for summer and fall. Winter should be for the experienced only.
Fees and permits: None
Canine compatibility: Dogs must be on leash.
Trail surface: Trail in is worn and wide. Both peaks are wet and eroded. Large scrambles up Cliff. Plenty of rocks. The Calamity Trail toward Lake Colden is wide and rugged. Well worn with some trail management. You'll find stone stairs, boardwalks, and plenty of mud.
Land status: Central High Peaks Wilderness
Nearest town: Newcomb, NY

Water availability: Water is well available if you have a filter. There are such sources as Calamity Brook, Lake Colden, and Redfield Brook.
Amenities available: Some portapotties at the trailhead. Many camping spots along the way such as Lake Colden and Uphill Lean-to.
Maximum grade: 400 feet/0.2 miles: going up Cliff's main face; 1,300 feet/1.3 miles: Redfield ascent
Special considerations: It's going to be rough. Definitely bring gaiters and Gore-Tex.
Sunrise or sunset: Neither. These are the last peaks you want to be on for sunset.
Route type: Out-and-back
Views: Redfield has partial views in every direction, while Cliff has no views on the summit. Only going up the cliff scrambles can you catch a glimpse.

FINDING THE TRAILHEAD

From I-87 exit 29, head west on Blue Ridge Road for 17.4 miles to Tahawus Road. Turn right, proceed for 6.3 miles, and make a left at the High Peaks trails sign. Follow to the end. The trailhead is less than a mile past the old blast furnace. **GPS:** 44.08621°N / 74.05554°W

THE HIKE

Mount Redfield, at 4,606 feet, was named by Verplanck Colvin to honor William C. Redfield, a scientist, explorer, and early Adirondack enthusiast. Redfield's enthusiasm and observation contributed to the first great period of American science. Cliff Mountain is known for its imposing precipices and "shrinking" height, from an initial 4,000 feet in 1895 to 3,944 feet on the 1999 map. Despite its features, it has been overlooked by climbers and writers. Even brothers Bob and George Marshall, with guide Herb Clark, missed Cliff Mountain in their pursuit of climbing all Adirondack 4,000-footers and later returned to climb it. Verplanck Colvin named Cliff in 1872 while viewing its east face

Summit view from Mount Redfield.

from Redfield. Arthur Hopkins possibly made its first true ascent in 1917. Both Mount Redfield and Cliff Mountain hold significant places in Adirondack exploration and their unique features provide hikers with challenging and rewarding experiences, showcasing the natural beauty and history of the area.

This hiking begins at the well-known southern High Peaks trailhead Upper Works. Upon reaching the new hikers' parking lot, you're likely to find parking even on busy weekdays. Close to the parking area stands MacNaughton Cottage, where Teddy Roosevelt embarked on his midnight ride. Proceed along the gravel road to the old parking lot, a brief 5-minute walk, to locate the sign-in. Once you've signed in, set out on your trek. You'll swiftly cross the Hudson River, arriving at the first sign just 0.4 miles in. A left turn here reveals a stunning view of Henderson Lake, but stay right to remain on the Calamity Brook Trail. After 0.2 miles, another trail sign appears; keep right as a left turn would lead to Indian Pass. For the following 1.2 miles, navigate varied terrain while adhering to the red trail markers. At 1.8 miles from the car, you'll come across another trail intersection, the Calamity Crossover Trail. Avoid turning left, and instead, stay right, crossing the bridge and following directions toward Lake Colden. The trail maintains a relatively flat profile for an additional 0.5 miles before becoming significantly steeper. Hike 1.1 miles past the previous sign to encounter the Calamity Brook campsites, approximately 2.9 miles from the car. Continue along the trail for another 1.5 miles until you reach the David Henderson Memorial, an intriguing site to explore and learn from. This memorial commemorates Henderson's accidental self-inflicted gunshot wound, which inspired the names Calamity Mountain, Lake, Brook, and Trail. Positioned 4.4 miles from the beginning, the memorial marks a poignant spot.

In 0.25 miles, you'll arrive at Flowed Lands, where another sign-in box awaits. Just beyond, a rewarding spur trail presents an outstanding view of the Flowed Lands. At the sign-in box, veer left, following the trail in the direction of Lake Colden. Over the next mile, you'll circumnavigate the Flowed Lands, trek through the woods, surmount a small hill, pass the Mount Marshall turnoff, and then reach Lake Colden Dam 5.6 miles from your car. Upon reaching the dam, you will be greeted with a steep ladder, walking you down to the dam itself. This is a great spot to take a photo of the lake and Mount Colden in the distance. The dam is also another great spot to take a lunch break.

Continue past the dam, turning right and following the trail markers. You'll encounter several camping signs in this area, but keep following the primary footpath. A few hundred feet past a turn sign pointing toward Mount Colden, you will come to a beautiful suspension bridge over the Opalescent River. After crossing, turn left and proceed along the path for 1.3 miles.

During this stretch, you'll have spectacular cliff-edge views of Opalescent gorges, encounter wooden stairs and boardwalks, and navigate plenty of rocks. The trail gradually climbs 500 feet in elevation. At the end of the 1.3-mile section, you will reach Uphill Lean-to, the highest elevated lean-to in the park. This spot is ideal for resting or spending the night, as it boasts a great river source just beyond it. Approximately 50 feet beyond the turn into the camp, you will see a massive stack of rocks. Turn right here to embark on the trail leading to both Mount Redfield and Cliff Mountain. The initial short stretch takes you to the fork for each peak, approximately 0.15 miles or 5 minutes away. Be aware that there are no trail markers beyond this point. Shortly, you should arrive at the split for the two peaks. A thin, barkless tree with scrap metal at its base currently marks the fork. If you miss it, you might unintentionally start climbing Redfield. However, it's advisable to tackle Cliff Mountain first, as it poses a greater challenge and demands more energy. If you end up only being able to do one due to time or energy, it would be better to get this one out of the way. You may not have time to get Cliff if you start with Redfield. It is also safer to have as much daylight as possible for Cliff, as it poses more dangerous terrain.

As you commence the trail to Cliff, you'll be immediately greeted by an expansive mud field. Prioritize your safety and efficiency by sticking to the far left around the mud, where clean, raised paths are available. Once you've navigated this section, the trail continues through a trench with wooden logs, which is part of the old Twin Brook Trail. Eventually, veer right and ascend into a steeper section. Gradually, you'll climb up to the first "cliff," which you can scale either to the left or right, depending on the conditions. The second and third cliffs become increasingly challenging with each ascent. In these sections, adhere to the edges and rely on vegetation and roots for support. The third section also involves cutting across one of the faces. This demanding part of the mountain requires concentration, and it's on these small exposed faces that you'll find the only views. After surpassing the third cliff, climb over a few deep, muddy pockets. Navigate through these, and you'll approach the top of the first saddle. The trail eases beyond this point. This first hump is a mere 7 feet shorter than the true summit. From here, you can spot the true summit through the trees, 0.3 miles away. The trail descends 140 feet into the saddle col before briefly steepening, then gently arriving at the viewless summit of Cliff Mountain, regrettably boasting some of the least impressive views of any mountain. From here, return the way you came to the fork for your trip up Redfield. This ascent is the longer of the two, totaling 1.3 miles to the top one-way with 1,300 feet of vertical gain.

As you start your ascent, the trail weaves in and out of Uphill Brook. This brook offers some of the purest water to drink, sourced from mountain runoff and Moss Pond, the second-highest body of water in the park. The climb up Redfield can be confusing, so stay vigilant. The trail goes in and out of the brook multiple times before staying right and paralleling the brook. The trail remains consistent for most of the time, with only one or two steep scrambles up onto ledges. Eventually, the brook will diminish and disappear around the halfway point. From here, the trail continues in the same fashion. After

MOUNT REDFIELD AND CLIFF MOUNTAIN

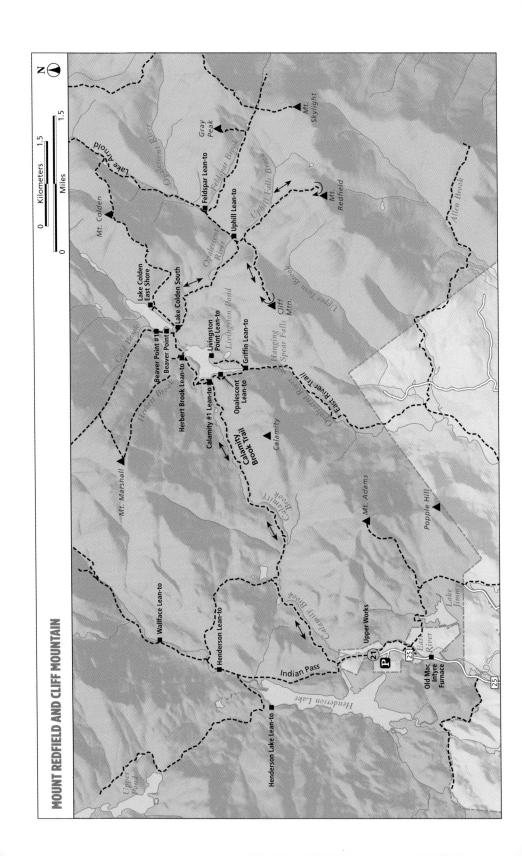

N

Kilometers
0   1.5   1.5

Miles
0   1.5

Mt. Colden

Lake Arnold

Opalescent River

Gray Peak

Feldspar Lean-to

Feldspar Brook

Uphill Lean-to

Mt. Skylight

Uphill Falls Brook

Mt. Redfield

Lake Colden East Shore

Lake Colden South

Opalescent River

Livingston Pond

Livingston Point Lean-to

Griffin Lean-to

Cliff Mtn.

Upper Twin Brook

Hanging Spear Falls

Coll Brook

Beaver Point #1

Beaver Point

Herbert Brook

Herbert Brook Lean-to

Calamity #1 Lean-to

Opalescent Lean-to

Calamity Brook Trail

Calamity

East River Trail

Opalescent River

Mt. Marshall

Calamity Brook

Mt. Adams

Popple Hill

Wallface Lean-to

Henderson Lean-to

Indian Pass

Calamity Brook

Upper Pond

Henderson Lake

Henderson Lake Lean-to

Upper Works

21

P

25

Old Mac Intyre Furnace

East River

Lake Jimmy

25

what might feel like the longest 1.3 miles you have ever hiked, you will finally reach the summit of Mount Redfield. If you continue just past the summit sign, you will be greeted with a panoramic view of the southern region. In the distance, you can see Allen Mountain, and just below you is a remote pond called Sky Pond (although Sky Pond doesn't appear on maps). Your author has also bushwhacked from Allen to this viewpoint multiple times, and it has never been faster, nor worth it. Once you have taken in the views (assuming you have them), make your way back down the 1.3-mile trail to the fork where you started. From there, it is 7.1 miles back to the car.

MILES AND DIRECTIONS

0.0 Start at the Upper Works Trailhead parking lot.

0.1 Sign-in box.

0.4 Turn right at the first sign.

0.5 Turn right at Indian Pass/Calamity Trail sign.

1.8 Keep right, crossing bridge at Crossover/Calamity Trail sign.

2.4 Steeper trail section starts.

2.9 Pass Calamity Brook camps.

4.4 David Henderson Memorial.

4.6 Reach Flowed Lands sign-in box.

5.6 Arrive at Lake Colden Dam.

5.7 Pass Mount Colden Trail sign. Continue Straight.

7.0 Reach Uphill Lean-to, turning right at the large rock stack.

7.1 Split for Redfield (left) and Cliff (right).

8.0 Cliff summit.

8.9 Return to fork. Continue to Redfield.

10.2 Reach summit of Redfield.

11.5 Return to fork, hiking back to trailhead.

18.6 Arrive back at the Upper Works Trailhead.

OTHER ROUTES

VIA ADIRONDACK LOJ—19.2 MILES, 4,100 FEET

Although longer than Upper Works, this could be a viable option if you find yourself staying in Lake Placid, saving you 3 hours of driving. Begin your hike at the HPIC at Heart Lake/Adirondack Loj. Take the standard hikers' trail into Marcy Dam. Follow the trail as if you were hiking to Avalanche Lake. Keep following signs to Avalanche Lake. Navigate through Avalanche Lake, following signs toward Lake Colden, staying on the left side of the lake. You will reach a sign before Lake Colden giving you the left or right option. Navigating to the left side of Lake Colden is faster. Navigate this trail, passing Colden, and eventually you will come to the Mount Marcy Trail. Turn left here, hiking 1.3 miles to Uphill Lean-to. Refer to the hike description for the remainder of the two climbs.

22 MOUNT SKYLIGHT AND GRAY PEAK

Nestled in around Mount Marcy, Gray Peak and Mount Skylight are two remarkable mountains offering unique views and diverse landscapes. These peaks can also be paired with Marcy. Gray Peak, named after the 19th-century botanist Asa Gray, and Skylight, named for its distinctive rock formation resembling a dormer window, are paired very well and have a fun history behind them. Although challenging to reach, they are both very rewarding.

Start: Adirondack Loj
Elevation gain: 4,500 feet
Summit elevation: Mount Skylight, 4,920 feet; Gray Peak, 4,840 feet
Distance: 18.2 miles
Difficulty: 5 out of 7, difficult
Hiking time: 10–12 hours
Seasons/schedule: Recommended for early summer, as this is when the forests and plant life are at full bloom and vibrant.
Fees and permits: $15 to park at Adirondack Loj
Canine compatibility: Dogs must be on leash.
Trail surface: The trail is well-worn, having a variety of large rocks, bogs, and boardwalks. You will encounter the infamous "floating logs" on the back side of Colden. This is a terribly maintained bog.
Land status: Central High Peaks Wilderness

Nearest town: Lake Placid, NY
Water availability: Water is well available if you have a filter. There are such sources as Marcy Dam, Lake Arnold, and Feldspar Brook.
Amenities available: The Adirondack Loj, Info Center, and the Hungry Hiker. Many tent sites and privies at Marcy Dam. Feldspar campsites.
Maximum grade: 500 feet/0.35 miles: Gray ascent; 600 feet/0.5 miles: Skylight ascent
Special considerations: These peaks can be hiked with Marcy as well. Consider doing the MSG loop if you have it in you.
Sunrise or sunset: Although remote, Skylight has an outstanding sunrise.
Route type: Out-and-back
Views: Skylight has some of the best views of any mountain. See for yourself. Gray, on the other hand, has some good views from outcroppings.

FINDING THE TRAILHEAD

Adirondack Loj is located 1.5 miles southeast of Lake Placid on NY 73; turn down Adirondack Loj Road and drive for 5 miles. Popular and often packed; arrive early. Weekdays are generally not full prior to 9 a.m. but can be full before 6 a.m. on weekends. Marcy Dam Truck Trail at the end of South Meadows can be used if parking is full. **GPS:** 44.18313°N / 73.96445°W

THE HIKE

On September 16, 1872, Verplanck Colvin and guide Bill Nye faced dense fog, treacherous ledges, and impenetrable dwarfed balsam on a journey from Mount Marcy to Gray Peak. They successfully reached Gray Peak's summit and descended into the valley, discovering Lake Tear of the Clouds. Contrary to previous beliefs, they found the lake fed into the Hudson River, revealing it as the highest source in the state. Almost a year later, Colvin and Old Mountain Phelps made the first ascent of Skylight, admiring its beautiful

Hikers on the summit of Skylight as viewed from Gray Peak.

summit. Gray Peak, described as a shameless imposter among the High Peaks, rises only 135 feet from the col separating it from Mount Marcy. In 1939, the Adirondack Mountain Club harshly criticized Gray Peak, stating it "hardly looks worth climbing" and has the worst dwarf balsam among the peaks. They even mentioned the lack of a place to sit. Despite its past reputation, Gray Peak is now a beautiful destination.

As you embark on your hike, you'll enjoy a leisurely stroll toward Marcy Dam, passing through gentle hills, spruce forests, and varied terrain. After 1 mile, you'll reach the first trail sign, which indicates the intersection for the MacIntyre Range (straight) and Marcy Dam (left). Turn left here, with Marcy Dam just 1.3 miles away. The trail will maintain its character for the next stretch until you reach Marcy Dam. Upon arriving at Marcy Dam, you'll see the collapsed dam straight ahead, the main trail to the left, and a spur trail to the right, leading toward the dam opening. Keep left and cross the bridge, then turn right once you're on the other side. A short walk later, you'll find yourself at the opposite end of the dam, where you'll encounter a second sign-in register. It's a good idea to sign in here as well. Continue past the sign-in, and soon you'll come across another trail sign, directing you toward Marcy. At this junction, you have two options: turning right leads to Avalanche Lake and Colden, while turning left takes you along the Van Hoevenberg Trail toward Marcy. Continue along the trail to the right, enjoying the next 1.1-mile stretch leading to the Avalanche camps. As you approach the end of this section, you'll cross a wooden bridge. A mere 100 feet later, you'll find a campsite on the right and the next intersection on the left. At this junction, you will see multiple signs pointing straight ahead for Avalanche Lake (1 mile) or to the left for Lake Arnold (1.5 miles). Follow the directions for the Lake Arnold route, and be prepared for an increased level of difficulty over the next 1.5 miles. The trail features increasingly rocky terrain that will challenge your footing. After completing the first mile of this section, you'll come across another trail sign located near a stream. This sign points toward "Indian Falls." Be sure to continue past this sign in the direction of Lake Arnold, following the blue markers that guide your path. As you proceed, the following 0.5-mile stretch will become progressively more rugged, with the possibility of wet conditions depending on recent weather. Upon reaching the picturesque Lake Arnold, sitting at about 3,700 feet, your 1.5-mile climb will gradually come to an end. You will arrive at the turnoff for Mount Colden. You will continue past this sign, heading straight. From this point, your next stretch of trail is 1.5 miles long, and it will be a tough one.

The trail beyond this point becomes increasingly rugged, climbing slightly more to 3,830 feet before cresting shortly after Lake Arnold. As you crest, you're greeted with a glimpse of Mount Redfield in the distance. From here, the trail dips down about 250 feet before leveling off at a gentler angle. It's crucial to read this next portion of the guide carefully. At about the halfway mark on this stretch, or 0.9 miles in, you'll cross the Opalescent River. There are numerous crossing spots, with the main one indicated by trail markers on the other side. If the water is too high or the crossing isn't convenient, a better spot may be just before the main crossing section. After crossing, you should be able to connect to a herd path that leads you back to the main trail. About a quarter-mile after the river crossing, you'll arrive at the infamous "floating logs." The trail will gradually worsen until you come to what seems like a dead end. One thing to note is that there are rumored plans by the DEC to fix this area of the trail eventually. This guide is to help aid in the event that there is no crossing. Roughly 30 feet before this dead end, you will find an open/herd path on the right. Your goal is to circumnavigate this bog. If you find the trail, be cautious and stay close to the bog, always within eyesight. If followed correctly, this herd path should bring you along the side, feeding you back onto the main trail. You should not be off-trail for more than a few minutes.

After successfully navigating the area, let's continue. About 0.4 miles from the bog, you should arrive at the Feldspar Lean-to on the right and the camping spots on the left. As you move past these, you will come to a small crossing at Feldspar Brook, a great spot to refill water. Cross the river, turning left, and follow the signs toward Mount Marcy. This next section up to Lake Tear of the Clouds is 1.2 miles long, climbing 1,000 feet. This climb is relatively straightforward. At the end of this section, you will be greeted with Lake Tear of the Clouds. The trail up to Gray is only marked by a cairn at the very beginning of the lake. It should be on the left as you approach the lake. This climb up to Gray is short but steep, with a round trip of just under a mile. Cross the little outlet at the cairn to begin your climb.

The trail is quite evident; however, about 0.25 miles up, you will come to a spot that seems like you could go left or right around a covered cliff face. Do not go left, as it is a dead end. Instead, turn right and climb a scramble with a fantastic view. Beyond this point, it's clockwork getting to the top. Right before you summit, you will find a small rock on your right with a stunning view to the south and a 4-foot ledge drop. Right after this drop, you will turn the corner and see the Gray Peak sign. Welcome to the summit. Just before the sign is another large rock that you can hop up on to see a great view out to the north.

Just past the sign, you can find a good view looking toward Marcy, where you might even see people up there. Carefully make your way back to Lake Tear. Once you arrive, continue the trail left toward Four Corners. Be vigilant for a massive rock, right as you start hiking. This rock has a weird spiral glyph on it with an uncertain origin story. What we do know for sure is that it is old and not naturally occurring. Some rumors suggest

The infamous "floating log" section.
Watch your step! JEFF DAHL

it could have Native American indications pointing to the source of the Hudson River, but we may never know the truth. As you leave Lake Tear, the trail continues for another 0.25 miles until you reach Four Corners. This is the intersection that would take you left up Marcy, straight into Panther Gorge, or right up Skylight. Take the trail right, following the sign for 0.5 miles to Skylight. This ascent involves a 600-foot gain. The trail up Skylight is mild in terrain and well-traveled. Eventually, you will pass the white alpine vegetation sign. From here, the path will bring you above the trees and the path will be marked by blazes and white string. One of Skylight's most prized features is its incredible vegetation. Please be very vigilant with the trail markings to ensure you stay on the designated footpath. This is certainly one of the most beautiful summits of the entire Northeast. Eventually, the trail will top out on the rocky nub up high. Welcome to the summit! From here, you can see around thirty-two of the forty-six high peaks.

You can take two different ways back to the trailhead. The shorter way would be back up and over the Lake Arnold approach, as described in the guide, or the slightly less rugged, but longer route through Avalanche Pass. Whichever way you choose, enjoy and stay safe.

MILES AND DIRECTIONS

0.0   Start at Adirondack Loj.

1.0   Turn left at Marcy Dam sign.

2.3   Arrive at Marcy Dam, turning left to go around to the other side.

2.4   Turn right at intersection split for Van Hoe Trail to Marcy or Avalanche Lake/Colden.

3.5   Reach Avalanche Camp, turning left, following signs to Lake Arnold.

4.5   Pass Marcy Brook with turn sign toward Indian Falls; continue straight.

5.0   Reach Lake Arnold, continuing straight.

6.0   Cross Opalescent River.

6.3   Cross the floating logs.

6.7   Reach Feldspar Camps/Brook.

7.9   Arrive at Lake Tear of the Clouds.

8.3   Summit of Gray Peak.

9.1   Reach Four Corners.

9.6   Summit of Mount Skylight; turn around and head back the way you came.

18.2   Arrive back at Adirondack Loj.

OTHER ROUTES

UPPER WORKS—20.5 MILES, 4,200 FEET

Begin your hike at the Upper Works Trailhead. Park at the new hikers' parking lot near MacNaughton Cottage. Walk along the gravel road to the old parking lot and sign in. Follow the Calamity Brook Trail, crossing the Hudson River (0.4 miles), and keep right at trail signs (0.2 miles and 1.8 miles). Hike 1.1 miles to Calamity Brook campsites (2.9 miles from the car) and continue 1.5 miles to David Henderson Memorial (4.4 miles).

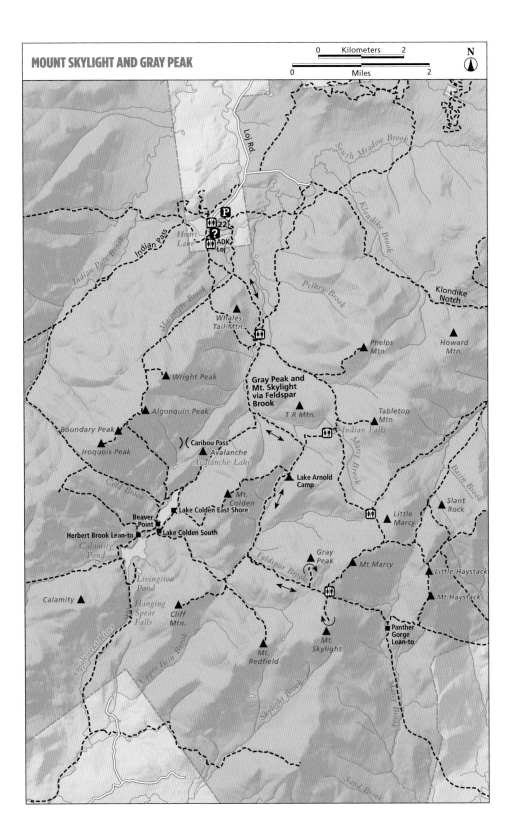

MOUNT SKYLIGHT AND GRAY PEAK

Kilometers 0 — 2

Miles 0 — 2

N

Loj Rd.

South Meadow Brook

Klondike Brook

P

22

?

ADK Loj

Heart Lake

Indian Pass

Indian Pass Brook

MacIntyre Brook

Pelkey Brook

Klondike Notch

Whales Tail Mtn.

Phelps Mtn.

Howard Mtn.

Wright Peak

Gray Peak and Mt. Skylight via Feldspar Brook

T R Mtn.

Tabletop Mtn.

Indian Falls

Algonquin Peak

Boundary Peak

Iroquois Peak

Caribou Pass

Avalanche

Avalanche Lake

Cold Brook

Marcy Brook

Basin Brook

Lake Arnold Camp

Mt. Colden

Lake Colden East Shore

Little Marcy

Slant Rock

Beaver Point

Lake Colden South

Herbert Brook Lean-to

Calamity Pond

Livingston Pond

Feldspar Brook

Gray Peak

Mt. Marcy

Little Haystack

Calamity

Hanging Spear Falls

Cliff Mtn.

Mt. Haystack

Opalescent River

Upper Twin Brook

Mt. Redfield

Mt. Skylight

Panther Gorge Lean-to

Muddy Brook

Skylight Brook

Sand Brook

After 0.25 miles, arrive at Flowed Lands and sign in. Veer left toward Lake Colden and hike 1 mile, passing Mount Marshall turnoff to reach Lake Colden Dam (5.6 miles). Cross the dam and follow the trail markers. After crossing a suspension bridge over the Opalescent River, turn left and hike 1.3 miles, enjoying cliff-edge views and climbing 500 feet in elevation, to reach Uphill Lean-to. Continue hiking for another 0.5 miles until you reach Feldspar Brook, turning right at the signs pointing toward Mount Marcy. From here, you can reference the hike description above for the remaining hike details from this point.

HOW WE GOT THE FORTY-SIX

The creation of the 46 High Peaks list began with Verplanck Colvin's topographical survey of the High Peaks, which initially identified forty-two peaks above 4,000 feet. Colvin's survey, conducted in the late 19th century, laid the foundation for the now-iconic list of mountains that would eventually become the Adirondack 46ers. As Colvin's survey gained attention, questions arose regarding the accuracy of the elevation measurements for some peaks. Doubts surrounding the true elevation of certain mountains fueled the controversy over which peaks should be included in the list. Eventually, Bob and George Marshall with Herb Clark embarked on an endeavor to be the first to climb a specific set of Adirondack peaks over 3,500 feet. They later reconsidered and decided to climb peaks over 4,000 feet instead. They devised their own rules for what constituted an Adirondack high peak: the 300-foot rise on all sides (prominence rule), and or the 0.75-mile end of a ridge (distance rule). They did not use a rule from a preexisting mountain list. This unofficial set of rules would later prove to be a highly challenged criteria. When they first created their list, they included one hundred peaks, which later became the Adirondack 100 Highest list. The distance rule allowed other "interesting" peaks to be added. They eventually decided to focus on climbing the forty-two peaks over 4,000 feet, as it was a manageable number.

Over time, as they climbed and further analyzed the peaks, four additional mountains—Gray, Couchsachraga, Cliff, and Blake—were found to satisfy their criteria for odd reasons, bringing the total to forty-six peaks. Russell Carson first recommended that Cliff and Gray Peak be added, partly out of concern that he did not want to see anyone claim they were the first to climb all peaks 4,000 feet and over, except for the three men. Russell's push for Gray Peak's inclusion was due to his admiration for Professor Asa Gray, a prominent American botanist after whom the mountain was named. Bob and George initially disagreed with the inclusion of Gray Peak, but ultimately conceded after further observations and discussions. Gray Peak was added to the ADK 42 and climbed by the trio on June 26, 1924. As they completed their climbs, the reputation of the High Peaks grew, and the 46er list gained popularity among hikers and outdoor enthusiasts. Despite initial skepticism regarding the inclusion of these additional peaks, the list of 46 High Peaks became widely accepted and remains a significant accomplishment for hikers in the Adirondack region to this day.

WHITEFACE AND ESTHER

Summit view from Whiteface Mountain overlooking Lake Placid.

23 WHITEFACE AND ESTHER MOUNTAINS

Whiteface and Esther are two high peaks well removed from the rest of the region. They are prominent in their location just north of Lake Placid. Whiteface has an incredible history and is easily accessible by hiking trail, or even the Veterans Memorial Highway. Esther also has a fun history. Both of these peaks are easier than others and can make for a fun day hike in the High Peaks.

Start: Atmospheric Science Research Center (ASRC)
Elevation gain: 3,700 feet
Summit elevation: Whiteface Mountain, 4,867 feet; Esther Mountain, 4,240 feet
Distance: 9.8 miles
Difficulty: 4 out of 7, moderate
Hiking time: 6–8 hours
Seasons/schedule: This hike is a great year-round hike. Great for winter if you have the right gear.
Fees and permits: None
Canine compatibility: Good hike for dogs; dogs must be on leash.
Trail surface: Trail is well worn, having a variety of surfaces. Rocky and muddy.
Land status: Wilmington Wild Forest/Whiteface (ORDA)
Nearest town: Wilmington, NY

Water availability: There is no water available on this hike naturally.
Amenities available: From May to Sept, you can find a fully operational weather station on the summit with a vending machine and a restroom in the lower part by the gift shop.
Maximum grade: Initial 1.1 miles/1,300 feet
Special considerations: This is a popular hike to finish your 46 on because people can drive to the top and meet you for the finish. Be prepared to see tons of people.
Sunrise or sunset: Whiteface is fantastic for both.
Route type: Out-and-back
Views: Whiteface has 360-degree views while Esther has minimal views through trees.

FINDING THE TRAILHEAD

From Lake Placid, take NY 86 to Wilmington's four-corner intersection. Turn left onto NY 431, continue for 2.4 miles, and turn left onto Atmospheric Science Research Center Road. Follow the one-way loop, then the trail and parking area are on your right. **GPS:** 44.39439°N / 73.85773°W

THE HIKE

Whiteface Mountain, potentially spotted from Montreal by French explorer Jacques Cartier in 1535, has long captivated the imaginations of those who have laid eyes upon it. Early settlers in the region, arriving as early as the 1790s, marveled at the mountain's majesty even believing it may have been the tallest peak in the region. The exact origin of the name "Whiteface" remains uncertain, but some theories suggest that it could be attributed to early settlers or explorers who named it based on the snowcapped peak's resemblance to a white "face" gazing toward the sky. Ebenezer Emmons, who made the first officially recorded ascent of Whiteface in 1836, also contributed to the naming discussion, offering insights into the appearance of white slides as a possible source of its

The trail up Whiteface near the summit at sunset.

name. Esther Mountain has a whole different story. See the sidebar below, "The Tall Tale of Esther McComb."

Whiteface Mountain offers four different ways to ascend its peak, but when combining both Whiteface and Esther, there are two popular routes: the ASRC and the Reservoir. For this guide, we will take the quickest and most traveled route, starting our hike at the ASRC. After finding the correct parking area as described in the finding the trailhead section, you'll see an unmarked rocky path leading straight into the woods. This initial trail is only 0.1 miles long and takes you to a gravel road. Be vigilant, as there are no signs marking the beginning of this trail.

Once you reach the gravel road, turn left and walk a short distance to reach the base of Marble Mountain. You will know you're at the right spot when you see signage on the left and an electrical box on the right. The first ascent of Marble Mountain is quite steep, yet consistent, covering 0.8 miles and climbing 800 vertical feet. Be sure to pace yourself during this climb to conserve energy for the rest of the hike. As you approach the summit of Marble Mountain, the trail will thin out and become less steep.

At the top, you'll find a small outcropping view on the left, and the continuing trail to the right. Shortly after moving forward, you'll encounter an intersection with a sign pointing left to the Reservoir. Turn right.. From this point, the next 1.2-mile trail section leads to the Esther Mountain turnoff and includes a 1,200-foot climb. The trail is relatively easy to follow and remains pretty straightforward, but there will be some rocky and muddy spots along the way that can be unpleasant. The trail will consistently climb for this section. The end of the section will be met by a long flat area right before the Esther turn. This turn will be marked with a large rock stack on the ground and the Esther Mountain sign pointing right stating, "Path is not maintained or marked." This out-and-back to Esther is approximately 1 mile long one way. This trail is the most rugged and challenging section of the entire hike. As you start toward Esther, the trail climbs about 100 feet up to Look Mountain, where a small view to the right is available for hikers to enjoy. After cresting the top, descend another 100 feet into the col between Lookout and Esther, navigating the rugged trail. As you make your way down the trail, you'll find wooden boards at the bottom, followed by muddy sections on the ascent to the summit. These muddy stretches can be quite difficult, so it's essential to remain vigilant and prepared. As you near the top of Esther Mountain, you'll discover a scenic view on your right, with Whiteface Mountain in the background. The true summit, marked by the Esther Macomb plaque, is just beyond this viewpoint. Welcome to Esther Mountain! From this vantage point, looking toward Whiteface, you'll see the entire Great Range to the left.

DID YOU KNOW?

The Whiteface Mountain Veterans Memorial Highway, dedicated to the memory of the men and women who fought in World War I, was decided by Governor Franklin D. Roosevelt. Construction began on December 25, 1931, following Roosevelt's ceremonial shoveling of dirt on September 11, 1929. Coinciding with the Great Depression, the highway's construction aimed to stimulate the Adirondack economy and create jobs. Costing around $1,250,000 at the time, it was considered one of the most ambitious road construction projects of the era. The road opened to the public on July 20, 1935. During its construction, there was only one death, which was when a workhorse named Paddy died from an accident carrying materials. There was a monument erected to commemorate the horse's efforts and sacrifices up top.

After taking in the views from Esther Mountain, retrace your steps back to the Esther intersection, and turn right to continue the 1.5-mile journey to Whiteface's summit. The first half of this section is relatively flat and easygoing, with a 100-foot climb over 0.7 miles. After briefly crossing the Whiteface Mountain ski trail, the steep climb resumes. Ascend 0.25 miles to the Memorial Highway toll road, which features a beautiful stone wall on your right just before reaching the road. Continuing the hike, you'll see the trail moving past the road up to the right. The final 0.5-mile stretch weaves through dense small pine forest and eventually takes you to the exposed ridgeline of Whiteface, above the tree line. Yellow blazes mark the trail, and it's crucial to stay on the path to protect the delicate alpine vegetation. Weather conditions in this section can vary greatly, ranging from pleasant and beautiful to terrifying and windy. During this final approach, you'll see the weather observatory ahead of you. The trail leads you to the left side of the weather station, past a small shack, and up to the summit rock. Congratulations, you've reached the summit of Whiteface! If you visit during summer daylight hours, you'll likely encounter many other hikers and a beautiful wooden deck surrounding the weather observatory.

You can even go inside to explore fascinating displays and exhibits, making the summit experience even more memorable. Be sure to take a photo by the famous Whiteface summit sign to commemorate your accomplishment. From the summit, you can also walk the stone stairs on the other side of the peak, descending to the castle and then returning to the road, which eventually connects back to the hiking trail. Alternatively, you can simply take the hiking trail back the way you came.

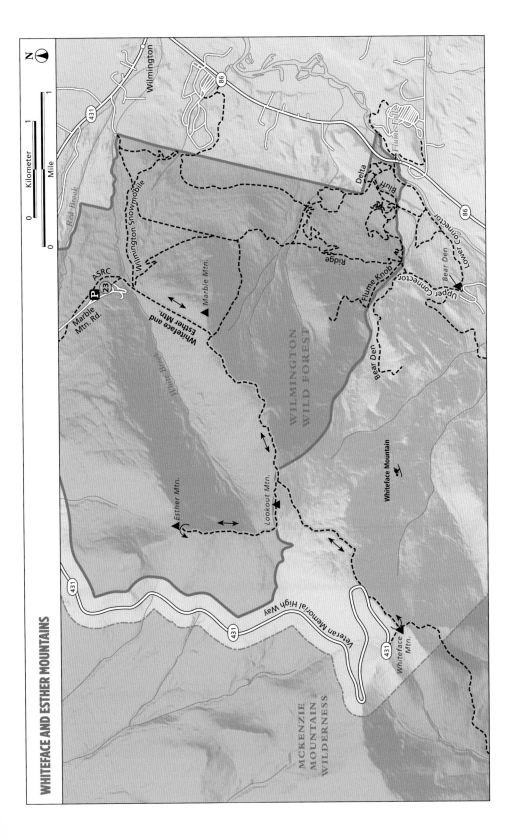

WHITEFACE AND ESTHER MOUNTAINS

MILES AND DIRECTIONS

0.0 Start at ASRC trailhead, following unmarked rocky trail.

0.1 Turn left onto the gravel path.

0.2 Start ascent up Marble Mountain.

1.0 Summit Marble, turning right up top, then turning right at the next sign.

2.4 Esther junction; turn right to Esther.

3.4 Esther summit; turn around.

4.4 Return to Esther junction, turning right toward Whiteface.

4.9 Pass over ski trail.

5.2 Climb up to the toll road, staying right following the trail.

5.6 Summit of Whiteface Mountain; turn around and head back the way you came.

9.8 Arrive back at the ASRC.

OTHER ROUTES

RESERVOIR TRAIL—12.0 MILES, 4,400 FEET

This trail is nearly the same as the ASRC, however, you start 700 feet lower in elevation with an added 2 miles. I've never understood why people would prefer this option, but it is still an alternative. The trail starts about a mile south of the ASCR on NY 431. You will find the signs for this on the road. Starting out, you will hike for 0.1 miles until you pass your first sign. Stay straight. After another 0.2 miles, you will pass your next sign. Stay straight, following the Wilmington Trail to Marble Mountain. After another 1 mile, you will pass a sign pointing to Marble Mountain (right). This climb is 0.8 miles, climbing 1,000 feet up to Marble. The trail will then join back up with the ASRC/standard route. Follow the main hike description for the remaining directions.

A panoramic sunrise from the summit of Whiteface.

CONNERY POND/WHITEFACE LANDING—13.5 MILES, 3,600 FEET

This approach from the southwest/Lake Placid side is less traveled and only recommended if your goal is to only summit Whiteface Mountain. However, this could be an option for those looking to thru-hike the two peaks. I must note that this is the most rugged approach to Whiteface and is certainly the most difficult. It would make the trip around 11.8 miles with 3,700 feet. The trail starts you out at the Connery Pond Trailhead. There are about six parking spots or so. This trail will be nice and cordial through the woods for about 2.5 miles to Whiteface Landing. Turn right, following the signs to Whiteface. From here, it is 3.5 miles to the summit. It is 1.1 miles to a lean-to where your primary ascent will start. From the lean-to, it is 2.3 miles with 2,700 feet of gain.

It is not uncommon to be above the clouds, especially in winter on Whiteface due to its prominence and unique weather patterns during that time of year.

THE TALL TALE OF ESTHER MCCOMB

Most high peaks come with a certain account of how they got their names; however, mountains like Santanoni, Whiteface, and Esther have somewhat uncertain origins, with Esther being the most elusive title. Here's how the story goes: Esther Mountain is named after a young girl named Esther McComb, or so the legend says. Esther was a 15-year-old girl with a burning ambition to climb Whiteface Mountain, despite her parents' disapproval. One day, she set out on her own to climb Whiteface, but she lost her way and ended up climbing the mountain that now bears her name. A search party found her the following morning, and her mother jokingly named the mountain "Esther" in honor of the misadventure. This name persisted and became part of the lore surrounding the High Peaks. The story of Esther McComb and her accidental climb has been passed down through a kind of "telephone game" over the years, leading to discrepancies and confusion. The story was first heard by Russell Carson from Charles Beede, a Keene Valley guide, who had heard it from Wallace Goodspeed, a former guide, in 1923. Goodspeed claimed to have heard the tale as a boy when he lived in the town of St. Armand, near the supposed home of the McComb family. Carson had difficulty verifying the story and its details when he was writing his historical sketches in the early 1920s. No one he corresponded with, no book or document he read, could provide a solid account of how Esther Mountain had received its name.

When he published his expanded sketches in *Peaks and People of the Adirondacks* (1927), he included the story of Esther McComb, citing Beede's account from Goodspeed as his source. The tale was then repeated and embellished in various publications, including Adirondack Mountain Club trail guides, and became ingrained in the lore of the mountains. Extensive research by Sandra Weber, author of *The Lure of Esther Mountain, Matriarch of the Adirondack High Peaks*, found no evidence of a McComb family in the area during the time of the alleged ascent. Instead, she discovered a family named Combs living in the town of St. Armand in the mid-19th century, but their arrival in the area came years after the supposed first ascent. Bob Marshall admired Esther McComb's adventurous spirit, which he saw as embodying the essence of Adirondack mountain climbing: embarking on adventures "for the sheer joy of climbing." By the early to mid-1900s, the name Esther Mountain became widely accepted. On July 30, 1939, a group of about twenty hikers, led by Ed and Grace Hudowalski, cofounders of the 46ers, trekked to the summit of Esther Mountain to honor the centennial of what they believed to be Esther McComb's first ascent in 1839. Margery Nash Ludlow of Troy crafted the bronze plaque, and Ed Hudowalski had meticulously cemented it to a rock at the summit. This plaque remains on Esther Mountain's summit, serving as a testament to the stories and legends that are an integral part of the Adirondack Mountains' rich history. Visitors who reach the peak can witness this tangible tribute to Esther McComb's enduring legacy, which still inspires climbers today.

The famous plaque for Esther McComb on the summit of Esther Mountain.

COLVIN RANGE

Midsummer-day view from the summit of Mount Colvin with Lower Ausable Lake in view.

24 MOUNT COLVIN AND BLAKE PEAK

These two peaks may just give you a new appreciation for the forty-six, especially once you get to Blake Peak. Tucked in the Ausable Lakes Valley, these peaks are moderately visited. Mount Colvin is a great day hike by itself, while Blake Peak should only be done if you are going for your forty-six. These peaks can also be joined with Nippletop and Dial Mountains for a longer day.

Start: Adirondack Mountain Reserve (AMR)/Ausable Club/St. Huberts
Elevation gain: 4,050 feet
Summit elevation: Mount Colvin, 4,057 feet; Blake Peak, 3,960 feet
Distance: 15.6 miles
Difficulty: 4 out of 7, moderate. Terrain overall is mild but very steep and has many challenges.
Hiking time: 9–11 hours
Seasons/schedule: This hike is generally hiked in summer/fall. This would be a more challenging winter climb.
Fees and permits: Free reservation required for parking at the AMR May–Oct.
Canine compatibility: Dogs are not allowed on AMR property, but they are allowed if this route is hiked from the Elk Lake approach and back.
Trail surface: Very well trafficked. About half of this hike is on the AMR Lake Road (gravel road). The other half is typical rough High Peaks terrain with rocks, mud, and slabs. Mixed rock and dirt surfaces with

scrambling up high. Lots of steep and rocky scrambles.
Land status: AMR property/Outer High Peaks Wilderness
Nearest town: Keene Valley, NY
Water availability: There are plenty of rivers down low but no water sources higher up.
Amenities available: Gill Brook has campsites and privies.
Maximum grade: Going up the second half of Blake and also back up Colvin
Special considerations: Bring lots of water. There is none at all after Gill Brook.
Sunrise or sunset: Colvin for sunset or sunrise is all right. Good light in the valley.
Route type: Out-and-back
Views: Colvin has a decent panoramic view from the summit while a spur trail nearby has a view to the south. Blake Peak, on the other hand, has one view while climbing up the mountain but nothing on summit—a terrible reward.

FINDING THE TRAILHEAD

AMR/St. Huberts is right across the street from Roaring Brook Falls Trailhead for Giant, labeled as St. Huberts Parking Area or the Adirondack Mountain Reserve. Approximately 7.5 miles from I-87. Reservations are needed May–October. **GPS:** 44.14970°N / 73.76806°W

THE HIKE

Mount Colvin and Blake Peak, nestled within the Adirondack Wilderness, both hold historical and sentimental significance. Named after Verplanck Colvin, Mount Colvin commemorates the man who dedicated himself to the survey of the Adirondack region and its preservation. Meanwhile, Blake Peak pays tribute to Mills Blake, Colvin's trusted

The Great Range from a viewpoint on the way to Blake from Colvin in the winter.

friend and assistant on the Adirondack Survey. Inextricably linked to Colvin's work, Blake endured harsh conditions to gather crucial data. These two peaks, standing close together, symbolize the unbreakable bond between Colvin and Blake, who devoted their lives to understanding and conserving the Adirondack Wilderness.

Upon your arrival at the AMR parking lot, you will commence your journey by walking up the gravel road that connects to it. This uphill path will guide you past the golf course and, after 0.5 miles, you will turn left at the tennis courts. Shortly thereafter, you will arrive at a sign-in area and a large wooden AMR gate via Lake Road. If this is your first visit to this location, you will inevitably establish a strong bond with the property during your 46er journey. The gravel road that you will walk leads to numerous other remarkable sites, including Indian Head, Rainbow Falls, Nippletop, and the Colvin Range. As you walk past the wooden gate, this road continues for 3.5 miles to the end; however, you will only cover 2 miles down this path. During this 2-mile section, you will pass the H.G. Leach Trail on the left, the Wolfjaws Bridge on the right, and eventually cross a wooden bridge. Just before your 2-mile section ends, the Gothics Trail via Beaver Meadow Falls Trail will appear on your right. The end of your 2-mile section is signified by a small dam on the left, accompanied by a wooden sign indicating the Gill Brook Trail. This is where you turn off Lake Road, following the sign pointing to Gill Brook Trail. For the next 1 mile, you will closely follow Gill Brook, weaving throughout the forest. You will see signs labeled "scenic" or "easy." Both options lead to the same trail, with one providing a gentler path and the other offering more picturesque surroundings. After completing 1 mile, you will arrive at the Gill Brook Cutoff sign. This signpost has several indications, but you will continue straight. Shortly afterward, you will pass another sign directing toward Indian Head on the right. Keep going straight past this sign. Soon, you will come across individual Gill Brook campsites on both your right and left sides. About 0.25 miles after the campsites, you will encounter the next Indian Head Trail sign. This is the most efficient trail to Indian Head if you wish to make a brief visit. I highly recommend it if you have the energy—it's better to visit it on the way back, in my opinion.

Over the next 0.6 miles following this sign, the trail becomes increasingly steeper, ultimately leading you to the Nippletop/Colvin intersection. This junction is marked with "Nippletop" to the left (1.9 miles) or "Mount Colvin" to the right (1.1 miles). From this point, it is nearly a 5-mile out-and-back trip to Blake, with no water and little cell

A glimpse of Blake on the descent from Colvin.

service. This is a great spot to take a break and refill your water before continuing on. The trail up to Colvin is indeed 1.1 miles and ascends around 900 feet, so it is relatively mild compared to other sections. The ascent begins steeply, then gradually levels off before getting steep again. You will encounter small muddy spots, drop-downs, scrambles, and a small wooden ladder followed by a scramble before reaching the summit. Upon arrival, you will be greeted by another trail sign pointing toward Blake. The summit of Colvin is right here at the highest point to the right. From this vantage point, you can clearly see Nippletop and its slide to the right, Giant in the distance, Lower Ausable Lake and Indian Head, and the entire Great Range to the left. A small summit marker is also present on the rock. Head back to the trail to continue your journey. From here, Blake Peak is 1.3 miles away. Be warned that the 2.6-mile round trip is challenging and may have you question why you are out there.

As you start your descent toward Blake, keep an eye out for an additional viewpoint located slightly off the trail to the right. The path gradually becomes steeper, demanding your hiking skills to tackle a series of ladders and rock scrambles. This distance down to the col is 0.8 miles. When you reach the bottom, you'll find a flat resting area with a downed log offering a much-needed break. Look for the sign pointing toward Blake Peak, just 0.5 miles away, and follow its direction. As the trail continues, it starts off gradually but becomes increasingly steeper and more technical during the latter half. The second half of this section will have you climbing a large hands-on scramble. This spot also offers the only view during the ascent, making it a rewarding point to pause and take in the scenery. Right after this challenging section, the trail flattens out and carries you across the summit top. Keep going until you see a trail sign indicating "Mont Colvin" and "Ridge to Pinnacle." This marks the summit of Blake Peak, a hard-earned accomplishment.

At the summit, you will find a small cutout into the woods with a large rock that you can sit on and rest. This is the peak of Blake, which, according to your author, is his least favorite of the High Peaks, on par with Cliff and Couchsachraga. However, you can take pride in overcoming its challenges and reaching the top. From here, unfortunately, you will have to backtrack up Colvin to make your way out of the wilderness. Retracing your steps, remember to pay attention to the trail markers and your surroundings to ensure you stay on the correct path. As you head back to your car, consider making a visit to Indian Head. This is a highly recommended detour that offers breathtaking, one-of-a-kind views.

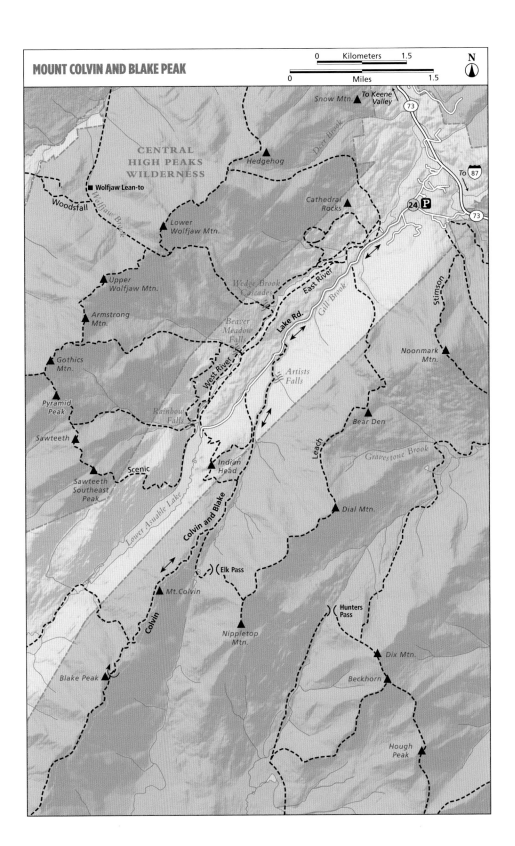

MOUNT COLVIN AND BLAKE PEAK

0 Kilometers 1.5

0 Miles 1.5

N

CENTRAL
HIGH PEAKS
WILDERNESS

Snow Mtn.

To Keene Valley

73

To 87

Hedgehog

Deer Brook

24 P

73

Woodsfall

Wolfjaw Lean-to

Wolfjaw Brook

Cathedral Rocks

Lower Wolfjaw Mtn.

Wedge Brook Cascades

East River

Stimson

Upper Wolfjaw Mtn.

Beaver Meadow Falls

Lake Rd.

Gill Brook

Armstrong Mtn.

Noonmark Mtn.

West River

Gothics Mtn.

Artists Falls

Pyramid Peak

Rainbow Falls

Bear Den

Leach

Gravestone Brook

Sawteeth

Scenic

Indian Head

Sawteeth Southeast Peak

Lower Ausable Lake

Colvin and Blake

Dial Mtn.

Elk Pass

Mt. Colvin

Hunters Pass

Colvin

Nippletop Mtn.

Dix Mtn.

Beckhorn

Blake Peak

Hough Peak

MILES AND DIRECTIONS

0.0 Start at AMR parking lot.

0.6 Reach AMR gate for Lake Road.

2.7 Turn at Gill Brook Trail sign on the left.

3.7 Pass a sign, continuing straight.

3.9 Pass an Indian Head sign, heading straight.

4.5 Pass another Indian Head sign, again heading straight.

5.3 Come to Nippletop/Colvin fork sign, staying right to Colvin.

6.4 Reach Colden summit. Head to Blake, descending back side of Colvin.

7.2 Reach the bottom col between Blake, following signs to Blake.

7.7 Reach Blake Peak summit; turn around.

15.6 Arrive back at the Ausable parking lot and gate.

THE MAN VERPLANCK COLVIN

In the heart of our wilderness, one man's passion and determination shaped the landscape and the region's future. Verplanck Colvin, a determined and adventurous spirit, embarked on a mission to survey the High Peaks, driven by a deep love for the wilderness and a desire to protect it for generations to come. Colvin's extensive survey of the High Peaks Wilderness not only produced detailed maps of the region but also documented the exploitation of the natural resources. Upon witnessing the devastation caused by lumbermen during his ascent of Seward Mountain in 1870, Colvin became determined to protect the forests from further damage. Colvin's incredible journey began with his first ascent and survey of Mount Marcy. This monumental task took months to complete, as he precisely measured the mountain and recorded the surrounding landscape. In the summer of 1873, Colvin embarked on a daring and remarkable journey to survey Mount Marcy amid unpredictable weather and treacherous terrain. Colvin and his dedicated team meticulously measured Marcy's height by extending a line of linear measurements from Lake

Verplanck Colvin in 1885.

Champlain to the summit. The final calculation determined the peak to be 5,344.311 feet above mean tide level in the Hudson, being 3 inches off from today's most accurate surveys. Verplanck Colvin's journey to survey Mount Marcy is a testament to his unwavering determination and passion for understanding and preserving the wilderness. His groundbreaking work laid the foundation for future explorers and conservationists, securing his lasting legacy in the Adirondack High Peaks region. Throughout his career, Colvin scaled and documented numerous high peaks, each ascent revealing new insights into the region's geology, ecology, and beauty. His unmatched knowledge of the wilderness and innate understanding of mountain terrain led him to discover a general law of symmetry regarding mountain slopes, a testament to his keen scientific mind and pioneering spirit.

25 NIPPLETOP AND DIAL MOUNTAINS

These two peaks are neighbors to Colvin and Blake and the Dix Rage. These peaks are moderately difficult and can also be paired with Colvin and Blake for a bigger day. This hike is along an entire ridgeline, making it a more comfortable descent than most other loops. These peaks are also recommended for anyone who is looking to have a longer day hike even without going after the forty-six. It is about the same difficulty as a day hike to Mount Marcy.

Start: Adirondack Mountain Reserve (AMR)/Ausable Club/St. Huberts
Elevation gain: 4,200 feet
Summit elevation: Nippletop, 4,620 feet; Dial, 4,020 feet
Distance: 14.2 miles
Difficulty: 4 out of 7, moderate. All-round challenging.
Hiking time: 8–10 hours
Seasons/schedule: This hike is generally hiked in summer/fall. This would be a more challenging winter climb but a good one.
Fees and permits: Free reservation required for parking at the AMR May–Oct.
Canine compatibility: Dogs are not allowed on AMR property, but they are allowed if this route is hiked Gravestone Brook to the northeast of Dial.
Trail surface: Very well trafficked. Mixed rock and dirt surfaces with

scrambling up high. Some steep and rocky scrambles.
Land status: AMR property/Outer High Peaks Wilderness
Nearest town: Keene Valley, NY
Water availability: There are plenty of rivers down low but no water sources higher up.
Amenities available: Gill Brook and Elk Pass have campsites and privies.
Maximum grade: 1,100 feet/0.6 miles: going up Nippletop from Elk Pass
Special considerations: Bring lots of water. There is none at all after Elk Pass.
Sunrise or sunset: Both peaks are great for sunset.
Route type: Loop
Views: Nippletop has some of the best views of any high peak. It also has views on both sides. Dial also has good panoramic views.

FINDING THE TRAILHEAD

AMR/St. Huberts is right across the street from Roaring Brook Falls Trailhead for Giant, labeled as St. Huberts Parking Area or the Adirondack Mountain Reserve. Approximately 7.5 miles from I-87. Reservations are needed May–October. **GPS:** 44.14970°N / 73.76806°W

THE HIKE

Nippletop and Dial Mountains stand out not only for their majestic beauty but also for their intriguing origins. Named during the 1800s, these peaks have since been entwined with Verplanck Colvin and Ebenezer Emmons. Using a barometer, theodolite, and stan-helio automatic signal, Colvin's original measurement was 4,656 feet. Emmons approximated Nippletop's height at 4,900 feet using leveling. Nippletop, with its distinct shape, earned its name as a natural reflection of its appearance when viewed from Elk Lake. Despite its rather candid name, it has remained steadfast, defying the efforts of Victorian

The sunset from Nippletop is one of the best in the High Peaks.

sensibilities to rename it. Dial Mountain, on the other hand, had a more convoluted naming history. It was initially dubbed as Dial by Emmons in 1837, but the name was intended for what is now known as Nippletop. However, the name failed to gain traction and was eventually transferred to the nearby peak along Nippletop's ridgeline, supposedly by Old Mountain Phelps. Dial got its name from Hunters Pass (the pass in between Nippletop and Dix) which was formerly known as "Gorge of the Dial," which Emmons named due to its directional view of and from Noonmark Mountain.

Upon your arrival at the AMR parking lot, you will commence your journey by walking up the gravel road that connects to it. This uphill path will guide you past the golf course and, after 0.5 miles, you will turn left at the tennis courts. Shortly thereafter, you will arrive at a sign-in area and a large wooden AMR gate via Lake Road. If this is your first visit to this location, you will inevitably establish a strong bond with the property during your 46er journey. The gravel road that you will walk leads to numerous other remarkable sites, including Indian Head, Rainbow Falls, Nippletop, and the Colvin Range. As you walk past the wooden gate, this road continues for 3.5 miles to the end; however, you will only cover 2 miles down this path. During this 2-mile section, you will pass the H.G. Leach trail on the left, the Wolfjaws Bridge on the right, and eventually cross a wooden bridge. Just before your 2-mile section ends, the Gothics Trail via Beaver Meadow Falls Trail will appear on your right. The end of your 2-mile section is signified by a small dam on the left, accompanied by a wooden sign indicating the Gill Brook Trail. This is where you turn off Lake Road, following the sign pointing to Gill Brook Trail. For the next 1 mile, you will closely follow Gill Brook, weaving throughout the forest. You will see signs labeled "scenic" or "easy." Both options lead to the same trail, with one providing a gentler path and the other offering more picturesque surroundings. After completing 1 mile, you will arrive at the Gill Brook Cutoff sign. This signpost has several indications, but you will continue straight. Shortly afterward, you will pass another sign directing toward Indian Head on the right. Keep going straight past this sign. Soon, you will come across individual Gill Brook campsites on both your right and left sides.

About 0.25 miles after the campsites, you will encounter the next Indian Head Trail sign. This is the most efficient trail to Indian Head if you wish to make a brief visit. I highly recommend it if you have the energy. Over the next 0.6 miles past this sign, the trail steepens considerably, leading you to the Nippletop/Colvin intersection. Here, you'll see "Nippletop" (1.9 miles) to the left and "Mount Colvin" (1.1 miles) to the right. It's an ideal spot to take a break and refill your water. Turning left, the trail takes you 0.5 miles into Elk Pass, passing a pond, a boardwalk, another pond, and arriving at the Elk Pass campsite at Nippletop's base. The ascent, a challenging 1,200-foot climb in just 0.8 miles, features steep scrambles and plenty of rocky terrain. Upon reaching an intersection, turn right, following the sign pointing to Nippletop (0.2 miles). You'll see the summit in the distance after a small hill. The trail descends slightly before ascending to the summit, marked by a dead end and a 270-degree view to the west. Behind you, there's another lookout to the east at the Dix Range and Hunters Pass.

Retrace your steps to the intersection, then continue along the ridge for 5.7 miles to Lake Road, which includes about six uphill sections, climbing a total of 1,000 feet on the descent. The trail initially descends and climbs slightly before the real descent begins 0.1 miles past the sign. You'll encounter three minor uphill sections until reaching Dial (1.9 miles from the intersection). The picturesque trail leads to Dial's summit, marked by a large rock to be straddled and climbed, offering a view similar to Nippletop's but from a lower perspective. From Dial, it's 1.7 miles to Bear Den and 3.8 miles to Lake Road.

Hiker stargazing from the summit of Nippletop.

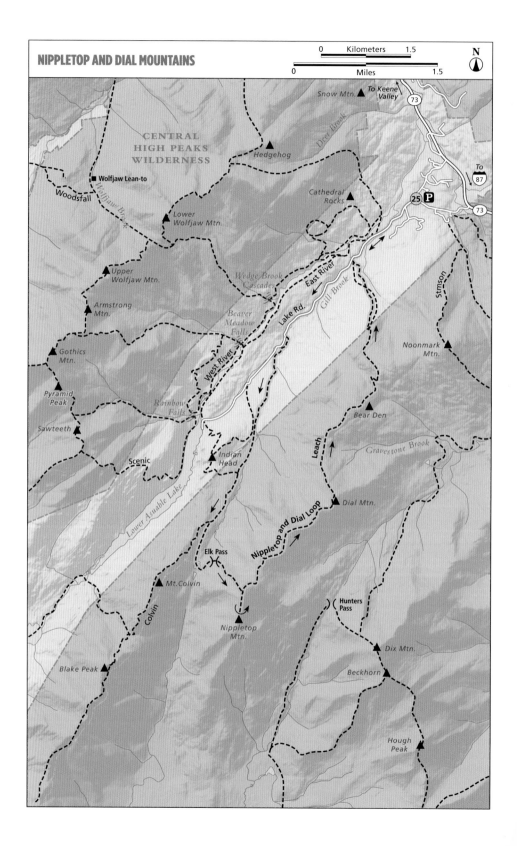

Kilometers

0   1.5

Miles

0   1.5

N

Snow Mtn.
To Keene
Valley

CENTRAL
HIGH PEAKS
WILDERNESS

73

To
87

Hedgehog

Deer Brook

Cathedral
Rocks

25   P

73

Woodsfall

Wolfjaw Lean-to

Lower
Wolfjaw Mtn.

Wolfjaw Brook

Wedge Brook
Cascades

East River

Gill Brook

Stimson

Upper
Wolfjaw Mtn.

Armstrong
Mtn.

Beaver
Meadow
Falls

Lake Rd.

Noonmark
Mtn.

Gothics
Mtn.

West River

Pyramid
Peak

Rainbow
Falls

Bear Den

Leach

Gravestone Brook

Sawteeth

Scenic

Indian
Head

Lower Ausable Lake

Dial Mtn.

Nippletop and Dial Loop

Elk Pass

Mt. Colvin

Colvin

Nippletop
Mtn.

Hunters
Pass

Dix Mtn.

Beckhorn

Blake Peak

Hough
Peak

Descending 1,000 feet from Dial, you'll briefly climb to Bear Den, followed by a 600-foot descent to the col and a steep ascent to Noonmark's Shoulder, or "The Burn Zone." This area suffered a 1999 wildfire that burned 90 acres, leaving behind burnt debris and a thriving black birch forest. The top offers scenic views of the ridge you just hiked down. The road is 1.6 miles away. Leaving the top, you'll traverse an eroded trail prone to flooding in wet conditions. The trail then descends into the Ausable Valley, crossing back onto AMR property and passing through hardwood forests before reaching Lake Road. The gate is 0.8 miles from this point. Sign out and return to the parking lot.

MILES AND DIRECTIONS

- 0.0 Start at AMR parking lot.
- 0.6 Reach AMR gate for Lake Road.
- 2.7 Turn at Gill Brook Trail sign on the left.
- 3.7 Pass a sign, continuing straight.
- 3.9 Pass an Indian Head sign, heading straight.
- 4.5 Pass another Indian Head sign, again heading straight.
- 5.3 Come to Nippletop/Colvin fork sign, staying left to Nippletop.
- 5.8 Reach Elk Pass, climbing Nippletop.
- 6.6 Reach Nippletop intersection (0.2-mile sign).
- 6.8 Summit of Nippletop. Descent the ridge to Dial.
- 8.7 Summit of Dial Mountain.
- 10.4 Reach Bear Den summit.
- 11.2 Reach Noonmark's Shoulder.
- 12.8 Reach Lake Road.
- 13.6 Return to AMR gate.
- 14.2 Arrive back at the St. Hubert's parking lot.

Stagelike view from the summit rock on Dial.

DIX RANGE

A gloomy winter day looking at Dix Mountain and Hough Peak (left) from Giant Mountain.

26 DIX MOUNTAIN

This route offers a single peak out-and-back journey to Dix Mountain. Regardless of the chosen path, hiking Dix Mountain is a demanding endeavor. The Dix Range is best suited for experienced hikers with proper gear. Dix Mountain, with its distinctive shape and impressive size, stands out among other peaks. Although it ranks among the more challenging trailed high peaks, Dix delivers breathtaking views, rivaling those from Marcy and Algonquin. Its remote nature and increased difficulty often result in fewer crowds compared to some of the more accessible high peaks.

Start: Round Pond/Dix Mountain
Elevation gain: 3,600 feet
Summit elevation: 4,857 feet
Distance: 14.6 miles
Difficulty: 4 out of 7, moderate. All-around challenging.
Hiking time: 8–10 hours
Seasons/schedule: This hike is generally hiked in summer/fall. It would be a more challenging winter climb but a good one.
Fees and permits: None
Canine compatibility: A leash is not required but recommended.
Trail surface: Very well trafficked. Rugged trail. Mixed rock and dirt/mud surfaces with scrambling up high. Even a small slide climb.

Land status: Outer High Peaks Wilderness (former Dix Mountain Wilderness)
Nearest town: Keene Valley, NY
Water availability: There are plenty of rivers down low but no water sources higher up.
Amenities available: Some campsites at Round Pond and Bouquet Forks Lean-to.
Maximum grade: 1,500 feet/0.75 miles: ascent to Dix from the slide
Special considerations: Expect a very difficult climb to the top.
Sunrise or sunset: Both.
Route type: Out-and-back
Views: This mountain does not lack in views in the slightest. You won't want to leave the summit.

FINDING THE TRAILHEAD

 Round Pond is situated on NY 73 from Keene Valley, 5 miles past Keene Valley on the right side when driving south. **GPS:** 44.13203°N / 73.73197°W

THE HIKE

Old Mountain Phelps describes Dix's summit appearance as follows: a "sharp, narrow, curved, uneven ridge covered with balsam brush from two to four feet high, and as thick as hair on a spaniel dog; a look at it reminds one of a look at an old poor cow doubled up to lick her hip, and for a man to travel it with a knapsack on would be like ants taking a big egg and traveling the cow's back." In 1807, an unknown surveyor named "Rykert" climbed Dix Mountain, making it the second recorded high peak ascent. He established boundaries between Keene and North Hudson in the Totten and Crossfield Purchase. Professor Ebenezer Emmons named the peak after John A. Dix, New York's secretary of state, in 1837. Dix, born in 1798, was a War of 1812 veteran, lawyer, journalist, and proponent of a statewide geological survey.

The trail going up Dix after the Thumb Slide.

As stated previously, parking spaces are limited. From the lot, walk up the road a short distance to an incline leading into the woods, where the sign-in register is located. Round Pond is about 0.5 miles from the register. Once you reach the pond, turn right and follow the counter-clockwise path around to the other side. The best part about this approach to Dix is its straightforward nature. At the end of the pond, the first ascent starts, climbing 700 feet over 0.8 miles. Your next objective is the intersection of the Old Dix Trail, with signage for AMR and Noonmark. At this three-way intersection, bear left and continue straight toward Dix, which is 4.9 miles away. From this intersection, the trail will lead you along the North Fork Bouquet River, up and around some marshland, over Gravestone Brook (which could be marked by a cairn or survey tape), passing Bouquet River Lean-to, and eventually bringing you to the Thumb Slide. Make sure to strictly follow the blue trail markers during this entire trek. Approximately 6.3 miles from your car or 3.9 from the last trail sign, you will arrive at the Thumb Slide. Upon arrival, you will see the trail continuing up the slide itself, marked by yellow blazes and cairns. Be very vigilant about where the trail goes, as it should only follow the slide for around 100 yards or so. The trail will then reconvene back into the woods. Please note that many

A panoramic view from the summit of Dix.

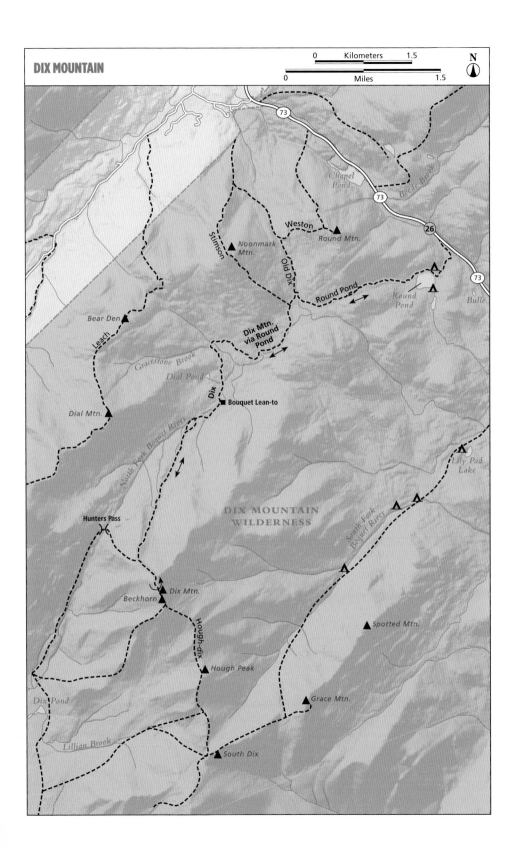

0   Kilometers   1.5

0   Miles   1.5

N

Chapel Pond

73

73

26

73

Weston

Round Mtn.

Stimson

▲ *Noonmark Mtn.*

Old Dix

Round Pond

Round Pond

Bulle

Bear Den ▲

Leach

Gracestone Brook

Dial Pond

Dix Mtn.
via Round
Pond

Dix

■ Bouquet Lean-to

Dial Mtn. ▲

North Fork Boquet River

Lily Pad Lake

DIX MOUNTAIN
WILDERNESS

South Fork Boquet River

Hunters Pass

Beckhorn

▲ Dix Mtn.

Hough-dix

▲ *Spotted Mtn.*

Dix Pond

▲ Hough Peak

▲ *Grace Mtn.*

Lillian Brook

▲ South Dix

people have made the mistake of following the slide for too long. The next section is a challenging ascent of 1,500 feet in just 0.75 miles. Slow and steady wins the race.

About 0.4 miles from the summit, you will come to the Hunters Pass Trail intersection on your right. Keep left, following the last 0.4 miles to the summit of Dix Mountain. The summit is marked by a survey disk embedded in the rock. From this vantage point, you can see nearly every high peak to the west, all of Vermont to the east, and on a clear day, you may even be able to see some of the White Mountains and Mount Washington. You can also see the nearby Beckhorn, a fun little walk and view spot with a massive flat rock the size of a condo. Take a rest, eat some lunch, and then head back to your car the same way you came.

MILES AND DIRECTIONS

- **0.0** Start at the Round Pond Trailhead.
- **0.1** Sign-in box.
- **0.6** Round Pond.
- **2.4** Reach Old Dix Trail intersection, keeping left.
- **4.0** Cross Gravestone Brook.
- **4.7** Pass Bouquet River Lean-to.
- **6.3** Reach the Thumb Slide.
- **6.9** Pass Hunters Pass Trail.
- **7.3** Reach summit of Dix Mountain; turn around.
- **14.6** Arrive back at the Round Pond Trailhead.

OTHER ROUTES

DIX MOUNTAIN VIA ELK LAKE/BECKHORN—13.2 MILES, 3,400 FEET

Find the trailhead near the end of Elk Lake Road and sign in at the trail's start. This well-maintained trail has few deviations. After 1.8 miles, you'll leave Elk Lake property and maintenance becomes less frequent. At 2.2 miles, pass the Slide Brook and Macomb Slide turnoff marked by a cairn, with the Slide Brook Lean-to nearby. Continue on the path, passing more campsites. After 0.8 miles (3 miles total), reach the Lillian Brook Trail, marked by a small cairn. Continue straight for another 0.3 miles where you will come to the Lillian Brook campsites. Continue past this for another 0.8 miles where you will come to a sign indicating Dix Mountain via the Beckhorn. This turnoff is 4.3 miles from the start. Turn here. The climb up to the Beckhorn is 2.1 miles in length with 2,500 feet of climbing. The trail will progressively get harder the higher you climb up. After 2.1 miles, you will come to the top of the Beckhorn marked by a massive flat cut rock. Follow the trail left and up around the rock, turning left on the trail for 0.25 miles, where you will reach the summit of Dix Mountain.

27 MACOMB MOUNTAIN, SOUTH DIX, GRACE PEAK, AND HOUGH PEAK

Although these four peaks are commonly paired with Dix Mountain, you may want to consider this particular bunch if you want to split up the Dix Range into two different trips. Leaving out Dix makes the trip surprisingly easier. Adding Dix will complete the full Dix Range traverse.

Start: Elk Lake Trailhead
Elevation gain: 4,050 feet
Summit elevation: Macomb Mountain, 4,405 feet; Hough Peak, 4,400 feet; South Dix, 4,060 feet; Grace Peak, 4,012 feet
Distance: 12.8 miles
Difficulty: 4 out of 7, moderate. All-around challenging.
Hiking time: 9–11 hours
Seasons/schedule: This hike is generally hiked in summer/fall.
Fees and permits: None
Canine compatibility: A leash is not required but recommended.
Trail surface: Very well trafficked. Rugged trail. Mixed rock and dirt/mud surfaces with scrambling up high. Even a small slide climb.
Land status: Outer High Peaks Wilderness (former Dix Mountain Wilderness) and Elk Lake Lodge Property
Nearest town: North Hudson, NY
Water availability: There are a few rivers down low but no water sources higher up.
Amenities available: Some campsites and lean-tos, and Elk Lake Lodge for guests.
Maximum grade: 900 feet/0.35 miles (steepest in the High Peaks): Macomb Slide; 700 feet/0.3 miles: Lilian Brook Trail
Special considerations: Due to the nature of Macomb Slide, it is best to go down it rather than up.
Sunrise or sunset: This range isn't really friendly to either, but being on Macomb at sunset is very nice.
Route type: Lollipop loop
Views: Each peak has good views to some degree.

FINDING THE TRAILHEAD

Take exit 29 on I-87 and head west toward Newcomb on Blue Ridge Road. After 4 miles, turn right onto Elk Lake Road, marked with a sign for Elk Lake Lodge. The trailhead is near the end of this road. Two miles before the trailhead is Clear Pond, which is alternate parking. **GPS:** 44.02083°N / 73.82784°W

THE HIKE

The surrounding Elk Lake is steeped in history and natural beauty. Early explorers to the region were captivated by the sight of majestic elk roaming the lush landscapes. The lake was once known as Mud Pond, but the abundance of elk eventually inspired a name change to reflect the area's natural charm. Prior to the establishment of the lodge, the land around Elk Lake was owned by Finch, Pruyn and Company, which used Adirondack Park's abundant timber resources for paper production. In the early 20th century, ownership of the land was transferred, and the lodge was established as a rustic retreat for those seeking to experience the natural beauty and tranquility of Elk Lake and its surrounding

Macomb (right), South Dix (center), and Hough (left) as seen from Nippletop at sunset.

forests. The lodge has had a significant impact on the conservation of the area, with its owners consistently demonstrating a commitment to preserving the land and its rich biodiversity. In the 1960s, the lodge's owners negotiated a groundbreaking conservation easement with the state, protecting a swath of land around Elk Lake and its islands today.

As you drive onto the property, keep the preservation of this land in mind. This guide takes you to Hough Peak first, as it will disperse your energy better throughout the varied elevation terrain. Find the trailhead near the end of the road, with the sign-in at the beginning of the trail. This trail is a straight shot without many deviations. As you start hiking, the trail remains well-maintained until you venture out of Elk Lake property 1.8 miles in. After that, the trail is still maintained but not as often. At 2.2 miles in, you'll pass the Slide Brook and Macomb Slide turnoff marked by a cairn. Here, you can see the Slide Brook Lean-to right off the trail after crossing a small bridge. Continue straight on the initial path, passing a couple more campsites. The trail remains the same. You'll hike another 0.8 miles (3 miles total) until you arrive at the Lillian Brook Trail, marked similarly to the Slide Brook turnoff by a small cairn. Be on the lookout. Turn right here. From here, it's a 1.6-mile ascent to the col between Hough and Pough Peaks. The initial ascent is gradual, climbing around 700 feet in elevation. There will be another turn 1.3 miles up this trail at around 3,200 feet.

After 0.7 miles along this path, you'll pass over a small stream. After 1.3 miles, you'll come to a fork where the trail splits. Stay left here. Turning right leads to another cutoff trail that feeds you in between Macomb and South Dix. Continuing on, the last 0.3 miles up is brutal, with about 700 feet of climbing in this short distance, making it one of the steepest unofficial trail sections in the High Peaks. Upon reaching the top, you'll find a trail junction; turn right to Pough and left to Hough. The trail to the summit is 0.3 miles, with 500 feet of climbing. The summit is marked by a yellow disk on a tree.

From here, you'll get a gorgeous perspective of the Beckhorn, which blocks the true summit of Dix. Upon returning, you will pass where you came up, then continue up and over Pough Peak. From where you came up initially, South Dix is 0.5 miles away. After ascending Pough, you'll dip back down before climbing again to reach the summit of South Dix. Be cautious here: Right before the summit of South Dix, there's a trail split. Stay left. Soon after, you'll reach South Dix, marked by another yellow disk on a tree. As you head toward Grace Peak, there's a view spur trail on your right. This is the only view from this peak. The trail to Grace is gradual, with Grace 1 mile away. The first 0.8 miles

MACOMB MOUNTAIN, SOUTH DIX, GRACE PEAK, AND HOUGH PEAK

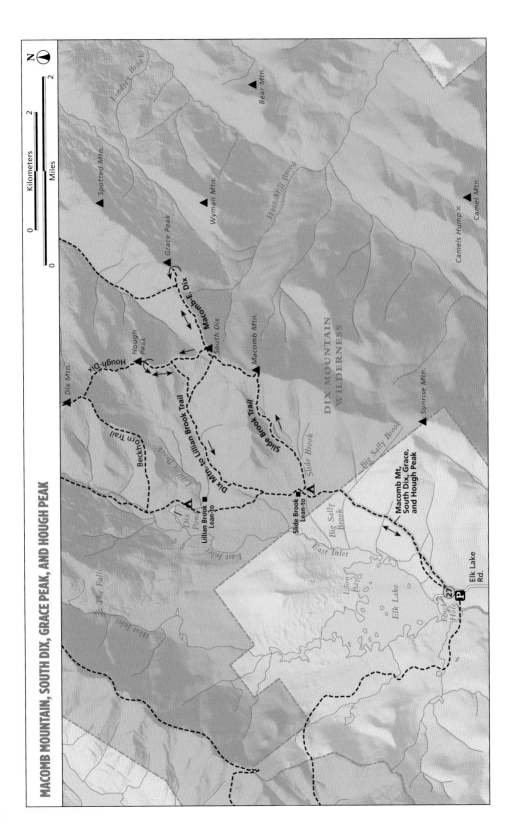

is all descent before climbing the majority in the last quarter-mile. At the bottom of this descent to Grace, there's a large rock you can crawl under or walk around. The ascent up to Grace is marked by some steep scrambles. As you climb up, the summit is marked by a massive rock perched on the high point. Climb this rock to summit Grace Peak. If you feel like going off-trail slightly, there are a series of spur trails on the summit that take you further north. These spots will give you clear views of Dix, Grace Slide, and Keene Valley.

Now, make your way back to South Dix. Continue past South Dix to the trail split from earlier, then turn left. This trail carries you over exposed rock above the trees. As you descend, be vigilant of where the trail goes. As you look toward Macomb, the trail takes you toward a direct approach of that mountain, with maybe a few leftish deviations. The trail down on this exposed rocky section should have some cairns to mark your path. As you near the bottom, the trail will reenter the woods, and you will see the cutoff trail that takes you back to Lillian Brook. Do not accidentally take this path; keep left to continue toward Macomb. The ascent up Macomb is straightforward, covering 0.5 miles with around 600 feet of climbing.

Upon reaching the top, you'll see the summit sign and the beautiful panoramic view with Elk Lake in the distance. Take a good look, because that is where you are walking back to. To leave the summit, continue past the sign, descending steeply into the trees. As you navigate down, this top section before the slide is precarious, with loose soil, rocks, and roots, as well as a couple of drop-downs. It gets very steep. After 0.25 miles, you will be funneled to the top of Macomb Slide, where you can stand on a rock to catch a wide view of the slide. Your descent down the slide will be dicey but easier than going up. The path will have you stay primarily on the right side of it, with cairns leading you down. Stay vigilant. Near the bottom, look for a ramp-like hill marked with a cairn on the right. This path takes you off the slide and over the small brook. Once back on the trail, the path will be straightforward back to the Slide Brook Lean-to. From the bottom of the slide, it's 1.2 miles back to the Elk Lake Trail. Once back on the trail, it's another 2.2 miles back to the trailhead.

MILES AND DIRECTIONS

0.0   Start at Elk Lake Trailhead.

2.2   Reach Slide Brook.

3.0   Reach Lillian Brook Trail, turning right.

4.3   Reach fork for cutoff, staying left.

4.6   Top of trail ridge turning left up to Hough.

4.9   Summit of Hough. Turn back to South Dix.

5.7   Reach summit of South Dix.

6.7   Reach summit of Grace Peak.

7.7   Return to South Dix, turning left toward Macomb.

7.9   Reach col of Macomb and trail split for cutoff, staying left.

8.5   Reach summit of Macomb. Descend to the slide.

9.4   Reach bottom of the slide.

10.6   Return to Slide Brook campsites, turning left onto the Elk Lake Trail.

12.8   Arrive back at the trailhead.

28 GRACE PEAK

This route to Grace Peak is an uncommon approach, but in recent years it has started to gain attention. The only reasons why one may want to consider this hike is if you need to get Grace Peak by itself or if you want to have a long, hard wooded, and unique day hike. This is an unmarked path and is not maintained. It is entirely a herd path by nature and requires some navigational skills.

Start: NY 73 at the North Fork Bouquet River crossing
Elevation gain: 2,800 feet
Summit elevation: 4,012 feet
Distance: 12.2 miles
Difficulty: 3 out of 7, moderate
Hiking time: 8-10 hours
Seasons/schedule: This hike is generally hiked in summer/fall.
Fees and permits: None
Canine compatibility: A leash is not required but recommended.
Trail surface: Although infrequently traveled, the trail is in good condition. Rugged trail. Not much traffic. Mixed dirt/mud surfaces and rocky up high.
Land status: Outer High Peaks Wilderness (former Dix Mountain Wilderness)

Nearest town: Keene Valley, NY
Water availability: The trail follows the South Bouquet River most of the time.
Amenities available: A few designated campsites along the way.
Maximum grade: The last mile climbs 1,300 feet.
Special considerations: This is not a trail for beginners. This is directionally challenging because it is a herd path.
Sunrise or sunset: Grace Peak is good for sunrise, but it is not recommended for a first-time hike.
Route type: Out-and-back
Views: Grace Peak has good views in every direction.

FINDING THE TRAILHEAD

Traveling on NY 73 from Keene Valley, the trailhead is situated a little over 6 miles past Keene Valley on the right side. If coming from I-87, the trailhead is 4 miles away. This spot is indicated by a nice stone bridge that you drive across. There is pull off at this bridge as well. On Google Maps, this spot is also known as "Five Mountain Loop Trailhead." **GPS:** 44.11301°N / 73.70892°W

THE HIKE

East Dix was officially renamed Grace Peak in 2014 in honor of Grace Hudowalski (#9). Grace was the first woman to climb all forty-six high peaks and served as a longtime historian for the 46ers. The renaming campaign began in the early 2000s and aimed to recognize Grace's enthusiasm for the Adirondacks and her mentorship to thousands of people. To start the hike, find the trailhead and choose the path on the left side of the river. While both sides are accessible, the left is easier and shorter. There's also a sign-in on this side. As you walk the path, you'll notice many trails leading to other features in the area. After 0.25 miles from the sign-in, you'll reach your first intersection. Turn right to cross the bridge instead of going left toward Shoebox Falls. Just past the bridge, you'll intersect with the trail from the other side. Turn left here. From this point, there are no other additional trails, and it's a straight shot into the woods. After about 0.6 miles, cross over the North

A view of Grace, South Dix, Macomb, and Hough from Giant.

Fork Bouquet River. Then, 0.3 miles later, pass your first campsite on the left, Lillypad Pond, totaling 1.9 miles from the start. From Lillypad Pond, the summit is approximately 4.2 miles away. About 0.6 miles beyond Lillypad Pond, you'll encounter the South Bouquet Fork River, which you'll parallel for almost the remainder of the hike. You'll pass more campsites at miles 2.8, 3.0, and 3.9. After the last campsite, the trail stays close to the river. Stay vigilant, as the trail crosses the river multiple times, occasionally marked by a cairn and sometimes not. At 5.2 miles, the trail begins to aim toward the peak and ascend more steeply. At 5.7 miles, you'll approach Grace Slide, which can be climbed to reach the summit. However, it can be very slick and slimy when wet, so exercise caution.

If you choose the trail, stay to the right side of the slide, avoiding it altogether. Past this section, the trail climbs steeply and eventually connects with the Grace Peak Trail from South Dix. The summit is only 0.1 miles away. Before the final climb to Grace, you'll encounter a large rock you can crawl under or walk around. The ascent up to Grace involves some steep scrambles. The summit is marked by a massive rock perched on the high point; climb this rock to reach Grace Peak's summit. For those interested in venturing slightly off-trail, there are a series of spur trails on the summit leading farther north. These spots offer clear views of Dix, Grace Slide, and Keene Valley. After enjoying your time at the summit, return to the trailhead via the same route.

MILES AND DIRECTIONS

0.0   Start at the trailhead, sign in, and take the left path along the river.

0.25 Reach intersection, cross the bridge and turn left.

1.5   Cross over North Fork Bouquet River.

1.9   Pass Lillypad Pond campsite.

2.5   Reach South Bouquet Fork River.

2.8   Pass additional campsites along the trail.

3.0   Pass additional campsites along the trail.

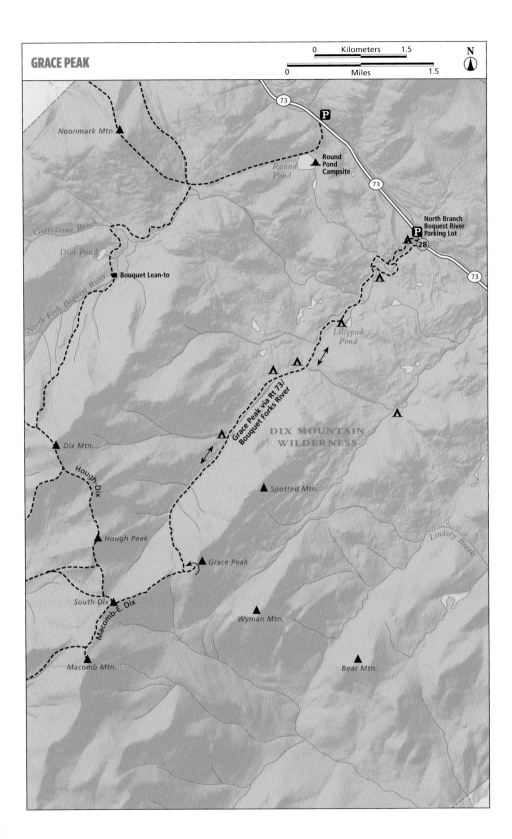

Kilometers

Miles

N

73

P

Round
Pond

Round
Pond
Campsite

73

North Branch
Boquest River
Parking Lot

P

28

73

Noonmark Mtn.

Gravestone Brook

Dial Pond

Bouquet Lean-to

North Fork Boquet River

Lillypad
Pond

Grace Peak via Rt 73/
Bouquet Forks River

DIX MOUNTAIN
WILDERNESS

Dix Mtn.

Hough-Dix

Spotted Mtn.

Lindsey Brook

Hough Peak

Grace Peak

South Dix

Macomb-E. Dix

Wyman Mtn.

Macomb Mtn.

Bear Mtn.

A panoramic view up the valley from Grace Peak looking toward Dix in March.

3.9 Pass additional campsites along the trail.

5.2 Trail begins to steeply ascend toward the peak.

5.7 Reach Grace Slide; opt for trail to the right, avoiding the slide.

6.0 Join Grace Peak Trail from South Dix; summit is 0.1 miles away.

6.1 Reach summit of Grace Peak. Explore spur trails for views; turn around.

12.2 Arrive back at the trailhead via the same route.

SANTANONI RANGE

Santanoni rising up as viewed from Panther Peak.

29 SANTANONI, PANTHER, AND COUCHSACHRAGA PEAKS

The Santanoni Range is known for its rugged trails, remote location, and diversely challenging three high peaks: Santanoni, Panther, and Couchsachraga. This range should only be considered by the well-seasoned High Peaks hikers. This range is also generally saved for the latter half of the 46er journey.

Start: Santanoni Range/Bradley Pond Trailhead
Elevation gain: 4,500 feet
Summit elevation: Santanoni Peak, 4,607 feet; Panther Peak, 4,442 feet; Couchsachraga Peak, 3,820 feet
Distance: 16.1 miles
Difficulty: 5 out of 7, difficult
Hiking time: 9–11 hours
Seasons/schedule: This hike is generally hiked in summer/fall.
Fees and permits: None
Canine compatibility: A leash is not required but recommended.
Trail surface: This area is certainly "dismal wilderness." The trails can be somewhat navigationally challenging and present some of the nastiest muddy terrain you will encounter during the entire 46. Very rugged. Tons of rocks, roots, and mud.
Land status: Outer High Peaks Wilderness (former Western High Peaks)

Nearest town: Tahawas/Newcomb, NY
Water availability: Water can be found all along at Santanoni Brook and Bradley Pond. There is none up on the range.
Amenities available: Santanoni Lean-to and the Bradley Pond Campsite.
Maximum grade: 1,700 feet/1.3 miles: ascent of Express Trail
Special considerations: This is a very wet range. Bring Gore-Tex boots and gaiters. Trekking poles are definitely recommended.
Sunrise or sunset: Santanoni is great for sunrise. Panther is great for sunset.
Route type: Lollipop loop
Views: Each peak has views to some degree. Some say Santanoni has the best views, while others say Panther.

FINDING THE TRAILHEAD

From I-87 exit 29, head west on Blue Ridge Road (CR 84) toward Newcomb. Turn right onto Tahawus Road and make a left at the High Peaks trails sign after 6.3 miles. The Santanoni/Bradley Pond parking lot will be on your left after 2 more miles or about 1 mile before Upper Works. **GPS:** 44.069°N / 74.0617°W

THE HIKE

The Santanoni Range features three peaks that are part of the forty-six high peaks: Santanoni, Panther, and Couchsachraga. The name Santanoni is believed to be a corruption of the words Saint Anthony, who was the patron saint of the Saint Regis and Abenaki natives. There is also speculation that the name is derived from Native dialect, calling it *Sandanona* or *Si-non-bo-wanne*. Santanoni appeared on maps in 1838. The range's Panther Peak, first identified on the 1901 USGS map, derived its name from the common practice of naming topographic features after animals, likely based on the eastern cougar (which by the way still elusively roams these woods). The first ascent of Panther Peak is credited to Daniel Lynch, an Adirondack land surveyor, in 1904. The Marshalls and Herb Clark first climbed Couchsachraga in 1924. Originally considered over 4,000 feet in elevation, the 1954 USGS survey later reduced its elevation to 3,820 feet. Couchsachraga, pronounced *Kook-suh-krah-guh* is the smallest peak in the original forty-six and is now known for its remoteness, bog, and lack of views. This name is an ancient Indigenous name for the region in between the Santanoni Range and Seward Range, where the Cold River lies. It can be translated to "the great dismal wilderness" or "beaver hunting grounds."

The nice part about this hike is the beginning. Starting from the parking lot, you'll follow Santanoni Road, a comfortable walk spanning 1.8 miles with a modest 200 feet of elevation gain. After 1.8 miles, you'll come across the Bradley Pond Trail turnoff, marked by two yellow arrows and blue trail markers. Turn right here, and you'll be guided to the base of Santanoni and Henderson Mountains along a 1.9-mile trail. During this section, you'll cross a wooden bridge, start climbing, and encounter rougher terrain as you gain 900 feet to reach an elevation of approximately 2,800 feet. It's generally easier to complete the hardest peak first, and this approach maximizes your chances of successfully finishing all three. The Santanoni Express Trail turn is at the 3.7-mile mark from the start and marked by a large rock cairn. It can be easy to miss, but it's somewhat conspicuous. Turn left here and cross a small stream, which is your last water source before descending. Refill if needed. From this point, the trail reenters the woods briefly before guiding you to a small marshland.

Numerous routes have been forged through this spot, so choose the best path for you and reconnect with the trail on the other side. Your ascent up the Express begins, covering 1,700 feet over 1.6 miles. This route is quite degraded, with mud, loose rocks, and roots, making it fairly steep. The trail feels consistent for about 0.8 miles, after which you'll encounter an awkward 50-foot scramble that can be treacherous when wet. Choose your best line and proceed with caution. Just beyond this point, the trail eases, offering your first glimpse of Santanoni's summit in the distance. You're only 0.3 miles from the top trail at this juncture. Eventually, you'll arrive at the Santanoni Trail, where you'll turn left and hike 0.1 miles to the true summit. Before reaching the summit, there's an exceptional viewpoint on the left, which will be your primary summit vista. Just beyond this is the true summit, marked by a wooden sign and a large rock. From here, the traverse to Times Square is 1.1 miles. This traverse is where people can get confused or lost, so please stay vigilant. If you think you may have lost the path, retrace your steps back to where you last knew the true trail was. As you start, you'll be able to see the rest of the range, with Panther in the distance and "Couchie" down and off to the left. The trail will descend 400 feet into the in-between of these peaks, and remember that there are no trail markers. You'll encounter descents on scrambles, muddy spots, and potentially thick blowdown. As you near the end of this 1.1 miles, you'll be greeted with a view out to the left. Eventually, you'll hike uphill and come to a rock with a small cairn indicating the path to Couchsachraga. If you missed it, retrace your steps and look for it.

Tackling Couchsachraga second is recommended, ensuring maximum daylight. This challenging out-and-back is 3.2 miles, with 1.6 miles to Couch. Ensure sufficient energy, water, food, and daylight, as this section can take hikers 3 to 4 hours. You'll immediately encounter two mud pits before entering a consistently rugged and dismal trail that descends to 3,500 feet. At 0.4 miles down, enjoy a pleasant view of the vast expanse and distant Seward Range. The bottom is about 0.6 miles away from this point. As you

A sunset summit view from Panther Peak looking toward Couchsachraga.

SANTANONI, PANTHER, AND COUCHSACHRAGA PEAKS

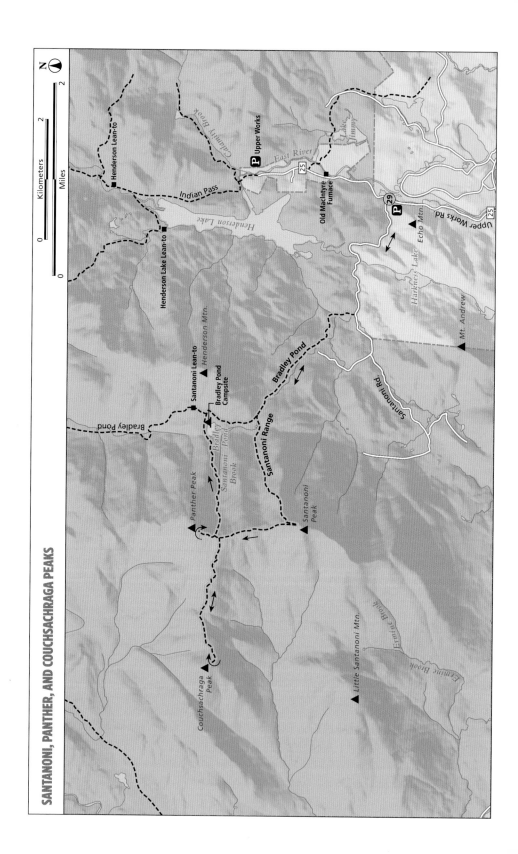

N

Kilometers
0   2

Miles
0   2

Henderson Lean-to

Cahanny Brook

Indian Pass

Henderson Lake Lean-to

Henderson Lake

Upper Works

East River

Old MacIntyre Furnace

25

29

Harkness Lake

Echo Mtn.

Upper Works Rd

25

Mt. Andrew

Santanoni Lean-to

Henderson Mtn.

Bradley Pond Campsite

Bradley Pond

Bradley Pond

Santanoni Brook

Santanoni Range

Santanoni Peak

Panther Peak

Couchsachraga Peak

Santanoni Rd.

Little Santanoni Mtn.

Ermine Brook

Ermine Brook

approach the bottom, Couchsachraga becomes prominent, and the trail features steep scrambles. At the bottom, you'll find the Couchsachraga Bog. Crossing it unscathed is rare. Identify the dead center of the bog, stepping over a large log if it's the correct spot. Take a direct, straight approach without deviating. The center has many dead branches, tree limbs, and hidden logs beneath the muck. Remember, you'll need to cross it again on the return. From here, the summit is 0.5 miles away, with a 300-foot climb. Notable scrambles lead to the top, the largest right before the summit. At the summit, an open space and wooden sign welcome you. Enjoy a partially obstructed 360-degree treetop view. Along the mountaintop, a few vantage points offer glimpses of the range. Retrace the 1.6 miles back to Santanoni Trail.

Once back on the trail, celebrate before continuing to Panther. Head north or left to Times Square, marked by a rock cairn and faint "TS" engraving. At the intersection, go straight toward Panther instead of right, which leads back to Bradley Pond. Panther is only 0.25 miles away with 150 feet of climbing. Cross two muddy sections before reaching the summit face, which requires a hands-on scramble above the tree line. At the summit, find the sign and enjoy unobstructed views in all directions except the Central High Peaks area. Return to Times Square and begin the 1.6-mile descent to Bradley Pond on a rugged trail. Cross Panther Brook (or Santanoni Brook, according to some maps) and reach the bottom. Pass Bradley Pond and rejoin the Bradley Pond Trail, following signs to the trailhead. It's a 2.5-mile hike to Santanoni Road and an additional 1.8 miles back to the trailhead.

MILES AND DIRECTIONS

0.0 Start at the parking lot, and follow Santanoni Road.

1.8 Reach Bradley Pond trail turnoff, and turn right.

3.7 Arrive at Santanoni Express Trail turn, marked by a rock cairn, and turn left.

5.3 Finish ascent up the Express, reach Santanoni Trail, and turn left.

5.4 Reach Santanoni summit.

6.5 Complete 1.1-mile traverse to Times Square.

8.1 Arrive at Couchsachraga summit.

9.7 Return to Santanoni Trail from Couchsachraga.

9.8 Reach Times Square from Santanoni Trail.

10.0 Arrive at Panther summit.

10.2 Return to Times Square from Panther, hiking down.

11.8 Reach Bradley Pond from Times Square.

14.3 Arrive back at Santanoni Road from Bradley Pond Trail.

16.1 Reach the trailhead and parking lot.

SEWARD RANGE

Sunrise from Donaldson Mountain.

30 SEWARD, DONALDSON, AND EMMONS MOUNTAINS

The Seward Range, renowned for its remote location, rugged trails, and the diverse challenges posed by its three high peaks—Seward, Donaldson, and Emmons, along with occasionally Seymour—should be reserved for experienced High Peaks hikers. As a result, navigating through this range can be a true test of one's hiking abilities, and offers a more secluded and adventurous experience. Typically, this range is tackled during the latter stages of the 46er journey.

Start: Seward Trailhead/Blueberry Trail
Elevation gain: 4,000 feet
Summit elevation: Seward Mountain, 4,361 feet; Donaldson Mountain, 4,140 feet; Emmons Mountain, 4,040 feet
Distance: 16.0 miles
Difficulty: 5 out of 7, difficult. (Adding Seymour would make this a 6 out of 7.)
Hiking time: 10–12 hours
Seasons/schedule: This hike is generally hiked in summer/fall.
Fees and permits: None
Canine compatibility: A leash is not required but recommended.
Trail surface: This range is unmarked and not nearly as traveled as other ranges. Very rugged. Tons of rocks, roots, and mud.

Land status: Outer High Peaks Wilderness (former Western High Peaks)
Nearest town: Tupper Lake, NY
Water availability: Water is very scarce. Water can be found flowing at the bottom of Seward Mountain Trail.
Amenities available: Blueberry and Ward Brook Lean-tos and Calkins campsites.
Maximum grade: 2 miles/2,100 feet: ascent of Seward
Special considerations: This is a very wet range. Bring Gore-Tex boots and gaiters. Trekking poles are definitely recommended here.
Sunrise or sunset: This range is not recommended, but Donaldson isn't terrible for sunrise.
Route type: Loop
Views: Each peak has views to some degree, but don't expect too much.

FINDING THE TRAILHEAD

From Saranac Lake, take NY 3 toward Tupper Lake. After approximately 12.5 miles, turn left onto Coreys Road, marked with a sign for the Seward Range. The trailhead is at the end of this road about 5.5 miles. **GPS:** 44.19166°N / 74.26352°W

THE HIKE

The Seward Range, particularly Mount Seward, once held a reputation for being considerably taller than it actually is. In 1837, Ebenezer Emmons estimated Mount Seward's elevation at around 5,100 feet. However, its true height of 4,331 feet was discovered in 1870 by Verplanck Colvin and his guide Alvah Dunning. The region has also experienced drastic changes due to logging activities by the Santa Clara Lumber Company. Although it has been over 80 years since the last timber was cut and sledded off the mountains, the woods are still recovering from the damage. The once tall trees and old-growth forest

The sunrise from the summit of Donaldson.

surrounding the Seward Range have since disappeared, but travelers who visited the region before the Civil War saw those woods in their primitive state. Today, remnants of the logging industry can be seen at every corner of this range.

Today, we'll embark on a clockwise journey, starting with the most challenging mountain, Seward, and descending via the Calkins Trail to efficiently disperse our energy throughout the day. This route also helps us avoid the tedious descent down Seward. Our adventure begins on the Blueberry Trail, a straightforward trail with few deviations. We will cover 5.2 miles to reach the base of Seward Mountain, passing several key points such as the horse trail cutoff at mile 0.8, the turn to Calkins Brook Truck Trail at mile 1.3, the Blueberry Lean-to at mile 4.8, and connecting to the Ward Brook Truck Trail at mile 5.0.

At the 5.2-mile mark, we'll turn right for Seward Mountain, which is located next to a wooden bridge and marked by a cairn with metal. The ascent to Seward's summit spans 2.3 miles and entails a climb of 2,300 feet. The trail starts gradually, weaving through the woods and along the river. About 0.5 miles in, you'll cross a small stream, a good opportunity to refill your water. As you proceed, the terrain becomes rockier and steeper, eventually becoming pure rocks. This is one of the rockiest trails in the High Peaks. Near the top, you will find a rare Adirondack switchback. This point also gives you a great view out to the north. Shortly after this, you will arrive at the top of Seward which is marked by a wooden sign. There is also another view just past the summit.

From Seward's summit, you'll continue to Donaldson, located 0.8 miles away. The journey will involve navigating steep scrambles, loose terrain, some views, and an abundance of rocks. The trail will take you up a hill and then down again before starting up to Donaldson. Approximately 0.1 miles before Donaldson, you'll pass the Calkins Brook Trail, which you'll use for your return journey, but not just yet. Soon after this point, you'll climb a scramble that brings you to the summit spur. Be vigilant, looking left for a spur trail that will take you up to a raised area to Donaldson's summit, which is marked by a wooden sign. From here, you can enjoy a decent view through the trees toward the east. Next, we'll proceed along the trail to Emmons, which is 0.9 miles away. The traverse to Emmons will require navigating several mud pits, and will also pass another

SEWARD, DONALDSON, AND EMMONS MOUNTAINS

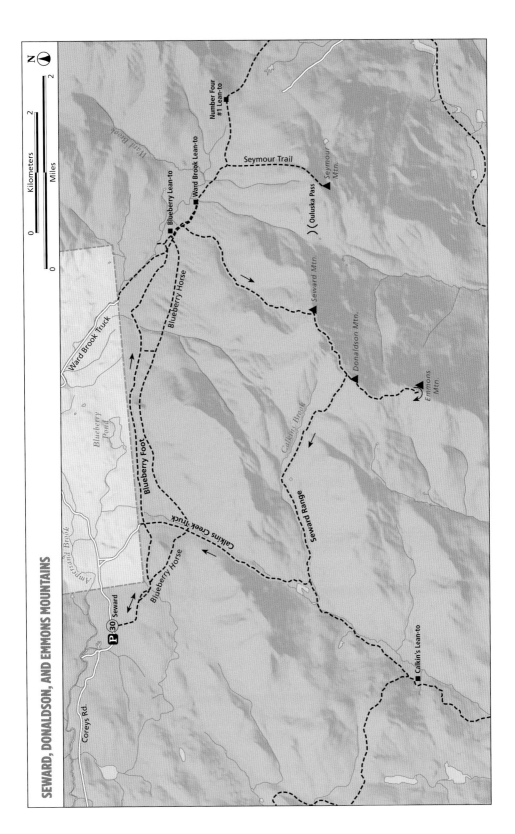

Coreys Rd.

Ampersand Brook

Blueberry Pond

Ward Brook Truck

P 30 Seward

Blueberry Foot

Blueberry Horse

Calkins Creek Truck

Blueberry Horse

Blueberry Lean-to

Ward Brook Lean-to

Ward Brook

Number Four #1 Lean-to

Seymour Trail

Ouluska Pass

Seymour Mtn.

Seward Mtn.

Donaldson Mtn.

Emmons Mtn.

Calkins Brook

Seward Range

Calkin's Lean-to

N

0   2   Kilometers
0   2   Miles

viewpoint 0.2 miles past Donaldson. From this vantage point, you can see Long Lake and the rest of the journey to Emmons. The trail will then drop about 300 feet before bringing you back up to Emmons. Just before reaching Emmons, you'll need to hop up a 6-foot scramble. Immediately after this, you'll arrive at Emmons's summit, marked by a sign but devoid of views. Make your way back to the Calkins Brook Cutoff trail, located just beyond Donaldson (1 mile from Emmons).

As we begin our descent on the Calkins Trail, you'll encounter loose dirt and some muddy patches along the 2.6-mile trail down to the truck trail. This narrow path will lead us around blowdown and will eventually come to Calkins Brook just over halfway down. At the bottom, you'll cross the brook, looking for

The descent off Seward in the wintertime looking toward Emmons.

cairns to the other side, and continue along a herd path to the intersection marked by rocks and metal. Turn right here on to the truck trail. You are 3.2 miles from the trailhead at this point. We'll walk along the wide truck trail for 1.8 miles where you will pass a campsite on the right. At this point, you can either turn left to take the horse trail shortcut, which will save you a few minutes, or continue straight on the Blueberry Trail. Either option is fine; just make sure to eventually turn left. Once you reconnect with the Blueberry Trail, we'll hike the remaining distance back to the trailhead, completing your adventure.

MILES AND DIRECTIONS

0.0 Start at the trailhead parking lot, and follow Blueberry Trail.

0.8 Pass the horse trail cutoff on your right.

1.3 Pass the turn to Calkins Brook Truck Trail.

4.8 Pass the Blueberry Lean-to.

5.0 Connect to Ward Brook Truck Trail.

5.2 Turn right for Seward Mountain, next to a wooden bridge.

7.5 Reach Seward summit.

8.2 Pass the Calkins Brook Trail (0.1 miles before Donaldson).

8.3 Arrive at Donaldson summit.

9.2 Reach Emmons summit.

10.2 Return to Calkins Brook Cutoff trail, just beyond Donaldson.

12.8 Reach the truck trail at the bottom of Calkins Trail.

14.7 Pass a campsite on the right; turn left to take the horse trail shortcut or continue straight to the Blueberry Trail.

16.0 Arrive back at the trailhead and parking lot.

31 SEYMOUR MOUNTAIN

Seymour is sometimes paired with the three other Seward Mountains but can certainly be hiked by itself if one so chooses. This mountain is the definition of "a walk in the park," not because it's easy but because it requires a lot of flat forested miles. Seymour is rough, rugged, and ragged, hence why it was given the name Ragged Mountain before its current name.

Start: Seward Trailhead/Blueberry Trail
Elevation gain: 2,800 feet
Summit elevation: 4,120 feet
Distance: 14.6 miles
Difficulty: 4 out of 7, moderate. Very steep and slablike terrain.
Hiking time: 8–10 hours
Seasons/schedule: This hike is generally hiked in summer/fall.
Fees and permits: None
Canine compatibility: A leash is not required but recommended.
Trail surface: This trail is unmarked and not nearly as traveled as other peaks. Very rugged. Tons of rocks, roots, and mud.

Land status: Outer High Peaks Wilderness (former Western High Peaks)
Nearest town: Tupper Lake, NY
Water availability: Water is scarce. Water can be found flowing at the bottom in various streams.
Amenities available: Blueberry and Ward Brook Lean-tos.
Maximum grade: 0.45 miles/1,030 feet: second half of Seymour ascent
Special considerations: Bring Gore-Tex boots and gaiters.
Sunrise or sunset: This mountain is not recommended for either, but sunrise is decent.
Route type: Out-and-back
Views: Seymour has good views.

FINDING THE TRAILHEAD

From Saranac Lake, take NY 3 toward Tupper Lake. After approximately 12.5 miles, turn left onto Coreys Road, marked with a sign for the Seward Range. The trailhead is at the end of this road about 5.5 miles. **GPS:** 44.19166°N / 74.26352°W

THE HIKE

Seymour Mountain's first ascent remains uncertain between Arnold Guyot and Ernest Sandoz in 1863 or Verplanck Colvin and his team in 1872. The mountain was named after politician Horatio Seymour, the last New York governor to have a high peak named in his honor. The current route to the summit is unmarked, unmaintained and has changed over time. Originally, it followed a thin slide on the mountain's north side. However, as vegetation covered the slide, a new steep path developed just west of it. This path has now become one of the most eroded and muddy trails in the Adirondacks. But over the years, dozens or so paths have been forming around the muck. Our adventure begins on the Blueberry Trail, a straightforward path with few deviations. We'll cover 5.8 miles to reach the base of Seward Mountain, passing several key points such as the horse trail cutoff at mile 0.8, the turn to Calkins Brook Truck Trail at mile 1.3, the Blueberry Lean-to at mile 4.8, and connecting to the Ward Brook Truck Trail at mile 5.0. At the 5.2-mile mark, we'll pass the turn for Seward Mountain, the Ward Brook Lean-to at mile

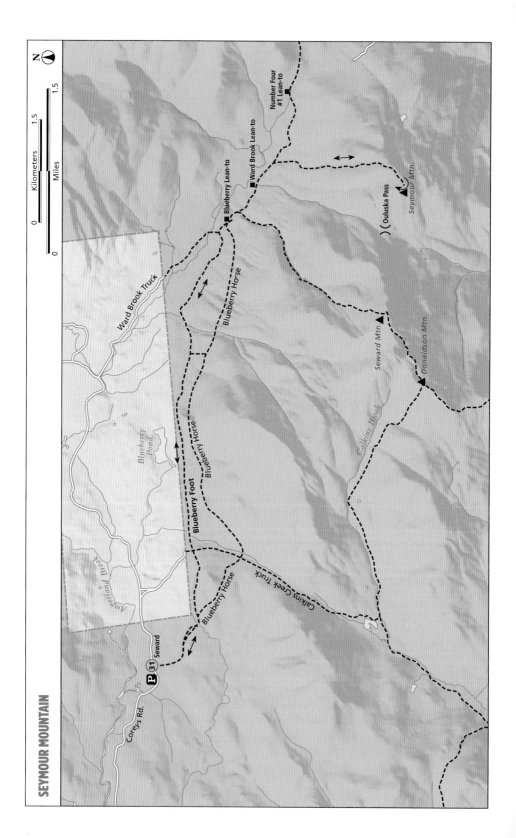

SEYMOUR MOUNTAIN

The view from the ledge near the summit of Seymour looking at Seward.

5.7, and finally the turn for Seymour at 5.8 miles, indicated by a stack of rocks and some metal. The ascent of Seymour is rather straightforward, spanning about 1.5 miles.

There aren't any deviations off the trail, but reaching the top is challenging. This trail has everything a High Peaks trail offers: mud, eroded paths, rocks, and slab climbing. The initial part of the trail is casual, leading to a muddy area with multiple paths formed over time. Navigate through this section as needed. The trail, like other High Peaks trails, gradually becomes steeper. The second half of the ascent is one of the steepest in the Adirondacks, transitioning into slab terrain. Most of the dirt has eroded away, leaving roots over slippery wet rock. You'll likely need your hands to climb some sections. Nearing the summit, the trail flattens out, and you'll climb one last steep section before reaching Seymour's summit. Just before the summit is a fantastic viewpoint on a ledge rock overlooking the Seward Range. At the summit, you can enjoy an eastern view by going just beyond the sign. Once you've taken in the sights, head back down the way you came, carefully retracing your steps to the trailhead.

MILES AND DIRECTIONS

0.0   Start at the trailhead, and follow the Blueberry Trail.

0.8   Pass the horse trail cutoff on your right.

1.3   Pass the turn to Calkins Brook Truck Trail.

4.8   Reach the Blueberry Lean-to.

5.0   Connect to the Ward Brook Truck Trail.

5.2   Pass the turn for Seward Mountain.

5.7   Reach the Ward Brook Lean-to.

5.8   Turn for Seymour, marked by a stack of rocks and metal.

7.3   Reach Seymour summit and enjoy the view.

8.8   Return to the bottom of Seymour.

14.6   Arrive back at the trailhead.

ALLEN MOUNTAIN

Spur trail view from Allen summit looking toward Skylight, Marcy, Panther Gorge, and Haystack.

32 ALLEN MOUNTAIN

Sitting alone in the southern High Peaks, Allen is the longest out-and-back of any stand-alone high peak in the Northeast. This hike is challenging in every regard and should be approached with caution. This remote mountain offers a test of endurance, skill, and navigation prowess. It is highly recommended you go with a friend who has hiked Allen before.

Start: East River Trailhead
Elevation gain: 3,600 feet
Summit elevation: 4,340 feet
Distance: 19.6 miles
Difficulty: 5 out of 7, difficult
Hiking time: 12–14 hours
Seasons/schedule: This hike is generally hiked in summer/fall.
Fees and permits: None
Canine compatibility: A leash is not required but recommended.
Trail surface: This trail is long, rugged, and muddy.
Land status: Central High Peaks Wilderness
Nearest town: Tahawus/Newcomb, NY
Water availability: Water can be found at the Opalescent River and Skylight Brook at the base.
Amenities available: No campsite or privies.

Maximum grade: 1,050 feet/0.5 miles: upper half of Allen Mountain ascent
Special considerations: Wait until you feel like you can hike this in 1 day. Go with a friend, and expect it to be long and hard. If you have bad footwear, bring microspikes for the slide up Allen. It's very slimy. This route involves a mix of unmarked herd paths, overgrown areas, and river crossings, with challenging, steep climbs and slippery, eroded sections, demanding careful navigation.
Sunrise or sunset: Don't bother.
Route type: Out-and-back
Views: This hike has breathtaking views of the Great Range, Panther Gorge, and the surrounding wilderness.

FINDING THE TRAILHEAD

East River Trailhead is 0.5 miles before Upper Works. Follow Blue Ridge Road (CR 84) west from I-87 exit 29 toward Newcomb. Travel for 17.4 miles until you reach the intersection with Tahawus Road (CR 25) after the train tracks. Turn right and continue for 6.3 miles, then make a left at the High Peaks trails sign. Just past the Boreas River Bridge, the trailhead is on the right. **GPS:** 44.08120°N / 74.05516°W

THE HIKE

Allen Mountain remains a test of endurance and spirit for hikers seeking solitude and a challenge. With an elevation of 4,340 feet, Allen's remoteness and lack of marked trails have earned it a reputation as one of the most challenging among the forty-six high peaks. And it is arguably the most remote 4,000-footer in the Northeast. Located in the southern High Peaks, Allen somewhat connects to Skylight Mountain via an irregular ridge and is characterized by dense forests of birch, spruce, and fir trees, along with numerous streams and wetlands that create a diverse and thriving ecosystem. Named in 1869 after Reverend Frederick B. Allen, an Episcopal minister, Allen Mountain has a rich history that is closely connected to the development of the Adirondack region. The

A still morning photo of Lake Sally in October.

first recorded ascent of Allen Mountain took place more than 50 years later in 1921, by brothers Robert and George Marshall along with their guide, Herbert Clark. Historically, this mountain was commonly climbed from the east side, but today it is climbed from the west.

The trail begins with a pleasant walk through the woods on a fairly wide path. After a couple hundred yards, it bears right at the Hudson River, following it for a hundred feet before leading you to a metal suspension bridge. Exercise caution while crossing the somewhat lopsided bridge, which has not been replaced since high waters nearly destroyed it in 2019. After crossing, the trail continues for about 0.3 miles until you reach Lake Jimmy. Stay alert, as the trail will eventually turn left into the woods. If you continue straight, you'll hit a dead end at the lake where a crossing used to be before 2011; however, some debris should block the trail. The path veers left into the woods, following a herd path that navigates clockwise around the lake. As you go around the lake, you'll encounter boardwalks, and muddy and marshy land, eventually reaching the other side where the bridge originally connected. The trail remains wide and easy to follow. About 0.3 miles past the lake, you'll pass the abandoned Mount Adams fire tower ranger shack on the left; the trail then veers right. Shortly after, you'll pass the Mount Adams Trail turnoff on the left, 1.2 miles from the start, marked by a sign. Continue straight past this point.

Over the next 0.5 miles, the trail features varied muddy terrain before arriving at Lake Sally. As you approach the lake, there's another intersection for a logging path, directing you to stay left. You'll parallel Lake Sally for 0.4 miles, and once the lake disappears, the trail remains unchanged for another 0.3 miles before reaching another logging path junction, 2.7 miles in. This will merge you onto another path, guiding you to stay left as well. Over the next 1.4 miles, the trail becomes easier, remaining relatively flat and easy to walk. Enjoy the lovely views of marshland and your first glimpse of Allen Mountain way off in the distance. The next challenge is the water crossing of the Opalescent River, 4.1 miles in.

A beautiful rebuilt bridge that once stood here was swept away in 2019. If the water is low enough, you can cross directly where the bridge used to be by hopping on rocks.

Alternatively, you may find sections for rock-hopping a bit farther down the river on the right. There's a 50-50 chance of crossing without getting wet (assuming you don't fall in), but it's not unlikely that you may need to remove your boots and socks to ford the river. Once on the other side, the trail becomes much more rugged, leading you into a denser wooded area. Over the next 1.2 miles, the path remains relatively easy to walk and travel. During this stretch, you'll pass by more marshland, catch another glimpse of Allen, cross a river, and eventually pass the East River Trail to Lake Colden 1.3 miles after the Opalescent crossing. The trail continues straight through more rugged woods. After another 0.5 miles, the trail will lead you onto a larger logging road where you'll turn left, walk briefly, and then turn right into an older ranger trailhead. The parking lot is 5.8 miles in. You'll walk to its end, and from there, you are 2.8 miles from the base of Allen. It's crucial to be vigilant after this point, as the trail features varied terrain, leading through rough, rugged woods and wide-open hardwood on dirt and rocky surfaces. Over the next

Hikers cross the bridge over the Hudson.
JONATHAN'S MOM

2 miles, you'll start climbing in elevation, but this is not Allen Mountain. Instead, it is a miscellaneous high point within the valley. During these 2 miles, the trail will have you ascend 600 vertical feet before descending on the other side. This section can be challenging to follow, so stay alert and retrace your steps if needed. Eventually, the trail will crest over the hill, descending 200 feet in elevation before crossing a small river.

About 0.1 miles after this little river crossing, you'll arrive at another primary river crossing at Skylight Brook. Most of the time, this crossing is manageable and easy, making it an excellent spot to refill water. Although the trail will gradually start ascending Allen from this point, the true base of the mountain is farther ahead. Skylight Brook is 8 miles in. The trail, composed of dirt and roots, will lead you uphill, paralleling Skylight Brook on your left for around 0.5 miles before veering right and bringing you to the base of Allen. The true base is marked by a flat-walled waterfall, which should be an obvious point of interest. From here, the summit is 1.2 miles away, with a nearly 1,600-foot climb. From here, the real challenges begin. Expect the ascent to take an hour. The route primarily follows Allen Brook, making the trail inherently wet. You'll encounter numerous rocks, mud, roots, and dead tree limbs to navigate around, over, and under, as well as sections where you'll have to cross flowing water. As you climb higher, glimpses of the summit may appear ahead of you.

Around 70 percent up the mountain, you'll encounter the infamous Allen Mountain slide. The surface can be treacherous, often covered in wet red slime depending on prior conditions. Ensure you step on dry spots and stay close to trees when possible. Halfway up the slide, the trail crosses to the other side. Climbing the slide offers great views of the

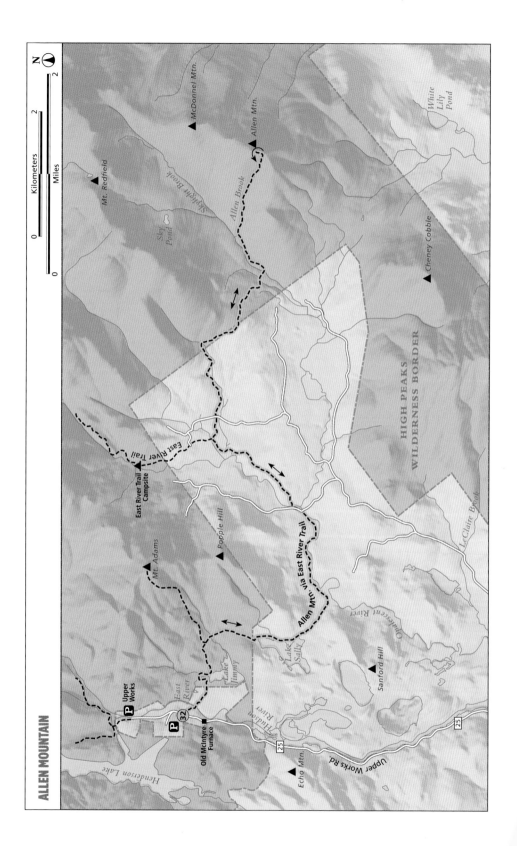

ALLEN MOUNTAIN

N

Kilometers
0   2

Miles
0   2

Henderson Lake

Upper Works **P**

P

Old McIntyre Furnace

32

25

Upper Works Rd

25

Echo Mtn.

East River

Lake Jimmy

Lake Sally

Hudson River

Sanford Hill

Crescent River

Mt. Adams

Popple Hill

East River Trail Campsite

East River Trail

Allen Mtn. via East River Trail

LeClaire Brook

HIGH PEAKS
WILDERNESS BORDER

Mt. Redfield

Sky Pond

Skylight Brook

McDonnel Mtn.

Allen Brook

Allen Mtn.

Cheney Cobble

White Lily Pond

Santanoni Range and the distance you've traversed. Once at the top of the slide, the trail leads back into the woods, remaining incredibly steep. Expect one or two scrambles, relying on surrounding vegetation for assistance. Gradually, the summit comes into view as the trail levels off. You'll turn left for the final approach to the summit, continuing along the ridge. Just before the top, there's an excellent viewpoint to the west. Approaching the summit, you'll climb another 40-foot section, the "nubble" of Allen. At the top, you'll find the summit sign. The view is relatively obscured; the sign stands about 7 feet high, but in winter, it can be as little as 6 inches off the ground or even buried in snow. For a better view, follow a herd path beyond the sign to see the entire Great Range, Skylight, Panther Gorge, and many other high peaks. The summit of Allen is 9.8 miles from the start. To return to the start, retrace your steps 9.8 miles back to the East River Trailhead. Good luck!

The sunset from the remote Twin Brook Slide on the backside of Mount Redfield looking back at Allen Mountain.

MILES AND DIRECTIONS

0.0   Start at East River Trailhead.

0.1   Turn right at Hudson River, and cross metal suspension bridge.

0.5   Trail turns left into woods near Lake Jimmy.

0.8   Reach other side of Lake Jimmy.

1.2   Pass abandoned ranger shack and Mount Adams Trail, and continue straight.

1.8   Turn left at logging path fork, arriving at Lake Sally shortly after.

2.7   Reach another logging path junction, and stay left.

4.1   Cross Opalescent River.

5.2   Pass the East River Trail to Lake Colden, continuing straight.

5.7   Turn left onto a larger logging road, then turn right into an older ranger trailhead.

5.8   Reach parking lot, and walk to its end.

8.0   Cross Skylight Brook.

8.5   Reach base of Allen marked by a flat-walled waterfall.

9.4   Reach Allen Mountain slide.

9.7   Summit Allen Mountain, following herd path for better views; turnaround.

19.6   Arrive back at East River Trailhead.

OVERNIGHTS AND TRAVERSES

Hiker ascending the cliff section up Saddleback while doing the Great Range Traverse.

33 GREAT RANGE TRAVERSE

For adventurous hikers seeking one of the most demanding challenges in the Adirondacks, the Great Range Traverse is the perfect endeavor. It can be hiked over several days at various campsites or attempted in one single outing. This is the Adirondacks' version of New Hampshire's Presidential Traverse. The pinnacle of the route is Mount Marcy, the highest peak at 5,344 feet. Throughout the journey, hikers will encounter some of the East's most rugged terrain, featuring several steep scrambles, many ladders, and pounding rocky descents. The abundant summits along the trail offer breathtaking mountain vistas at almost every turn.

Start: Adirondack Loj; End: Rooster Comb parking lot
Elevation gain: 9,400 feet
Summit elevation: Mount Marcy, 5,344 feet; Haystack, 4,960 feet; Basin, 4,827 feet; Saddleback, 4,515 feet; Gothics, 4,736 feet; Armstrong, 4,400 feet; Upper Wolfjaw, 4,185 feet; Lower Wolfjaw, 4,175 feet; Hedgehog, 3,389 feet; Rooster Comb, 2,762 feet
Distance: 23.0 miles
Difficulty: 7 out of 7, extremely difficult
Hiking time: 13–18 hours
Seasons/schedule: This hike is generally hiked in summer/fall.
Fees and permits: $15 to park at Adirondack Loj
Canine compatibility: Difficult for dogs; dogs must be on leash.
Trail surface: Due to its popularity, this route is well eroded from foot traffic. It consists of some of the East's most rugged terrain.
Land status: Central High Peaks Wilderness

Nearest town: Lake Placid, NY/ Keene Valley, NY
Water availability: There is barely any water on the route, so bring plenty of water (3.5 liters recommended).
Amenities available: The Adirondack Loj, Info Center, and the Hungry Hiker. Many tent sites and privies along the route.
Maximum grade: Many steep and technical sections such as the Gothics Cables and Saddleback Cliffs
Special considerations: Properly plan bail trails if you need to escape the range for any reason. Make sure you are logistically covered in every way. As stated previously, this is a long and rocky hike. Bring good footwear and lots of water. This is not the hike you want to mess up, so plan accordingly and don't be afraid to turn around.
Sunrise or sunset: I recommend starting this hike as a sunrise on Mount Marcy.
Route type: Thru-hike
Views: The best of the best

FINDING THE TRAILHEAD

Start: Adirondack Loj. Follow Adirondack Street next to Ausable Inn for about a mile, turning right onto Johns Brook Lane. Parking is limited; additional parking is available on the street in Keene Valley. Weekdays are generally not full prior to 9 a.m., but it can be full before 6 a.m. on weekends. **GPS:** 44.18911°N / 73.81561°W

Finish: Rooster Comb Trailhead. Situated just outside the entrance to Keene Valley, this trailhead is on the left if you're coming from I-87 or on the right as you depart Keene Valley heading toward I-87. It's approximately a quarter-mile south of the Noonmark Diner—a fantastic dining option! **GPS:** 44.185440°N / 73.786710°W

Hiker ascending Mount Marcy for sunrise while doing the Great Range Traverse.

THE HIKE

Chances are if you are seeking to do this traverse, then you are a well-seasoned hiker and more than likely have hiked in the High Peaks multiple times. Sometimes this is a first traverse for many who have never been to the Adirondacks. Whichever you are, this is certainly a test of endurance, the mind, and your feet. There are multiple ways this traverse can be done, however, this is the traditional route. It is worth noting that you are more than likely starting this hike out in the dark, especially if you choose to hike Mount Marcy for sunrise. Either way, this description is a comprehensive breakdown of the trail. This trail starts out at the end of Parking Lot Number 1, right in front of the High Peaks Info Center.

Start your hike toward Marcy Dam. At the first sign, a mile in, turn left. Cross the dam, sign in at the register, then follow signs for Marcy. The path gradually steepens and becomes rocky. Pass the Phelps Mountain sign, cross a bridge, ascend a steep part, and turn right at the Mount Marcy Ski Trail cutoff. Pass Tabletop Mountain, arrive at Indian Falls, and follow the blue markers left. After 1.4 miles, turn right at the Hopkins Trail sign. Reach Marcy's shoulder after 0.6 miles, turn right, and continue toward Marcy. The final half-mile ascent is steep but stunning. At the summit, enjoy panoramic views.

Next, descend half a mile to the Van Hoevenberg Trail intersection and follow the Range Trail. The next mile is steep and exposed, leading to Haystack's sub-peak, then to a trail intersection pointing to Haystack's summit. Climb Little Haystack, then follow the path through the forest and up to the peak of Haystack. Return to the Range Trail intersection and head to Basin, which is 1.2 miles away. Fill up on water here as sources are scarce beyond this point. Arrive at Basin's summit, then descend to Saddleback. The trail between these peaks is steep and technical, so proceed with caution.

Cross Saddleback's ridgeline to the Orebed Trail intersection, then follow signs to Gothics, which is steep and involves cables for climbing. Pass Gothics West Peak and reach the summit of Gothics, then descend to the Armstrong intersection. Armstrong is a mild climb away. Continue on the trail to Upper Wolfjaw, which features a steep descent and a long ladder. Summit UWJ and continue on to LWJ toward the Upper Wolfjaw Notch, a sub-summit 0.3 miles away from the actual summit. The next section is steep and tricky. At the col, follow signs to Lower Wolfjaw. The ascent is steep with rocky scrambles, but the summit is marked by a large rock. Follow the signs to Hedgehog and Rooster Comb. The initial descent from Lower Wolfjaw is very steep. Reach the intersection of the W. A. White Trail after 1.5 miles and turn left toward Hedgehog Mountain, and then to Rooster Comb. The trail ends at the Rooster Comb parking area, 2.2 miles away.

MILES AND DIRECTIONS

0.0 Start at Adirondack Loj.

1.0 Turn left at Marcy Dam sign.

2.3 Arrive at Marcy Dam, turning left to go around to the other side.

2.4 Turn left toward Marcy at Van H./Avalanche Pass sign.

3.6 Pass Phelps Mountain sign.

3.8 Cross bridge.

4.7 Arrive at Indian Falls. Follow blue trail markers.

6.4 Pass Hopkins Trail sign, turning right, continuing to follow the blue markers.

6.9 Reach Phelps Trail intersection, turning right to Marcy.

7.4 Summit of Mount Marcy, 5,344 feet.

7.9 Return to the last Van Hoevenberg Trail intersection, and continue straight on the Range Trail.

8.5 Reach the bottom between Marcy and Haystack, and turn right following blue trail markers toward Haystack.

9.0 Reach sub-peak of Haystack, then dip down 150 feet to intersect with Range Trail.

9.5 Summit Haystack, and return to Range Trail intersection.

10.0 Back to Range Trail to Basin.

10.5 Pass Sno-Bird Campsite and Shorey's Shortcut intersection.

11.2 Summit Basin, and descend to Saddleback.

12.2 Summit Saddleback, and continue on Range Trail.

12.6 Reach intersection sign for Orebed Trail or Range Trail for Gothics, and follow signs to Gothics (0.5 miles away).

13.1 Summit Gothics, and continue north.

13.5 Reach intersection for Beaver Meadow Trail or Armstrong, and turn left following ADK Range Trail signs.

14.0 Summit Armstrong.

14.8 Reach top of Upper Wolfjaw, following spur trail to rock summit.

15.1 Arrive at Upper Wolfjaw Notch, and begin descent.

GREAT RANGE TRAVERSE

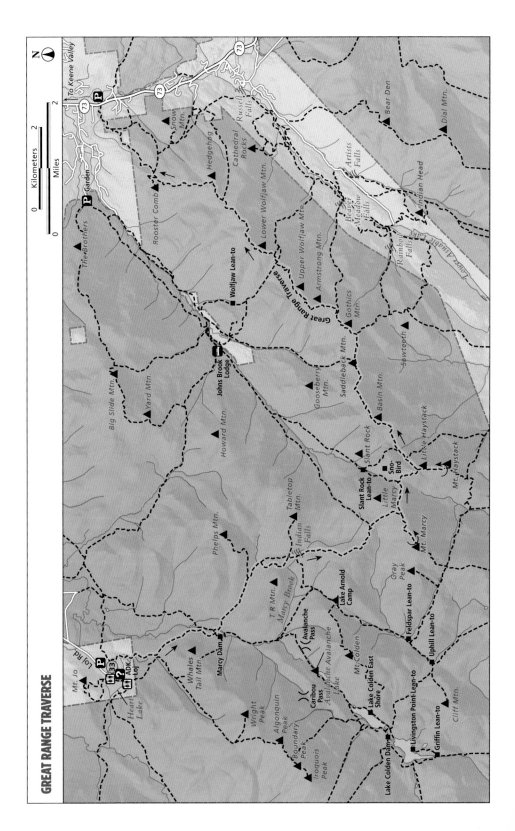

N

Kilometers
0   2

Miles
0   2

To Keene Valley

P 73

73

73

P Garden

Snow Mtn.

Rooster Comb

Hedgehog

The Brothers

Cathedral Rocks

Russell Falls

Lower Wolfjaw Mtn.

Wolfjaw Lean-to

Upper Wolfjaw Mtn.

Armstrong Mtn.

Artists Falls

Bear Den

Dial Mtn.

Indian Head

Beaver Meadow Falls

Great Range Traverse

Gothics Mtn.

Rainbow Falls

Lower Ausable

Yard Mtn.

Big Slide Mtn.

Johns Brook Lodge

Howard Mtn.

Gooseberry Mtn.

Saddleback Mtn.

Basin Mtn.

Sawteeth

Little Haystack

Slant Rock Lean-to

Slant Rock

Little Marcy

Sno-Bird

Mt. Haystack

Tabletop Mtn.

Phelps Mtn.

Indian Falls

Mt. Marcy

Gray Peak

Lake Arnold Camp

Feldspar Lean-to

Uphill Lean-to

T R Mtn.

Marcy Brook

Mt. Jo

Loj Rd

P

73

?

ADK Loj

Heart Lake

Wright Peak

Algonquin Peak

Whales Tail Mtn.

Marcy Dam

Caribou Pass

Avalanche Pass

Avalanche Lake

Mt. Colden

Lake Colden East Shore

Lake Colden Dam

Livingston Point Lean-to

Griffin Lean-to

Cliff Mtn.

Boundary Peak

Iroquois Peak

15.8 Reach the col, pass a sign pointing to JBL, and stay left.

16.4 Reach Lower Wolfjaw summit.

17.8 Turn left at the W. A. White Trail intersection, following direction to Hedgehog Mountain (0.4 miles).

18.2 Summit Hedgehog.

19.7 Reach intersection sign for trail up Rooster Comb (1-mile out-and-back, optional).

20.2 Summit Rooster Comb (optional); turn around.

23.0 Arrive at Rooster Comb parking area.

FASTEST KNOWN TIMES BY BETHANY GARRETSON

Hiking the forty-six highest peaks of the Adirondack Mountains is an alluring challenge. As the challenge has evolved, a growing trend in the hiking and ultra-running communities is the pursuit of FKTs, or "fastest known times." This movement is a nod to the legendary conservationist and ultra-hiker, Bob Marshall, who not only found solace in the mountains but also sought competition, creating lengthy routes that combined multiple high peaks in a single day. However, in the 1960s and 1970s, preservationists and conservationists advocated for the high peaks to be enjoyed as wilderness rather than personal playgrounds. As a result, record-keeping was considered taboo and often kept under wraps. It wasn't until the 2000s, with the help of websites like fastest knowntime.com, that records became more publicized. In 2008, Jan Wellford secured his place in Adirondack history by breaking Ted "Cave Dog" Keizer's 46 supported record by 1 hour. He covered approximately 160 miles with 68,000 feet of vertical gain in 3 days, 17 hours, and 14 minutes, aided by a support crew. The following year, Wellford teamed up with Cory DeLavalle, and together they set the first-ever unsupported thru-hike of all forty-six mountains in 7 days, 14 hours, and 15 minutes without outside assistance.

As the stakes have risen and strategies evolved, records have continued to be broken. Currently, as of 2023, Ryan Atkins holds the overall supported record for the forty-six peaks at 3 days, 5 hours, and 52 minutes, while Matt Moschella holds the unsupported record at 4 days, 21 hours, and 51 minutes. In 2020, during the height of COVID-19, there was a surge of FKTs in the Adirondack High Peaks and an increase in women's participation in the sport. Alyssa Godeskey and Sarah Keyes competed for the supported record, with Godeskey ultimately securing it at 3 days, 16 hours, and 16 minutes. A month later, Bethany Garretson and Katie Rhodes became the first women to complete the unsupported thru-hike in 7 days, 4 hours, and 50 minutes. Other popular FKTs in the High Peak region include the Great Range and Bob Marshall Traverse. With every season comes the curiosity of which record times will be lowered and which will stand the test of time.

34 PINNACLE TRAVERSE

The Pinnacle Traverse is a way to see new trails and views that you might not see otherwise. It is very different from other hikes and also pretty remote. This hike has you going over two high peaks, Mount Colvin and Blake Peak.

Start: Adirondack Mountain Reserve (AMR)/Ausable Club/St. Huberts
Elevation gain: 4,300 feet
Summit elevation: Mount Colvin, 4,057 feet; Blake Peak, 3,960 feet; Pinnacle Peak, 3,346 feet
Distance: 17.8 miles
Difficulty: 5 out of 7, difficult. Terrain overall is mild but very steep and has many challenges.
Hiking time: 10–12 hours
Seasons/schedule: This hike is generally hiked in summer/fall.
Fees and permits: Free reservation required for parking at the AMR May–Oct.
Canine compatibility: Dogs are not allowed on AMR property, but they are allowed if this route is hiked from the Elk Lake approach and back.
Trail surface: Moderately trafficked. Mixed rock and dirt surfaces with scrambling up high. Lots of steep and rocky scrambles, with soft dirt trails the second half.

Land status: AMR property/Outer High Peaks Wilderness
Nearest town: Keene Valley, NY/ North Hudson, NY
Water availability: There are plenty of rivers down low but no water sources higher up.
Amenities available: Gill Brook has campsites and privies but nothing else.
Maximum grade: 700 feet: descent of Colvin; 500 feet: ascent to Blake
Special considerations: Bring lots of water. There is none after Gill Brook.
Sunrise or sunset: Colvin for sunset is all right.
Route type: Thru-hike
Views: Colvin has a decent panoramic view from the summit while a spur trail nearby has a view to the south. Blake Peak, on the other hand, has one view while climbing up the mountain but nothing on the summit—a terrible reward. There are various views along the main ridge.

FINDING THE TRAILHEAD

AMR/St. Huberts is right across the street from Roaring Brook Falls Trailhead for Giant, labeled as St. Huberts Parking Area or the Adirondack Mountain Reserve. Approximately 7.5 miles from I-87. Reservations are needed May–October. **GPS:** 44.14970°N / 73.76806°W

THE HIKE

This thru-hike of the Pinnacle Ridge is not common, but this is why I recommend it. It is unique, lightly traveled, and a great way to see new sights. It is slightly logistically challenging since it is a thru-hike, but definitely worth a weekend trip. It can be hiked in both directions. Just make sure you acquire a reservation at the AMR.

Starting from the AMR parking lot, your journey begins by ascending a gravel path past a golf course. Turn left at tennis courts after 0.5 miles, leading you to a large wooden gate that marks the entry point to sites like Indian Head and Nippletop via Lake Road. Over the next 2 miles, observe features such as the H.G. Leach Trail and Wolfjaws Bridge before encountering the Gothics Trail via the Beaver Meadow Falls Trail. The trail then meanders through the forest, following Gill Brook. Both "scenic" and "easy" signs guide you to the same trail, eventually leading to the Gill Brook Cutoff sign. Continue straight, passing a sign indicating Indian Head.

The trail steepens over the next 0.6 miles, culminating at the Nippletop/Colvin intersection. Here, you're given a choice: a 1.9-mile journey to Nippletop or a 1.1-mile trek to Mount Colvin. Ascend 900 feet over 1.1 miles to Colvin's summit, overcoming muddy spots, scrambles, and a small wooden ladder. Head to Blake Peak 1.3 miles away. The descent toward Blake offers another viewpoint. This challenging trail becomes steeper as it starts going up, leading you to the summit of Blake Peak, where a trail sign directs you toward "Ridge to Pinnacle." The route to Pinnacle requires traversing over four hills

A subpar but somewhat rewarding view from Pinnacle Peak Summit.

over approximately 2.7 miles. Notable points include Lookout Rock and 72 Steps. Upon reaching Pinnacle's summit, face a 7.5-mile journey back to Elk Lake. The descent includes a 2-mile stretch through lightly traveled terrain to the Elk Lake Trail. The trail toward Elk Lake climbs a ridge for 0.7 miles before descending into Elk Lake area, where you'll cross Guideboard Brook. Upon entering Elk Lake's private property, follow the main trail, ensuring you stay on the correct path. After crossing a wooden bridge, you'll emerge onto Elk Lake Road. This remarkable journey concludes as you walk the final stretch back to your vehicle.

MILES AND DIRECTIONS

0.0 Start at AMR parking lot.

0.6 Reach AMR gate for Lake Road.

2.7 Turn at Gill Brook Trail sign on the left.

3.7 Pass a sign, continuing straight.

3.9 Pass an Indian Head sign, heading straight.

4.5 Pass another Indian Head sign, again heading straight.

5.3 Come to Nippletop/Colvin fork sign, staying right to Colvin.

6.4 Reach Colden summit. Head to Blake, descending back side of Colvin.

7.2 Reach the bottom col between Blake, following signs to Blake.

7.7 Reach Blake Peak summit.

8.2 Reach Lookout Rock.

8.8 Reach the second hill, known as 72 Steps.

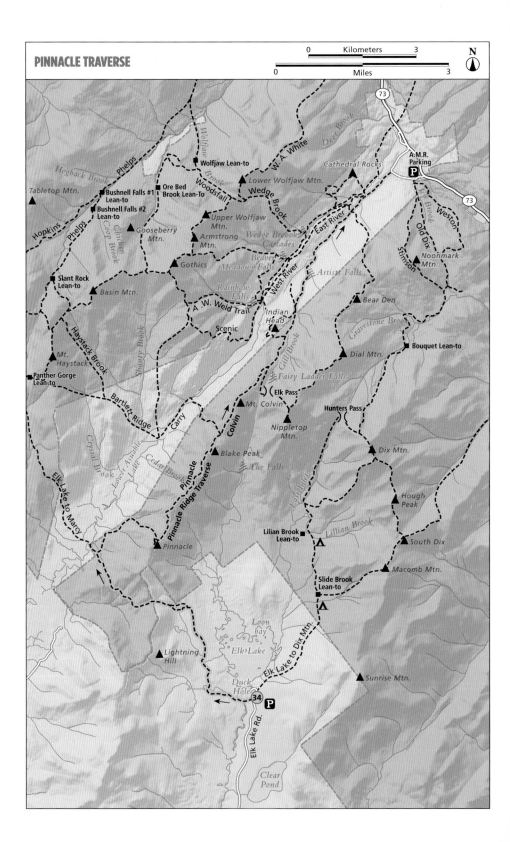

PINNACLE TRAVERSE

Kilometers 0 3
Miles 0 3
N

73

Phelps

Hogback Brook

Tabletop Mtn.

Wolfjaw Brook

Wolfjaw Lean-to

W. A. White

Deer Brook

Cathedral Rocks

A.M.R. Parking P

73 Weston

Bushnell Falls #1 Lean-to
Ore Bed Brook Lean-To
Bushnell Falls #2 Lean-to

Woodsfall

Lower Wolfjaw Mtn.

Wedge

Wolfjaw Brook

East River

Weston Brook

Old Dix

Hopkins Phelps

Chicken Coop Brook

Gooseberry Mtn.

Upper Wolfjaw Mtn.

Armstrong Mtn.

Wedge Brook Cascades

Beaver Meadows Falls

East River

Stimson

Noonmark Mtn.

Slant Rock Lean-to

Gothics

Rainbow Falls

West River

Artists Falls

Basin Mtn.

A. W. Weld Trail

Scenic

Indian Head

Bear Den

Gravestone Brook

Bouquet Lean-to

Haystack Brook

Shanty Brook

Gill Brook

Fairy Ladder Falls

Dial Mtn.

Mt. Haystack

Panther Gorge Lean-to

Bartlett Ridge

Carry

Crystal Brook

Lower Ausable Lake

Cedar Brook

Elk Pass

Mt. Colvin

Colvin

Nippletop Mtn.

Hunters Pass

Dix Mtn.

Elk Lake to Marcy

Pinnacle

Pinnacle Ridge Traverse

Blake Peak

The Falls

East Inlet

Hough Peak

Lilian Brook Lean-to

Lillian Brook

South Dix

Pinnacle

Slide Brook Lean-to

Macomb Mtn.

Lightning Hill

Loon Bay

Elk Lake

Elk Lake to Dix Mtn.

Sunrise Mtn.

Duck Hole

34 P

Elk Lake Rd.

Clear Pond

A view from Lookout Rock toward Upper Ausable Lake and the Great Range.

9.8 Reach the third hill on the range.

10.1 Trail turn for Pinnacle.

10.3 Reach Pinnacle summit and return to the trail, continuing to Elk Lake.

12.5 Arrive at Elk Lake Trail after descending from Pinnacle.

14.8 Cross Guideboard Brook, entering Elk Lake private property.

16.5 Pass the trail sign for Lightning Hill.

17.5 Cross a wooden bridge, then follow the trail up into the forest.

17.8 Arrive at Elk Lake Road.

35 BOB MARSHALL TRAVERSE

The Bob Marshall Traverse (BMT) is a challenging 35-mile thru-hike in the High Peaks. The traverse includes thirteen high peaks, featuring a demanding 15,500 feet of elevation gain. Over the years, the BMT has gained popularity among ultra-hikers and trail runners, symbolizing the early conservation movement in the United States and the perseverance required to protect America's wild spaces.

Start: The Garden Trailhead
Elevation gain: 15,500 feet
Summit elevation: Mount Marcy, 5,344 feet; Algonquin Peak, 5,114 feet; Mount Haystack, 4,960 feet; Skylight, 4,926 feet; Gothics, 4,736 feet; Basin Mountain, 4,827 feet; Saddleback Mountain, 4,515 feet; Big Slide, 4,240 feet; Armstrong, 4,400 feet; Upper Wolfjaw, 4,185 feet; Lower Wolfjaw, 4,173 feet; Iroquois Peak, 4,840 feet; Wright Peak, 4,580 feet; Mount Jo, 2,876 feet
Distance: 32.5 miles
Difficulty: 7 out of 7, extremely difficult
Hiking time: 16–20 hours
Seasons/schedule: This hike is generally hiked in summer/fall.
Fees and permits: $10 parking fee at parking lot for town of Keene Valley
Canine compatibility: Bringing your dog is not recommended unless the trip is going to last several days.
Trail surface: You'll experience every kind of terrain and surface available in the High Peaks.

Land status: Central High Peaks Wilderness
Nearest town: Keene Valley, NY
Water availability: There is a water station at Johns Brook Lodge and many rivers along the way but little to no water up on the Great Range section.
Amenities available: Johns Brook Lodge (for guests only), many privies and tent sites.
Maximum grade: Many steep grades; too many to count.
Special considerations: Come up with a good exit strategy if you need to bail in any section. (This is assuming this hike is attempted in 1 day.)
Sunrise or sunset: More than likely you'll be on Big Slide for sunrise and MacIntyres for sunset.
Route type: Thru-hike
Views: There are too many views to list them all.

FINDING THE TRAILHEAD

From Keene Valley follow Adirondack Street next to Ausable Inn for about a mile, turning right onto Johns Brook Lane. Parking limited; additional parking available on the street in Keene Valley. Weekdays are generally not full prior to 9 a.m. but can be full before 6 a.m. on weekends. **GPS:** 44.18911°N / 73.81561°W

THE HIKE

On a pristine day in the Adirondacks, Bob Marshall embarked on an unforgettable journey, traversing fourteen majestic peaks in a single day. His goal was to set the record of most high peaks done in a single day. First climbing Big Slide by 5 a.m., then having breakfast at JBL, climbing up to the Great Range, Herb Clark joining him for a cheerful lunch atop Mount Marcy, and Eugene Untermyer on the flashlight ascent of Mount Jo, Bob scaled the mountains, setting the bar and reveling in the breathtaking panoramas and unforgettable memories forged along the way. Unlike other hikes in this book, this hike will not be as comprehensive, due to the many intricate details that could be written about the route; considering this hike is for the experienced and knowledgeable hiker, I will give enough details to keep you going and get you where you need to be. Traditionally, this hike is 32 miles in length, not accounting for the distance it takes to hike to JBL from the Garden. JBL is where Bob Marshall started his watch, and where this hike also starts.

From the front porch of JBL, start heading back toward the direction of the Garden parking lot from which you came. On the way in, you passed a sign pointing up to Big Slide (2.3 miles). This sign is 0.4 miles from JBL. This is the center route up Big Slide where you will climb to your first summit. The trail up is pretty straightforward. After summiting Big Slide, descend back to JBL. At the tall sign in front of JBL, turn left for Lower Wolfjaw (LWJ), cross a bridge, and follow the trail. After 0.4 miles, follow signs to LWJ. Ascend to the Range Trail, and then climb to LWJ, marking 7.5 miles.

Descend back to the Range Trail, continue to Upper Wolfjaw (UWJ), and summit it. Traverse toward Armstrong. After a steep climb, a ladder, and reaching Armstrong's summit, descend to the intersection for Beaver Meadow or ADK Range Trail. Continue to Gothics.

At Gothics summit, pass through trees, ascend Gothics East Peak, and keep right at the next intersection, not toward Sawteeth. Descend the Gothics "cable route" to reach the intersection for Saddleback. Summit Saddleback at 11.2 miles. Follow yellow blazes, descend Saddleback's cliff, ascend Basin's shoulder, and climb Basin. Then, tread a demanding 0.7-mile trail to Haystack. Out-and-back Haystack, and head to Mount Marcy, 1.8 miles away. After reaching Marcy's summit (16.1 miles in), descend toward Skylight. After reaching Four Corners, out-and-back Skylight (17.2 miles in). From here, head toward Iroquois Peak. Pass Lake Tear of the Clouds, Gray Peak Trail, and reach Feldspar Brook (19.4 miles). Turn left for Lake Colden, pass Uphill Lean-to, and cross Lake Colden Dam (21.4 miles). Turn right after the dam and proceed for 0.5 miles to a sign for Algonquin and Boundary Peak. The steep, 2.3-mile trail to Algonquin will challenge you. Reach the intersection for Algonquin or Iroquois, and follow signs to Iroquois. Return and summit

An aerial view of Skylight, Marcy, and the Great Range.

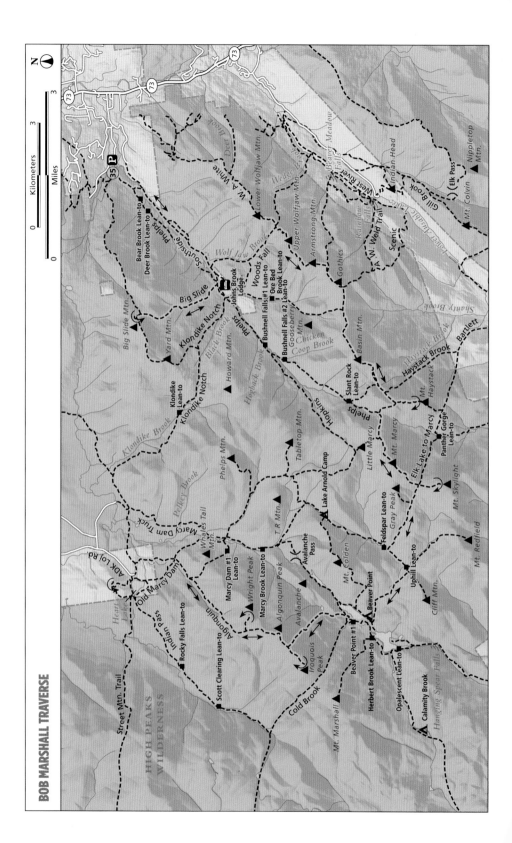

BOB MARSHALL TRAVERSE

Algonquin (25.9 miles). Descend Algonquin, reach the Wright Peak intersection trail, and out-and-back Wright Peak. From here, traverse 3.2 miles to Adirondack Loj, and finally, summit Mount Jo. Your epic 32.5-mile journey ends at the parking lot or Loj. Whether done in one or three days, it's a monumental accomplishment.

MILES AND DIRECTIONS

0.0 Start at Johns Brook Lodge (JBL).

0.4 Reach the sign to Big Slide, and turn toward Big Slide.

2.7 Reach Big Slide summit and return to JBL.

5.4 Turn left at the tall multi-sign in front of the lodge.

5.8 Reach the intersection for Short Job and Lower Wolfjaw, and follow to Lower Wolfjaw.

7.5 Reach Lower Wolfjaw summit.

8.8 Reach Upper Wolfjaw, and continue to Armstrong.

9.4 Reach Armstrong summit.

10.2 Reach Gothics summit.

10.7 Reach intersection for Orebed Trail or Range Trail for Saddleback.

11.2 Reach Saddleback summit.

12.1 Reach Basin summit.

13.4 Turnoff for Haystack out-and-back.

14.4 Continue from last point to Marcy.

14.8 Turn left following sign to Marcy (1.3).

16.1 Reach Mount Marcy summit.

16.7 Reach Four Corners.

17.2 Reach Skylight summit out-and-back.

18.0 Pass Lake Tear.

19.4 Pass Feldspar, turning left to Lake Colden.

19.9 Pass Uphill Lean-to.

21.4 Cross Lake Colden Dam.

21.9 Reach intersection for Algonquin and Boundary Peak.

24.2 Reach intersection for Iroquois Peak.

24.8 Reach Iroquois Summit.

25.4 Return to Algonquin intersection, and continue to Algonquin.

25.9 Reach Algonquin summit.

26.6 Reach Wright Peak intersection.

27.2 Reach Wright Peak summit.

27.7 Return to Wright Peak intersection and continue to Adirondack Loj.

30.9 Reach Adirondack Loj.

31.7 Summit of Mount Jo; return to Loj.

32.5 Arrive back at the parking lot or Loj to stop your time.

36 **HIGH PEAKS WILDERNESS TRAVERSE**

The High Peaks Wilderness Traverse connects its westernmost trailhead to its easternmost trailhead, via trail, via the most direct line. This route was originally conceived by Nick Arndt in 2020. This is a perfect route for those who may want to do a multiday thru-hike through the High Peaks but without an excessive amount of elevation gain.

Start: Seward Trailhead/Blueberry; trail end: The Garden Trailhead
Elevation gain: 6,300 feet
Summit elevation: 5,344 feet
Distance: 34.3 miles
Difficulty: 7 out of 7, extremely difficult (if done in 1 day)
Hiking time: 1–3 days
Seasons/schedule: This hike is generally hiked in summer/fall.
Fees and permits: None
Canine compatibility: This could be dog friendly if broken into a multiday hike. A leash is required in the Central High Peaks area.
Trail surface: Because you are going from the farthest point west to east, you will experience every kind of trail condition offered in the High Peaks. Very rugged. Tons of rocks, roots, and mud.

Land status: Outer High Peaks Wilderness and Central High Peaks Wilderness
Nearest town: Tupper Lake, NY/ Keene Valley, NY
Water availability: There are plenty of places along the way to refill water naturally.
Amenities available: Blueberry and Ward Brook Lean-tos, Bradley Pond Campsite, Calamity Brook Campsite, Lake Colden, Johns Brook Valley.
Maximum grade: Highest point is Mount Marcy.
Special considerations: Bring Gore-Tex boots and gaiters. Trekking poles are definitely recommended.
Sunrise or sunset: None.
Route type: Thru-hike
Views: Mount Marcy is the only high point with a view on this entire hike.

FINDING THE TRAILHEAD

Steward Trailhead: From Saranac Lake, take NY 3 toward Tupper Lake. After approximately 12.5 miles, turn left onto Coreys Road, marked with a sign for the Seward Range. The trailhead is at the end of this road about 5.5 miles. **GPS:** 44.19166°N / 74.26352°W

The Garden Trailhead: From Keene Valley, follow Adirondack Street next to Ausable Inn for about a mile, turning right onto Johns Brook Lane. Parking limited; additional parking available on the street in Keene Valley. Weekdays are generally not full prior to 9 a.m. but can be full before 6 a.m. on weekends. **GPS:** 44.18911°N / 73.81561°W

THE HIKE

This hike begins on the Blueberry Trail, leading us 5.8 miles to Seward Mountain's base, passing several landmarks like the Calkins Brook Truck Trail, Blueberry Lean-to, and Ward Brook Truck Trail. We reach the Seymour Trail at 5.8 miles and continue straight toward Duck Hole. After passing a marshland and continuing along the Northville-Placid Trail, we arrive at Duck Hole, then diverge onto the Preston Ponds Trail, following it 4.3 miles to Henderson Lake's north shore. We then connect to the Indian Pass

Preston Pond South.

Trail, and after a short distance, join the Crossover Trail, eventually reaching the Calamity Brook Trail. Following signs to Lake Colden, we pass Calamity Brook campsites and the David Henderson Memorial before arriving at Flowed Lands. Veering left toward Lake Colden, we navigate the Flowed Lands and reach Lake Colden Dam at 21.4 miles.

Next, we cross a suspension bridge over the Opalescent River and proceed along the path, climbing 500 feet in elevation. We reach Uphill Lean-to, an ideal resting spot, before continuing to Feldspar. From there, we turn toward Mount Marcy, scaling 1,000 feet to reach Lake Tear of the Clouds, where we continue toward Four Corners. We then ascend the steep trail to Mount Marcy's summit, descend the northeastern side to Van Hoevenberg Trail, and follow the Range Trail to Haystack. We descend to another intersection and follow the signs toward Johns Brook Lodge. Finally, we reach several landmarks including Slant Rock, Bushnell Falls, and JBL, eventually concluding our 34.3-mile hike at the Garden Trailhead.

MILES AND DIRECTIONS

0.0   Start at the parking lot for Seward Trailhead, and follow Blueberry Trail.

1.3   Reach Calkins Brook Truck Trail.

4.8   Arrive at Blueberry Lean-to.

5.0   Connect to the Ward Brook Truck Trail.

HIGH PEAKS WILDERNESS TRAVERSE

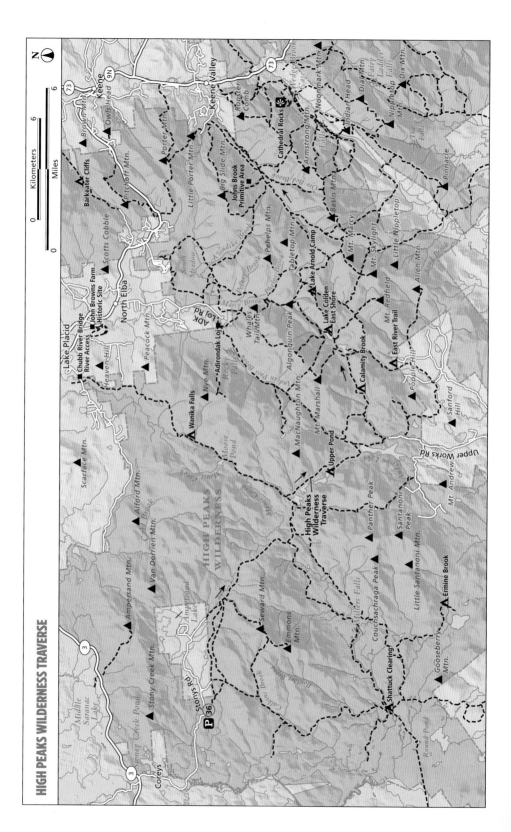

5.2 Pass the turn for Seward Mountain.

5.7 Arrive at the Ward Brook Lean-to.

5.8 Reach the turn for Seymour, indicated by a stack of rocks and some metal. Continue straight toward Duck Hole.

8.4 Reach a marshland, the condition of which may vary.

8.6 Reach the Northville-Placid Trail. Continue straight, following signs to Duck Hole.

10.3 Arrive at Duck Hole. Take a left at the trail sign-in.

10.7 Reach a bridge turn on your right; this is the Preston Ponds Trail heading southeast.

15.0 Arrive at the north shore of Henderson Lake. Pass a lean-to campsite.

15.7 Cross Indian Pass Brook and turn left onto the Indian Pass Trail.

16.0 Turn right onto the Crossover Trail to the Calamity Brook Trail.

17.6 Reach the Calamity Brook Trail. Turn left and follow the signs to Lake Colden.

18.7 Arrive at the Calamity Brook campsites.

20.2 Reach the David Henderson Memorial.

20.4 Arrive at Flowed Lands and sign in. Veer left, following the trail in the direction of Lake Colden.

21.4 Reach Lake Colden Dam. Continue past the dam, turning right and following the trail markers.

21.6 Reach a beautiful suspension bridge over the Opalescent River. Cross the bridge and turn left.

23.0 Reach Uphill Lean-to. Continue straight to Feldspar.

23.5 Arrive at Feldspar, and turn right following the signs toward Mount Marcy.

24.7 Reach Lake Tear of the Clouds. Continue straight toward Four Corners.

24.9 Arrive at Four Corners. Turn left following the signs to Mount Marcy.

25.7 Reach the summit of Mount Marcy. Continue northeast toward the Van Hoevenberg Trail.

26.2 Arrive at Van Hoevenberg Trail intersection. Continue straight, following signs toward Mount Haystack.

26.9 Reach the next intersection. Turn left following the signs to Johns Brook Lodge.

27.5 Arrive at Slant Rock.

29.3 Arrive at Bushnell Falls.

30.8 Arrive at Johns Brook Lodge.

34.3 Reach the Garden Trailhead, concluding your 34.3-mile thru-hike.

Nestled in the remote reaches of the Dismal Wilderness, the Cold River Loop is an immersive trek through the forests of the Western High Peaks region. Revered for its solitude, the area is so secluded that hikers often find themselves alone on the trail, even during the busy summer weekends. The Cold River Loop is not just a hike, it's an adventure that transports you into the history of this place and the heart of the wilderness, all while offering a unique blend of tranquility and challenge.

Start: Seward Trailhead/Blueberry Trailhead
Elevation gain: 3,000 feet
Summit elevation: No summit
Distance: 29.6 miles
Difficulty: 5 out of 7, difficult
Hiking time: 1–3 days
Seasons/schedule: This hike is generally hiked in summer/fall.
Fees and permits: None
Canine compatibility: This is a good loop for dogs. A leash is not required but recommended.
Trail surface: Very rugged.
Land status: Outer High Peaks Wilderness (former Western High Peaks)

Nearest town: Tupper Lake, NY
Water availability: Water is scarce and only available on the Cold River.
Amenities available: Blueberry and Ward Brook Lean-tos and Bradley Pond Campsite.
Maximum grade: None. It is all moderately flat.
Special considerations: This is a fantastic weekend getaway trip. Beautiful campsites and few people.
Sunrise or sunset: None
Route type: Loop hike
Views: None.

FINDING THE TRAILHEAD

From Saranac Lake, take NY 3 toward Tupper Lake. After approximately 12.5 miles, turn left onto Coreys Road, marked with a sign for the Seward Range. The trailhead is at the end of this road about 5.5 miles. **GPS:** 44.19166°N / 74.26352°W

THE HIKE

The Cold River, a rich source of untamed beauty, originates from Duck Hole, a location that, along with the river itself, bore the brunt of Hurricane Irene's destructive path in 2011. Despite the significant damage, state officials and local volunteers quickly sprang into action, restoring the trails and rebuilding the lean-tos, thus ensuring the area's continued allure for the adventurous souls. The Cold River Loop is a part of the 133-mile-long Northville-Placid Trail, and offers an enchanting journey through the wildest parts of Adirondack Park. As you traverse the trail, you'll be captivated by the verdant landscape punctuated by cranberry bogs and fruit bushes, all nestled within the dense, timeless forest. The trail also boasts several highlights. Big Eddy, a swimming hole birthed by a small waterfall on the Cold River, is a welcome reprieve on warm summer days. The Rondeau Hermitage offers a glimpse into the life of Noah John Rondeau, a man who lived in solitude here for 21 years during the 1950s.

A common Northville-Placid Trail marker along the Cold River.

The Cold River Loop is pretty straightforward and difficult to mess up. Our journey starts from the Blueberry Trailhead for Seward, following the Blueberry Trail. We can either take a shortcut via the horse trail at 0.8 miles or continue straight, eventually meeting the Calkins Truck Trail. Proceeding down this trail for 1.8 miles, we reach an intersection and turn right, continuing for about 7 miles toward the Cold River. Along the way, we pass another intersection, a lean-to, and a turnoff for Latham Pond before reaching the NPT intersection. At this point, we've covered about one-third of our journey. Turning left at the NPT, we encounter campsites and two Cold River lean-tos, marking miles 10.8 and 10.9. The trail continues in a rugged fashion until we reach the Seward Lean-to at mile 13.9. Farther down, we find the Ouluska Pass Brook Lean-to at mile 16.4, followed by the Noah John Rondeau Hermitage at mile 16.9. We then veer left, away from the Cold River, traversing a hardwood forest for 3.6 miles. At mile 20.0, we pass Mountain Pond, half a mile from the Ward Brook Truck Trail. Turning left at the truck trail, we head toward the Coreys Road trailhead, crossing over a tricky marshland and inclining slowly. The next landmarks include the Number Four #1 Lean-to and Seymour Mountain Trail turn, followed by improvements in trail conditions. We then pass the Ward Brook Lean-to, the turn for Seward Mountain, and the Blueberry Lean-to. After bypassing the Calkins Trail turn, we complete our 29.6-mile loop at Coreys Road.

MILES AND DIRECTIONS

0.0 Start at the Blueberry Trailhead for Seward, continuing onto the Blueberry Trail.

0.8 Option to take the horse trail shortcut to the right or continue straight.

1.3 Reach the Calkins Truck Trail if you took the shortcut.

1.8 Reach the Calkins Truck Trail if you continued straight.

3.4 Reach an intersection marked by rocks and metal; turn right.

4.9 Pass another intersection with a trail on the right, a cutoff trail to the Raquette River; continue straight.

COLD RIVER LOOP

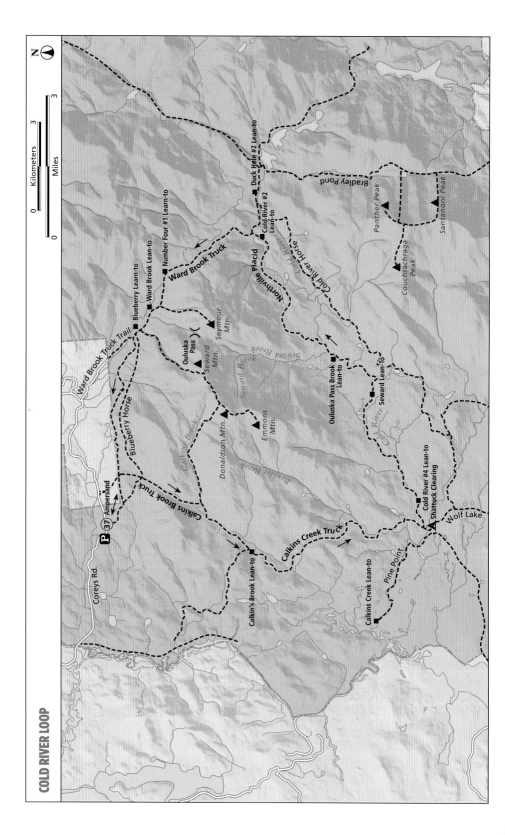

6.1 Pass the first lean-to; the trail bears left here and immediately crosses over a small stream.

9.8 Pass a turnoff for Latham Pond, and continue straight.

10.0 Reach the Northville-Placid Trail (NPT) intersection, and turn left.

10.8 Reach Cold River #3 Lean-to.

10.9 Reach Cold River #4 Lean-to.

13.9 Reach Seward Lean-to.

16.4 Reach Ouluska Pass Brook Lean-to. There is a challenging water crossing right before the lean-to.

16.9 Arrive at the Noah John Rondeau Hermitage; the trail immediately turns left at this point.

20.0 Pass Mountain Pond.

20.5 Reach the Ward Brook Truck Trail, and turn left.

21.1 Cross over a marshland; the trail will slowly incline after this.

23.1 Reach Number Four #1 Lean-to.

23.8 Pass the Seymour Mount Trail turn on the left.

24.8 Pass the Ward Brook Lean-to, then the turn for Seward Mountain.

25.0 Reach the connection of the Ward Brook Truck Trail with the Blueberry Trail.

25.2 Reach the Blueberry Lean-to.

28.0 Pass the Calkins Trail turn on the left.

29.6 Arrive back at the Coreys Road trailhead to end the loop.

THE MAYOR OF THE COLD RIVER

The Cold River region of the Adirondacks bore witness to an extraordinary man and his unique way of life. Noah John Rondeau, the self-proclaimed "Mayor" of Cold River, epitomized the spirit of wilderness independence. Despite having only an eighth-grade education, he was a man of many talents, adept at hunting, trapping, and survival, and known for his interests in astronomy and violin playing. Noah John wasn't just any hermit; he built a "village" atop a bluff near a former dam site on the Cold River. His wooden utopia included a "Town Hall," "Hall of Records," and several 12-foot-high teepees made of notched logs. The ingenuity of his construction was apparent in the design of the teepees, with logs notched at 2-foot intervals for easy breakage to feed his fires. Early 46ers, like the Dittmar and the Hudowalski families, befriended Noah John and often visited his hermitage. He was a gracious host, welcoming hikers and even guiding them up Couchsachraga. Despite his isolation, Noah John was a social individual. He stashed food and supplies along his traplines and paths, often retrieving a hidden jar of coffee or sugar as he walked. In 1947, Noah John's life took an unexpected turn when he was "discovered" by representatives of the New York Sportsman's Show. His 3-year stint as a celebrity saw him in the limelight of radio, television, and newspapers. But by 1950, weary and disillusioned, he returned to his Cold River sanctuary. However, the devastating "Big Blow" storm of 1950 abruptly ended Noah John's life as a hermit. Officials "closed" the woods due to storm damage, and Noah John was forced to leave his beloved Cold River for good. The remnants of his camp, including several teepees and part of his "city," can be seen today at the Adirondack Museum in Blue Mountain Lake, paying tribute to the legacy of the enigmatic "Hermit of Cold River."

BONUS HIKES

A beautiful late October day from Mt. Jo.

1 MACNAUGHTON MOUNTAIN— THE LOST 46ER

MacNaughton Mountain is a controversial yet highly sought out mountain among experienced hikers. It should be noted that this mountain is a real bushwhack. Despite not being an official 46er, it entices adventurers with its challenging trek through wild, untamed wilderness. The ascent is demanding, often threading through dense cripple-bush and blowdown, but reaching the summit is a rewarding endeavor.

Start: Adirondack Loj
Elevation gain: 2,900 feet
Summit elevation: 4,005.3 feet
Distance: 17.2 miles
Difficulty: 5 out of 7, difficult. It is a bushwhack.
Hiking time: 10–12 hours
Seasons/schedule: June–Oct.
Fees and permits: $15 to park at Adirondack Loj
Canine compatibility: This may be more demanding than normal for dogs; dogs must be on leash.
Trail surface: The trail to the Wallface Ponds is eroded and very muddy. MacNaughton is thick and forested.
Land status: Central High Peaks Wilderness
Nearest town: Lake Placid, NY

Water availability: There is some water on the route, but not much, so bring plenty of water (2.5 liters recommended).
Amenities available: The Adirondack Loj, Info Center, and the Hungry Hiker. Camping at Scott's Clearing.
Maximum grade: 800 feet over the last 0.6 miles to the top
Special considerations: Go with people or even with someone who has done this before. This requires genuine navigational skills and the ability to bushwhack. Don't forget your map and compass.
Sunrise or sunset: None.
Route type: Out-and-back/ bushwhack
Views: There are some views but not many.

FINDING THE TRAILHEAD

Adirondack Loj is located 1.5 miles southeast of Lake Placid on NY 73; turn down Adirondack Loj Road and drive for 5 miles. Popular and often packed; arrive early. Weekdays are generally not full prior to 9 a.m. but can be full before 6 a.m. on weekends. **GPS:** 44.18313°N / 73.96445°W

THE HIKE

MacNaughton Mountain, steeped in rich history and allure, is named after James Mac-Naughton, the grandson of the owner of McIntyre Iron Works. While it was initially omitted from the original roster of 4,000-footers, the 1950s USGS surveys confirmed its elevation, ensuring its recognition. Its challenging ascent, characterized by cripple-bush and blowdown, hasn't deterred 46ers, who are drawn to its secluded charm and limited views, dubbing it the "Lost 46er." More recent elevation data from a geographical survey have shed further light on MacNaughton's precise altitude. Utilizing a surveyor-grade GPS unit that was stationed on the summit for over an hour and communicated with two base stations, the measurement revealed an elevation of 4,005.3 feet. The accuracy

Full views can be found on MacNaughton. Looking toward the Wallface Ponds and Algonquin.

of the equipment and procedure was verified by a licensed surveyor, who confirmed that the tenth of a foot precision was justifiable. This information confirms that MacNaughton's elevation exceeds 4,000 feet. It also supports the superior accuracy of the contouring in the 1953 USGS series of topographic maps compared to the later 1979 metric series, which inaccurately portrayed a 4,000-foot contour on MacNaughton.

The beginning of this trail is located right next to the toll booth at the entrance. This trail sign will also indicate Mount Jo and Indian Pass. Start at this point. You will start out on a small gravel path, eventually taking you to the lake. It will have you turn right after a couple minutes. As you come to the lake, you will pass the ADK Mountain Club Flora and Fauna building on your left, with the Mount Jo Trail on your right. Continue walking straight, going around the lake. Continue on this trail for about 0.25 miles. Eventually you will come to the official sign-in registry. After signing in, continue walking the path. The ADK Mountain Club recently put new trail signs up to indicate the correct paths. From here, you will take the Indian Pass Trail 3.9 more miles to Scott's Clearing. Scott's Clearing is 4.5 miles from the Loj and is indicated on the signs as you hike in. Once you arrive, you will be met with a lean-to. This is a great place to resupply food, water, and clothing before going to the Wallface Ponds.

To continue, turn right once you get to the lean-to where you will then cross over a brief river. As you continue to follow the trail, just 0.3 miles from Scott's Clearing, you will come to another turn sign. Turn right here toward the river. This will be Indian Pass Brook. You will see what looks like a degraded stone cobble wall on the left and some spur trails leading straight or to the right. Take the path right and walk down to the river. There are multiple ways to cross, however to the right, downstream around 50 feet is where the true crossing is. This should be indicated by blue trail markers or a cairn. Once over, you will continue to take the path climbing up 2.6 miles to the Wallface Ponds. There will be multiple signs on this path indicating miles and directions to the ponds. One and a half miles up this path, you will be met with another brief river crossing and another degraded stone cobble wall on the left. Cross here, turning right at the trail. Between here and the ponds, the trail will have incredibly muddy sections, some of the muddiest on any ADK

MACNAUGHTON MOUNTAIN

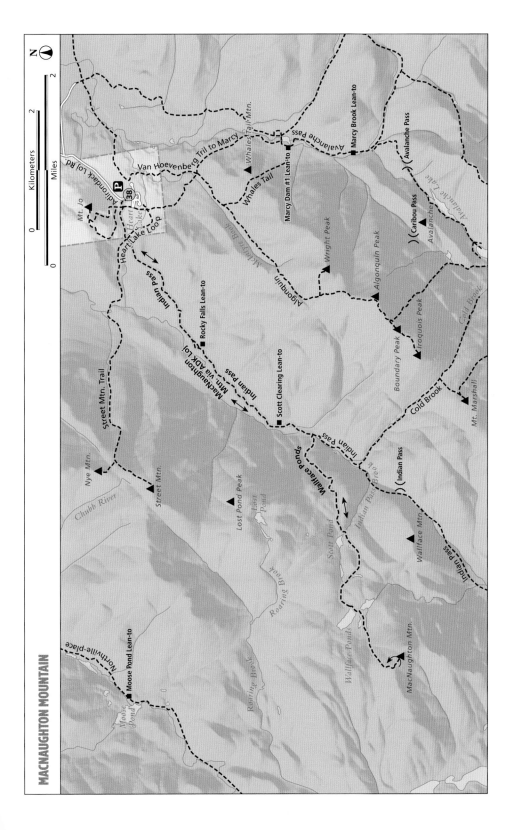

N

0 Kilometers 2

0 Miles 2

Mt. Jo

Adirondack Lot Rd.

Heart Lake

P 38

Van Hoevenberg Trl to Marcy

Heart Lake Loop

Whales Tail Mtn.

Whales Tail

Marcy Dam #1 Lean-to

Marcy Brook Lean-to

Avalanche Pass

Avalanche Pass

Avalanche Lake

Avalanche

Caribou Pass

Indian Pass

Rocky Falls Lean-to

Marcy Brook

Algonquin

Wright Peak

Algonquin Peak

Iroquois Peak

Boundary Peak

Cold Brook

Cold Brook

Mt. Marshall

Street Mtn. Trail

MacNaughton Mtn. via ADK Loj

Indian Pass

Scott Clearing Lean-to

Nye Mtn.

Chubb River

Street Mtn.

Lost Pond Peak

Lost Pond

Wallface Ponds

Indian Pass

Wallface Ponds

Scott Pond

Roaring Brook

Indian Pass Bro.

Indian Pass

Wallface Mtn.

Indian Pass

MacNaughton Mtn.

Northville-place

Moose Pond Lean-to

Moose Pond

Roaring Brook

trail. Stay vigilant, following the blue trail markers on the trees to navigate through. You will also pass a couple smaller ponds on the way. The very end of this trail will meet you with a dead end, a very large pond, and the trail markers will also stop.

This is where the route officially becomes a bushwhack. You are 7.4 miles in here. To continue forward, walk down to the water, cross the other side to the other shore of the pond, and navigate along the shore around 0.1 miles to the other side to the outlet in between the two ponds. Look for any indication at the outlet that looks like a path into the woods. From here, you will have to forge your own way heading directly southwest through the forest.

If followed correctly, the forest should give way to more hardwood. Keep heading southwest, looking for herd paths where other people may have been. Eventually you'll need to make a connection to the unknown drainage coming off MacNaughton. Near the drainage, you will find what looks like trails from what other people have made. Continue to follow any of these trails, which will take you in an eastward direction.. You will want to make sure you are within eye contact of this drainage for about 0.5 miles. As it thins out, you will eventually need to cross the drainage and start heading due southwest again. Stay vigilant as you continue to look for trails made by others over the years. As you get closer to the top, you may find yourself hiking what does seem like an unmarked trail. At the top, look carefully for the spur trail leading to where the summit sign is. Around 300 feet along the summit ridge, you can find another high point which is technically the true top and looks similar to the summit, but without a sign. On your return, the path down does not matter nearly as much, but try to retrace your steps the best you can. It is important that as you leave the summit you are heading northbound off the mountain. Find the drainage, and follow it out eventually bearing northeast back to the ponds and the trail.

MILES AND DIRECTIONS

0.0 Start at the trailhead next to the toll booth at the entrance, also indicating Mount Jo and Indian Pass.

0.5 Reach the official sign-in registry. Sign in and continue on the Indian Pass Trail.

2.3 Pass Rocky Falls.

4.5 Arrive at Scott's Clearing, marked by a lean-to. Resupply if necessary.

4.5 Cross a brief river right after the lean-to.

4.8 Reach a turn sign. Turn right toward Indian Pass Brook for another river crossing. Cross it downstream (right), and continue the path.

7.4 Reach the Wallface Ponds at the end of the marked trail.

7.5 Navigate around the shore of the pond to the outlet between the two ponds.

7.6 Reenter the woods.

7.8 Forge your own path, heading southwest through the forest toward an unknown drainage coming off MacNaughton. Stay close to the drainage.

8.3 Cross the drainage and head due southwest again.

8.6 Arrive at the summit ridge. Look for the spur trail leading to the summit sign; turn around by retracing your steps as closely as possible.

17.2 Arrive back at the trailhead.

2 SAWTEETH AND BLAKE PEAK LOOP

This less common route will bring you to lesser-hiked areas and unique trails. This is a difficult outing, yet rewarding. This hike will have you go in between Lower and Upper Ausable Lakes and up the infamous and rugged trail known as the "Elevator Shaft," having you hike three high peaks in total before returning to your car. Some of the trails offered on this route would not be visited unless someone were to do this particular route. That's one reason why this loop is fun and challenging.

Start: Adirondack Mountain Reserve (AMR)/Ausable Club/St. Huberts
Elevation gain: 5,800 feet
Summit elevation: Sawteeth, 4,100 feet; Mount Colvin, 4,057 feet; Blake Peak, 3,960 feet
Distance: 19.6 miles
Difficulty: 5 out of 7, difficult
Hiking time: 12–14 hours
Seasons/schedule: This hike is generally hiked in summer/fall and is not recommended for winter due to lack of foot traffic.
Fees and permits: Free reservation required for parking at the AMR May–Oct.
Canine compatibility: Dogs are not allowed.

Trail surface: This hike features mixed terrain with rocks, scrambles, and mud.
Land status: AMR property/Central High Peaks Wilderness
Nearest town: Keene Valley, NY
Water availability: There is little to no water, except in the brooks. Bring plenty of water.
Amenities available: None. No privy or campsites.
Maximum grade: 1,400 feet/0.8 miles: Elevator Shaft up to Blake/Colvin col
Sunrise or sunset: Neither.
Route type: Loop
Views: There are decent views on most of the high points.

FINDING THE TRAILHEAD

AMR/St. Huberts is right across the street from Roaring Brook Falls Trailhead for Giant, labeled as St. Huberts Parking Area or the Adirondack Mountain Reserve. Approximately 7.5 miles from I-87. Reservations are needed May–October. **GPS:** 44.14970°N / 73.76806°W

THE HIKE

On a map, this route will make plenty of sense. Maybe you never considered this route until reading this guidebook. Either way, you will find yourself starting at the AMR, which, like most hikes from here, will have you walk Lake Road 3.5 miles all the way to the end. Your first goal is to ascend and climb Sawteeth. This can be done either via the scenic route or the standard trail up the Weld Trail (see Hike 8). Whichever way you choose to get to Sawteeth's summit, look for the trail signs south of the true summit (beyond the summit viewpoint) where you will find a sign pointing down toward the Warden Camps. You will take this 2.3 miles all the way down the back side of Sawteeth. It should be noted that there is no exit back to the car this way. That's what makes this so fun and exciting. As you descend this trail, eventually you will cross back into AMR property. Near the bottom, you will cross a river then turn left on the trail, taking you to the outlet for Upper Ausable Lake. Please be mindful of the property. There will also be property signs pointing you toward the Lower Lake as well as Colvin and Blake. Once you arrive where the Upper Lake is, you will turn left toward the Lower Lake for 1 mile. At the end of this, turn right following the signs toward the Elevator Shaft Trail. This is a very steep and grueling ascent 0.8 miles to the intersection between Colvin and Blake, which will be marked by yellow trail markers. Once up at the top, turn right following the signs to summit Blake Peak. You will then head back down, continuing the trail up to Colvin, where you will eventually take the trail all the way back down to Lake Road, walking back to the car.

A sign at the Warden Camps points toward the Elevator Shaft route.

3 INDIAN HEAD

One of the most common and highly sought-out hikes within the Adirondacks certainly does not fall short of beauty. There are reasons why this is the most popular hike within the Adirondacks. Indian Head is a cliff outcropping standing 600 feet above Lower Ausable Lake. It gets its name because when viewed from either side, the cliff's shape resembles that of a Native American. This lake is also technically considered to be a fjord, one of the very few within the Northeast. This is a must-see spot if you're planning a trip to the Adirondacks.

Start: Adirondack Mountain Reserve (AMR)/Ausable Club/St. Huberts
Elevation gain: 800 feet
Summit elevation: 2,667 feet
Distance: 10.6 miles
Difficulty: 2 out of 7, mild
Hiking time: 3–6 hours
Seasons/schedule: This hike can be made in all seasons.
Fees and permits: Free reservation required for parking at the AMR May–Oct.
Canine compatibility: Dogs are not allowed.

Trail surface: There is a gravel road and maintained moderate trail.
Land status: AMR property/Central High Peaks Wilderness
Nearest town: Keene Valley, NY
Water availability: There is some water along the route but still pack what you need.
Amenities available: None.
Maximum grade: 400-foot climb right after the road ends
Sunrise or sunset: This hike is best at sunset.
Route type: Out-and-back
Views: This hike has fantastic views.

FINDING THE TRAILHEAD

AMR/St. Huberts is right across the street from Roaring Brook Falls Trailhead for Giant, labeled as St. Huberts Parking Area or the Adirondack Mountain Reserve. Approximately 7.5 miles from I-87. Reservations are needed May–Oct.
GPS: 44.14970°N / 73.76806°W

THE HIKE

This is best enjoyed as a loop of the available trails, providing an opportunity to witness the waterfalls and rivers such as Rainbow Falls and Beaver Meadow Falls. The hike commences on the AMR Lake Road after the gate sign in. You will walk the entirety of the road 3.5 miles to the end where you will be met with the footpath. There are alternate routes along the road that you can take, but I recommend going all the way to the very end. you will see a sign pointing toward Indian Head as well. The footpath begins flat, leading to the "Gothics Window," a viewpoint of Gothics through the trees. The trail then ascends steadily over steep terrain with many switchbacks to the crest of a ridge (0.8 miles from Lake Road) where a junction leads you to Indian Head. Eventually, the trail will bring you out to the cliffs where you are more than likely to be met with other people. To get the best view, descend the cliffs to the lower cliffs, where it will be fully unobstructed.

A gorgeous summer day view at Indian Head.

4 MOUNT JO

This is a well-known and a commonly hiked mountain. It is probably in the top five best hikes in all of the Adirondacks. If you are in the Lake Placid area, this is a ten out of ten recommendation, especially for a first mountain. It is also part of the Lake Placid 9er challenge. This hike boasts breathtaking panoramic views of the Central High Peaks and also has a very fun historical background. Upon visiting, you can also walk around the Heart Lake property visiting the info center, Loj, and lake. This hike is an ideal family adventure, offering the perfect opportunity for a picnic lunch.

Start: Adirondack Loj
Elevation gain: 700 feet
Summit elevation: 2,876 feet
Distance: 2.2 or 2.6 miles (depending on which route you take)
Difficulty: 1 out of 7, easy
Hiking time: 45–90 minutes
Seasons/schedule: This hike can be made in all seasons.
Fees and permits: $15 to park at Adirondack Loj
Canine compatibility: Dogs must be on leash.
Trail surface: The trail is rocky.

Land status: Adirondack Loj Property
Nearest town: Lake Placid, NY
Water availability: None. Pack enough water for the hike.
Amenities available: The Adirondack Loj, Info Center, and the Hungry Hiker.
Maximum grade: 600 feet/0.4 miles: most of the mountain
Sunrise or sunset: Sunrise is good.
Route type: Out-and-back or loop
Views: This hike features great views.

FINDING THE TRAILHEAD

Adirondack Loj is located 1.5 miles southeast of Lake Placid on NY 73; turn down Adirondack Loj Road and drive for 5 miles. Popular and often packed; arrive early. Weekdays are generally not full prior to 9 a.m. but can be full before 6 a.m. on weekends. **GPS:** 44.18313°N / 73.96445°W

THE HIKE

Start in the Loj parking lot. Walk back to the toll booth that you passed on the way in. Nearby is the beginning of the hike with a sign indicating Mount Jo. Take this route leading to a gentle, flat trail toward Heart Lake. The path navigates around the lake, passing by a cool cabin that showcases intriguing nature exhibits. With the lake to your left, proceed until you encounter a trail junction, where you should take a right following the Mount Jo signs. Continue on this trail for a quarter-mile until you reach another fork in the path. At this juncture, you have the option of taking the shorter yet steeper route to the right (recommended) or pursuing the lengthier, more gradual trail straight ahead. Depending on their preferences, many hikers opt to ascend using one trail and descend using the other. It's worth noting that the shorter path can have large and slippery rocks, possibly making the descent more challenging. If you're part of a large group, the longer trail may be more suitable due to its less steep nature. This trail is 0.3 miles longer. Near the top, the two trails converge again in a wooded area just before the summit, leading to a brief hike up to the peak.

A view from Mt. Jo in the fall.

5 MOUNT ADAMS FIRE TOWER

Out of the eighteen fire towers located within Adirondack Park, this is quite possibly the fan favorite. I personally think this is better than Hurricane Mountain. It is perfect for families and pets. Although it is quite the drive from anywhere, it is well worth it, even for a weekend trip.

Start: East River Trailhead
Elevation gain: 1,800 feet
Summit elevation: 3,520 feet
Distance: 5.0 miles
Difficulty: 2 out of 7, mild
Hiking time: 3-4 hours
Seasons/schedule: This hike is generally hiked in summer/fall.
Fees and permits: None
Canine compatibility: This is very dog friendly. A leash is not required but recommended.
Trail surface: This route is rocky and steep.

Land status: Outer High Peaks Wilderness
Nearest town: Tahawas/Newcomb, NY
Water availability: None. Pack enough water for the hike.
Amenities available: None.
Maximum grade: 1,500 feet/1.1 miles.
Sunrise or sunset: Both.
Route type: Out-and-back
Views: This hike has breathtaking views of the Central High Peaks and Vanderwhacker Wild Forest.

FINDING THE TRAILHEAD

The trailhead is 0.5 miles before Upper Works. Follow Blue Ridge Road (CR 84) west from I-87 exit 29 toward Newcomb. Travel for 17.4 miles until you reach the intersection with Tahawus Road (CR 25) after the train tracks. Turn right and continue for 6.3 miles, then make a left at the High Peaks trails sign. Just past the Boreas River Bridge, the trailhead is on the right. **GPS:** 44.08120°N / 74.05516°W

THE HIKE

Embarking on the trail, you'll find yourself strolling through a serene woodland setting on a relatively broad path. After a short distance of a couple hundred yards, the trail swings right toward the Hudson River, tracing its banks for about a hundred feet before leading you to a metal suspension bridge. Exercise care while crossing this slightly uneven structure, which hasn't seen any replacements since near destruction from high waters in 2019. Having crossed the bridge, the trail continues for roughly 0.3 miles until Lake Jimmy emerges. Pay attention here, as the trail soon takes a left turn into the forest. This should be marked by debris covering the trail, keeping you from going straight. If you keep going straight, you'll reach a dead end at the lake where there used to be a crossing prior to 2011. Instead, the trail diverts left into the woodland, following a path that curves around the lake in a clockwise direction. As you navigate around the lake, you'll come across boardwalks and patches of marshy, muddy terrain before reaching the opposite side where the bridge was originally located. The trail remains broad and easily navigable. Approximately 0.3 miles beyond the lake, you'll encounter the abandoned Mount Adams fire tower ranger shack on your left, after which the trail bends to the right. Shortly

A sunrise view from the fire tower on Mount Adams.

thereafter, you'll see the Mount Adams trail fork on your left, marked by a sign, about 1.2 miles from the beginning of your hike. The summit is 1.3 miles from here. Once the path diverges, it maintains a gentle incline through hardwood forest until a stream crossing. Here, the trail significantly steepens as it heads toward the summit. While the peak is shrouded in trees, obstructing the view, the fire tower provides an opportunity to ascend for a breathtaking panoramic view.

6 NOONMARK MOUNTAIN

Noonmark is an iconic mountain located in Keene Valley. It is a popular day hike for people looking to get breathtaking panoramic views of the High Peaks without climbing a high peak. Although this mountain is shorter in distance, it is pretty difficult to get up to the top, but it's still "beginner friendly."

Start: Adirondack Mountain Reserve (AMR)/Ausable Club/St. Huberts
Elevation gain: 2,200 feet
Summit elevation: 3,556 feet
Distance: 4.8 miles
Difficulty: 2 out of 7, mild
Hiking time: 3–6 hours
Seasons/schedule: This hike can be made in all seasons.
Fees and permits: Free reservation required for parking at the AMR May–Oct.
Canine compatibility: Dogs are not allowed.

Trail surface: This hike features steep dirt terrain and rock.
Land status: AMR property/Central High Peaks Wilderness
Nearest town: Keene Valley, NY
Water availability: None. Pack enough water for the hike.
Amenities available: None.
Maximum grade: 1,400 feet/1.1 miles
Sunrise or sunset: Both.
Route type: Out-and-back
Views: This hike has fantastic views.

FINDING THE TRAILHEAD

AMR/St. Huberts is right across the street from Roaring Brook Falls Trailhead for Giant, labeled as St. Huberts Parking Area or the Adirondack Mountain

A winter view from Noonmark Mountain.

Reserve. Approximately 7.5 miles from I-87. Reservations are needed May–October. **GPS:** 44.14970°N / 73.76806°W

THE HIKE

It should be noted that if you cannot get parking at the AMR, this hike can also be hiked from Round Pond just down the road toward I-87. From the AMR at the parking lot, traverse up the dirt road for approximately 0.25 miles until you reach the register marking the trailhead for Noonmark Mountain on your left. This will be indicated by a sign-in box. The initial section of the trail leads you through a private driveway for about 0.2 miles. Just before you reach a large barn at the end of the driveway, the foot trail diverts to the right. From here, the trail turns into a moderate difficulty level as it follows the path of an old forest road. Eventually you'll encounter a junction for Noonmark Mountain on the right. The trail's incline intensifies from this point. As you continue your ascent, the path becomes increasingly challenging, characterized by more rocky slabs and a trail adorned with beautiful cedar trees. The final stretch toward the summit is particularly steep, traversing over open rock where the panoramic views start to emerge. Reaching the summit, you'll be rewarded with a 360-degree view of the High Peaks region from the open rock vantage point. After your hike, you can go to the Noonmark Diner for breakfast, lunch, or dinner. Tell them I sent you. Best pie in the ADK.

A starry night from Mount Jo.

HIKE INDEX

Algonquin and Iroquois Peaks, 107

Allen Mountain, 201

Basin Mountain, 79

Big Slide Mountain, 53

Bob Marshall Traverse, 216

Cascade and Porter Mountains, 32

Cold River Loop, 224

Dix Mountain, 173

Giant and Rocky Peak Ridge, 42

Gothics and Armstrong Mountains, 63

Grace Peak, 181

Great Range Traverse, 207

Haystack, Basin, and Saddleback Loop, 91

High Peaks Wilderness Traverse, 220

Indian Head, 235

MacNaughton Mountain—The Lost
    46er, 229

Macomb Mountain, South Dix, Grace
    Peak, and Hough Peak, 177

Mount Adams Fire Tower, 240

Mount Colden, 128

Mount Colvin and Blake Peak, 162

Mount Haystack, 84

Mount Jo, 238

Mount Marcy, 96

Mount Marshall, 136

Mount Redfield and Cliff Mountain, 141

Mount Skylight and Gray Peak, 146

Nippletop and Dial Mountains, 167

Noonmark Mountain, 242

Phelps Mountain, 119

Pinnacle Traverse, 212

Porter Mountain from Marcy Field, 36

Rocky Peak Ridge from New Russia, 48

Saddleback Mountain, 75

Santanoni, Panther, and Couchsachraga
    Peaks, 186

Sawteeth and Blake Peak Loop, 233

Sawteeth via the Scenic Route, 69

Seward, Donaldson, and Emmons
    Mountains, 193

Seymour Mountain, 197

Street and Nye Mountains, 113

Tabletop Mountain, 123

Upper and Lower Wolfjaw Mountains, 58

Whiteface and Esther Mountains, 154

Wright Peak, 103

THE TEN ESSENTIALS OF HIKING

American Hiking Society recommends you pack the "Ten Essentials" every time you head out for a hike. Whether you plan to be gone for a couple of hours or several months, make sure to pack these items. Become familiar with these items and know how to use them. Learn more at **AmericanHiking.org/hiking-resources**

 1. **Appropriate Footwear**

 2. **Navigation**

 3. **Water** (and a way to purify it)

 4. **Food**

 5. **Rain Gear & Dry-Fast Layers**

 6. **Safety Items** (light, fire, and a whistle)

 7. **First Aid Kit**

 8. **Knife or Multi-Tool**

 9. **Sun Protection**

 10. **Shelter**